# THE VALENTINO COOKBOOK

# *Valenti*

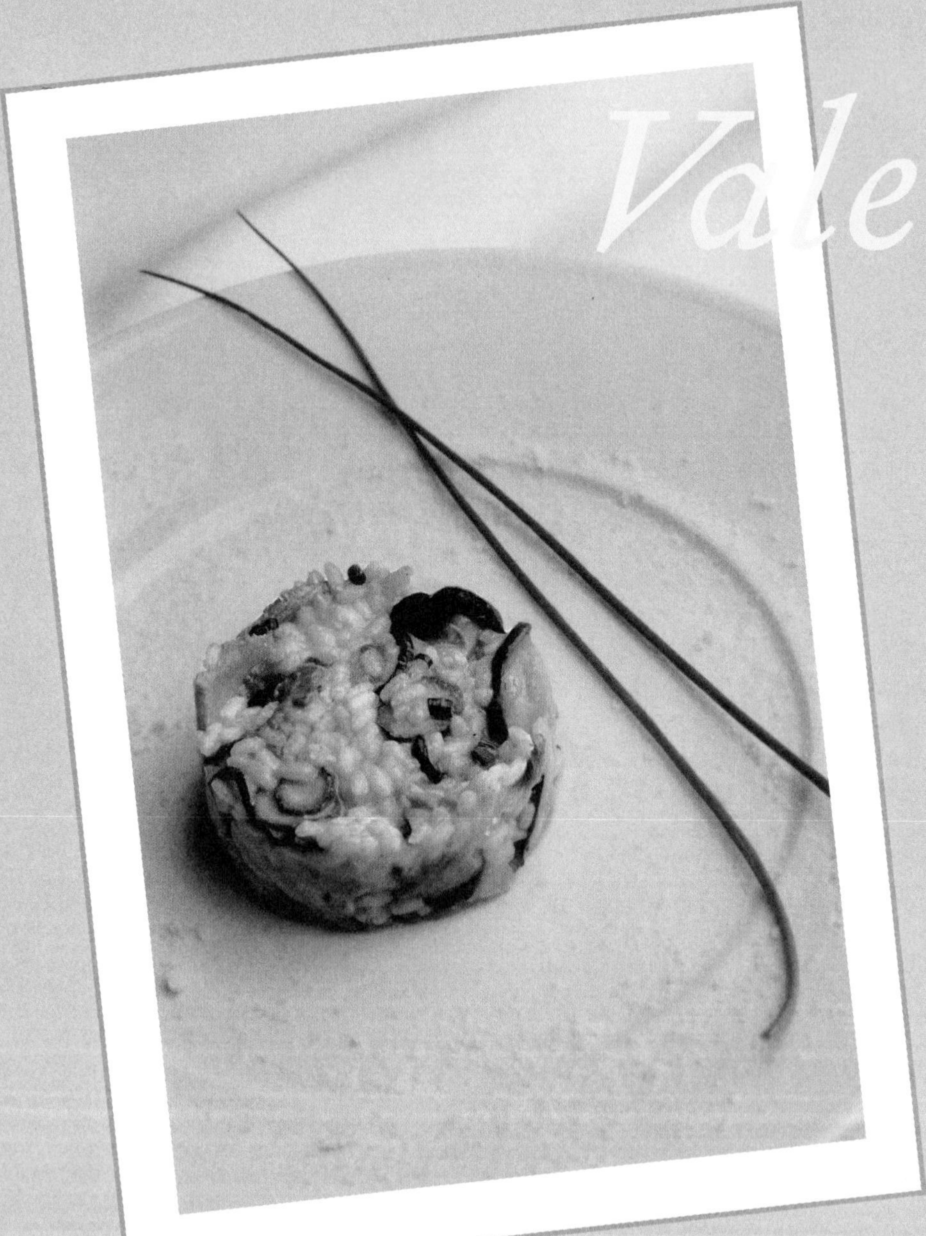

# THE VALENTINO COOKBOOK

*Piero Selvaggio*

*and Karen Stabiner*

PHOTOGRAPHS BY PATRICIA WILLIAMS

RECIPES BY ANGELO AURIANA AND LUCIANO PELLEGRINI

VILLARD  NEW YORK

All rights reserved under International and
Pan-American Copyright Conventions. Published
in the United States by Villard Books, a division
of Random House, Inc., New York,
and simultaneously in Canada by Random House of
Canada Limited, Toronto.

Villard Books and colophon are registered
trademarks of Random House, Inc.

ISBN: 0-679-45242-7

Villard website address: www.villard.com

Printed in the United States of America on acid-free paper

2 4 6 8 9 7 5 3

First Edition

*Book design by Barbara M. Bachman*

To the two most important women in my life:
my mother, Lina, who fed me,
taught me, and inspired me,
and my wife, Stacy, who encourages me
and provides love and support every day.

—*Piero Selvaggio*

To my parents, who fell in love over
a spaghetti casserole. To Larry and his
omelette, and Sarah and her pies.

—*Karen Stabiner*

# Acknowledgments

The chefs I work with—my extended family—challenge and inspire me, and I am always grateful to Angelo Auriana, who has been at Valentino for sixteen years, and to Luciano Pellegrini, who started at Primi, moved to Posto, and now, in his sixteenth year as well, runs the kitchen at Valentino Las Vegas. I thank Michelle Robie and Gianluca Fusto, the pastry chef at Valentino, and Jennifer Worthley, our catering manager, for their talent and hard work. And I must acknowledge the late Pino Pasqualato, chef at Valentino for four years, and Antonio Orlando, who followed Pino. They established a tradition of excellence.

I thank a handful of close friends who are also professional colleagues: Paola Di Mauro, Romano Tamani, Nadia and Antonio Santini, Franco Ruta, and Johanne Killeen and George Germon, all of whom graciously contributed ideas to this book. Maurizio Zanella introduced me to many memorable Italian restaurants. Carmela Speroni was a constant source of support.

I was lucky enough to work with Peter Gethers, whom I have known since he was a boy, and Shauna Toh and Amy Scheibe, who made sure that the spontaneity of the kitchen was translated into accurate recipes.

Teri Gelber made sure the recipes made sense. And Patty Williams gave them life with her beautiful photographs.

For my three boys—Giorgio, Giampiero, and Tancredi—I look forward to watching them grow, developing an appreciation of, and a respect for, people through great food and wine.

—P.S.

Angelo Auriana, Luciano Pellegrini, and Michelle Robie tolerated endless questions with great patience and charm. I enjoyed every moment I spent with them.

Thanks to Teri Gelber for her hard work on the recipes, and to Sue Clamage and Freddy Odlum, for turning everyone's efforts into a clean manuscript. And thanks to Jennifer Worthley, for being so organized.

Peter Gethers is enthusiastic and demanding, which is a productive mix, and Shauna Toh and Amy Scheibe offered wise advice along the way.

I am grateful to those who tried recipes at home, or ate them in our house, and made suggestions: Ginger Curwen and Jack Nessel, Vicky and Hummie Mann, Judith Owen and Harry Shearer, Marcie Rothman, Lucy Stille and David Shaw, and Dora Warren.

I was taught that the best food comes with side orders of love and conversation. I thank my husband, Larry Dietz, and my daughter, Sarah Dietz, for giving me good reason to cook. They make everything taste better.

—K.S.

# ✸ Contents

*Valentino*

# ✿ *A Life in Food and Wine*

ON FOOD

I have been a restaurateur for more than half my life. If you count my jobs in other people's restaurants, I have been in the business for over thirty-five years. And now, when I look back, I see that I was headed this way far earlier than I realized. I don't know if I believe in destiny. I do know that a mix of experience and luck can shape a life.

My childhood memories are always mixed in with images of food and wine, of my family at the table. Whether at my mother's table, eating *la cucina povera*, the robust food she made from simple ingredients, or at Valentino, savoring a newly discovered wine, the experience is the same. Good food and wine, always accompanied by spirited conversation—the gracious meal is the continuity in my life.

It is only now, with two restaurants in Los Angeles and one in Las Vegas, that I look over my shoulder and see the past clearly. I grew up in Modica, a small hillside town on the southeastern coast of Sicily, the middle child of three. My father drove a truck. My mother, like the other mothers in the neighborhood, kept house. When I was a little boy, the only thought I gave to food was that hers was good—simple, centered on seafood, pasta, and the fresh vegetables she bought daily—and the food at my boarding school was bad. The nuns lacked my mother's enthusiasm, and it showed; for years I could not eat *baccalà*—the dried, salted cod that was our alternative to fresh fish—because of the endless salty, tough servings I consumed as a boy.

My tastes were shaped by what was available, and by the special recipes handed down in my family from one generation to the next. Pasta, eggplant, and anything with ricotta, whether it was savory or sweet—these are the foods that still remind me of family dinners. I was starting to connect food with happiness; I just didn't know it yet.

I never set foot in a restaurant until I was sixteen years old. Then, on a day in 1963 that would change my life, my father, Giorgio, drove my mother, my older sister Angela, my baby brother Santo, and me to Catania to apply for our papers to travel to the United States. The drive took an hour and a half, and when we arrived we were hungry. But instead of buying some bread and cheese to eat in the square, my father had an idea. He remembered a truck stop where he had often eaten. This was an important occasion. He decided to spend the money on a restaurant meal.

The first thing I remember was the smell of good tomatoes, good basil, and garlic. And there were many tables, full of people I didn't know. Until then the only tables I knew were my mother's and the refectory tables at boarding school. I knew there were restaurants, but I couldn't visualize them.

I had a choice for the first time. It was a simple place, a one-page menu of ordinary things, and I stuck with pasta. What I was really interested in was the chef, this nice round person dressed all in white, with one big cauldron and a lot of colanders full of spaghetti. I saw more spaghetti than I'd ever seen in my life—he got an order, the colander went into the cauldron, that order came out, and the next one went in. Then he tossed the pasta with the sauce as though he were conducting an orchestra, waving his arms up and down. The next thing I knew there were twenty plates of pasta going out to the room. And I thought: Wow. Look at what this guy can do.

It was such an experience. And of course, the strangest thing of all—my mother never got up from the table.

From there we went to the consulate to get our papers. And all I remember was that the man spoke English as well as Italian. I was so impressed. He was like God—he was the one who would tell us if we could go to America or not. All that in one day. That meal was the beginning of our new life.

WE SETTLED IN BROOKLYN, in a neighborhood full of old and recent immigrants. So many things could have happened to me once I got there. I might have become a housepainter, like my uncles. But I was sent in another direction—my cousin, who worked in personnel at New York University, got me a job in the cafeteria in Hayden Hall. At seventeen I was washing pots and pans on the breakfast shift, six A.M. to two P.M. I knew about eggs, but the rest of it? Slabs of bacon, which was like pancetta but not; pancakes, these sweet, doughy things that took some getting used to; waffles and biscuits. I spoke no English, so I just kept to my job and watched, with fascination, as the cook turned out the food.

Soon after I began, a young man who worked in the administration office stopped by to see how I was doing. Julio was Puerto Rican, so we could communicate in Spanish, which I had begun to pick up in the cafeteria. He invited me to have dinner after work. "*Vamos a fuera para comer,*" he said, and I thought he literally meant "go out"—we would leave Hayden Hall and find a little stand on the street where we could get a snack. Instead he took me to a soda fountain where they served . . . well, I couldn't tell what they served. The waitress handed me a menu; I might as well have been reading Chinese! I waited to see what Julio would do.

He ordered, but I had no idea what. The only words I could manage were "Me, too" and "Coca-Cola." I waited to see what I was having for dinner.

Then it arrived: a patty of meat on round bread and these beautiful golden strips of potato. And ketchup! I waited. He poured the ketchup over the potatoes; so did I. I felt silly and happy, and every bite was memorable. I felt the way I had in Catania: Surely I was on the edge of an adventure.

But back in Brooklyn, I was heading nowhere. We all spoke Italian instead of English, and people ate food that belonged to neither country, like baked mostaccioli, which was like lasagne, only made with thick, short pasta. I was starting to pick up some English, and I was impatient to leave my past behind. I said to myself, "If I want to think of my life in a heroic way, I have to go on a real adventure." I decided I would take the bus across the country to California, to see my uncle, John Susino. I was so starved for something new that I never thought to be scared.

Uncle John was my mother's brother, and he had come to California in 1946, deserting a passenger ship where he worked as a waiter and finding a job at Chasen's restaurant in Los Angeles. He was a mythic figure to me. "Uncle John" was a majestic name in my family. We spoke of him as though he were a big businessman, even though he was only a waiter. My mother had explained to me that he was a very special waiter. He worked for movie stars.

That was enough for me. At seventeen I came to Los Angeles, and Uncle John became my legal guardian. His advice? Put on a jacket and tie (I only had one of each) and go look for a job as a busboy.

I didn't know what a busboy was, but I did as I was told. And so began my life in the restaurant business. I got a job as a room service waiter and busboy at the Beverly Hills Hotel, I enrolled in a community college, and found a room to rent for $35 a month. My real adventure, my life, had begun.

I loved all of it. Particularly when Uncle John got me hired for a catering job at Sonja Henie's house. There I was, holding a tray, serving food to Gregory Peck, Tony Curtis, and Elizabeth Taylor. I was in a complete fantasyland.

Then I got even luckier. I found a maestro, Aldo Lavagnini, an older gentleman who showed me the dignity inherent in the service business. He was the manager at The Marquis, a fairly formal continental restaurant on Sunset Boulevard, a jovial man who made service his profession and his pride. All through college I worked for him, advancing from waiter to captain, and from captain to his assistant. I got to see a new dimension of the restaurant business, as theater, where the audience—the customers—are part of the performance.

I left when I graduated, because I had promised myself that once I had a degree I would go on to bigger and better things. But I still had no idea what I wanted to do with my life. I was twenty-three, and very conscious that I had to do *something*. I just didn't know what.

Again, my life came to me. I had a friend, Gianni Paoletti, who was about ten years older than me and even more impatient. He had trained as a chef in England, moved to Los Angeles, and now he wanted to open his own restaurant. Would I be his partner?

Our own place. Were we crazy? Sure! It would mean my putting up $5,000, which was lots of money at that time, but I figured I was young enough to lose it and start over if I had to. If I didn't take a chance, I would be somebody else's employee forever. At least this way I would be able to say that for once in my life I was my own boss for a while.

One day he called me up and told me to meet him at a bar on Pico Boulevard in Santa Monica. When I got there I thought, Okay, this is halfway between him and me and now we're going to drive over to look at a restaurant together, in one car. I stood in front of the building and looked around: There was an auto mechanic on one side, a print shop on the other, a red-light motel across the street. This was not a street anybody would want to stroll down.

When Gianni arrived he explained that this was, in fact, the place where he wanted to open; he sometimes stopped in for a beer after work, and he knew the two owners were eager to sell. He took me inside, and things only got worse. There was a dark, long, ugly bar, a jukebox screeching, a bored waitress, and five coffee shop booths. The decorations on the wall were the kind of cardboard souvenirs sold for a dollar each when you're leaving Tijuana.

As soon as we got back outside I said to him, "Do you realize how dreadful this place is?"

"Yeah," he said, "but we don't have any money. It's a start."

I said I had to think it over, but the next day he announced that he was going to do it whether I did or not. That made me feel I had to take the chance. He had a wife and two kids, so much more to lose. Next thing you know, we were renting a beer bar. We went right to work. We painted the place, and brought in some chairs from both of our houses. The souvenirs came down. We scrubbed the kitchen and splurged and rented tablecloths—red undercloths with white ones on top.

Then there was the question of the name. We had catchy names, stupid names, Rome by Night, Rome by Day, Trevi Fountain, Gian-Piero for the two of us. Selvaggio Paoletti. We must have come up with fifty names before we got to Valentino. We liked it right away—it was romantic, we liked the musical sound, and it reminded us of Rudolph Valentino, which meant Italian, Hollywood, glamour, and sophistication. A very big name to live up to with a lot full of junked cars right next door.

It was my job to write out the menu. I still have it, framed, with "Continental Cuisine" lettered down the side, hanging in the hallway at today's Valentino. It reminds me of where I came from. In those days, the food was half Mamma and half my limited knowledge of more elegant dishes: manicotti with prosciutto and baked lasagne alongside a cobb salad and chicken breast Gina Lollobrigida. I even put the baked mostaccioli from my Brooklyn days on the menu. We had lots of energy, but not a lot of knowledge.

We sent out little invitations to everyone we knew, and at noon on December 4, 1972, we opened for business. It was a rainy, ugly day. Our first four customers were secretaries from the neighborhood who had walked by a couple of times on their way to buy a sandwich and asked us when we'd be open. When they walked in the door I couldn't help myself; I hugged each one of them and cried, "Welcome to Valentino. We are *so* glad you have come." We were in business.

Our friends all came, but there were very few real customers. Maybe eight lunches and a dozen dinners each day. And we were there twenty-four hours a day, me out front, Gianni in the kitchen with one helper, my brother-in-law Nino waiting tables, and one busboy. We did everything—ran the vacuum cleaner, learned bookkeeping, learned purchasing.

After two weeks, failure began to seem inevitable. I was very nervous, very tense and worried. So we worked harder and developed a philosophy: Worse comes to worst, at least we will eat well until we close.

Then, the week before Christmas, a man came in to eat, and I recognized him: He'd been there a few times before with his wife. He showed up late in the afternoon and asked for a menu—for his wife, who happened to be Lois Dwan, then the restaurant critic for the *Los Angeles Times*. He said, "I think this is a nice place, and Lois would like to write about it."

I was ready to kiss him. About a week later her column ran. She wrote about how her Christmas present to her readers would be three little restaurant jewels. One of them was Valentino. The review didn't help the other places—they went out of business soon after—but on Christmas Day, 1972, we had 110 people.

Suddenly we had a new problem. We couldn't handle that many customers. We had no idea what to do. All we *did* know was that we were hot. Los Angeles at that time didn't have a good trattoria, a middle-of-the-road place where people could eat good food and feel comfortable. So we were it.

Valentino was like a circus—overbooked, overcrowded, quite a few fiascos. But we hung on, and two years later we were a success. We both drove big leased Cadillacs and showed off hundred-dollar bills.

But then the disagreements started: Doing well meant we had to decide what to do next. I wanted to concentrate on Valentino. I was in the front of the house, and I saw we needed more room for people to wait, more room for wine storage. I wanted to buy the building, buy the junkyard next door, and really improve the restaurant. Gianni wanted to grow in other directions, including a partnership with another restaurateur, at another location. I told him he couldn't do both, because they would compete with each other.

We bought the building, and the space next door, but there was no patching up the relationship. Gianni left, I gave him an enormous amount of money I didn't have, and suddenly I owned Valentino, all by myself. I was twenty-seven.

The year that followed was the start of my real education. I began to see how much I needed to learn. I could kiss ladies' hands, and I was charming and warm, but it was a façade. Behind it was emptiness: no real knowledge of food, wine, or business. Surprisingly, there was very little competition—the food boom had not yet hit California—so the restaurant continued to do very well, but still I knew, in my heart, that I had work to do.

And then, one day, a dear customer took me aside to talk about the menu. "You know," he said, "you're not going very far with this kind of food."

That was all it took; I knew he was right. My first big adventure in life had been coming to America when I was seventeen. My second big adventure was to go back home to Italy, to learn what my native cuisine was all about. I left my brother-in-law in charge and got on a plane, not knowing what would happen, just knowing I had to do something.

I had made friends with Pino Khail, an editor at an Italian wine magazine, so I looked him up. He was based in Milan, which is where my education began. At a restaurant called Giannino I ate fettucine with porcini for the first time—though with my limited knowledge, I expected pasta with "little pigs" instead of mushrooms. I tasted truffles and different types of carpaccio. I experienced flavors and sensations I'd never encountered before. He took me to the father of great food, Gualtiero Marchesi, and I felt like I was in church.

My guide saw how shocked I was, how absolutely embarrassed to compare what we did at Valentino to what I was being served. This was another level of Italian food that I had never tasted before. I grew up at a boarding school, I had my first restaurant meal at a truck stop when I was sixteen, and as an immigrant my restaurant experience was limited to the neighborhood spaghetteria. I liked food, and I liked the business. But I didn't have a clue what the possibilities really were.

That trip created a bigger crisis, because I returned to Los Angeles realizing how much I didn't know. I vowed, "Some day I will be as good as them," as the artists whose food I had eaten in Milan, but I knew it was going to take a tremendous effort.

Where to start? I told the kitchen staff I didn't want any more heavy sauces. Less salt. Better-quality ingredients. I told myself that we needed a new chef. I had hired a friend to replace Gianni, but he made the same kind of heavy dishes we had always served, precooked everything, and just dished it out. Then I heard of a young man who had opened a restaurant in Treviso, a little town near Venice, that had only lasted six months because he had no business sense. He was just a good cook, and now he was very frustrated. He was available, and it was perfect timing.

Pino Pasqualato came in 1977, and Valentino began to change. The food was cleaner, the flavors were distinct, the sauces didn't drown the food. We started doing pasta that had a lighter style, like cappellacci, a small pasta filled with ricotta. We added poultry beyond chicken—quail, pigeon, and pheasant. And the cold dishes were great; he made a beautiful *cima alla Genovese*, a cold, stuffed veal breast that became one of our signature appetizers.

The transition was a gradual one that continues to this day. We still offer the old dishes—fettucine Alfredo, a dish called peasant spaghetti. But we revisit them, we interpret them in a new way. And I pull at everyone who works with me, to make each person grow.

That includes me. I am always impatient with the menu, eager to make changes. I opened a second restaurant, Primi, in 1985 because I wanted a restaurant where people could eat the way I like to eat—tasting lots of little courses, instead of the more formal Italian meal. I brought my memories of my mother's cooking forward, and developed a menu that concentrated on colorful, intensely flavored appetizers and an array of pastas. *Primi* means first course, but at Primi every course was a first course; we threw sequence out the window. The best way to eat there was to order ten different things and put them on the table, and that way even if you didn't like one taste you had plenty of others to choose from. The menu evolved over time, and you could put together a regular meal there, but it was always possible to pick and choose.

Primi closed in June 2000, but we carried its lessons to the other restaurants. Tasting is what I still do. If I am hungry at Valentino I go to the pantry to see what there is—a piece of cheese, marinated peppers from the night before, little bits of this and that. Or at three o'clock I go to the pasta station to see what is available. My idea of a perfect meal? A dish of beautifully cooked pasta, plain, maybe a sprinkle of pepper or cheese. That's it. I eat pasta every day. It is what connects me to my past.

My third restaurant, Posto, which opened in 1992, reflects another tradition—the rustic cooking that the chef, Luciano Pellegrini, and I love. We serve simple, straightforward food, lots of grilling, lots of strong flavors. And now that Luciano has gone to Las Vegas, to our second Valentino, we are guaranteed another round of exciting change.

Not even the original Valentino is immune. In 1987, in the midst of what I called "pizza time" at Los Angeles restaurants, I could have shut down Valentino, or taken it apart, put in a pizza oven, and made it a casual restaurant. But then it wouldn't have been mine anymore. So we took a calculated gamble and dressed it up instead: Gone were the leather booths and dark-wood trim, the clubby look that we created after I became the sole owner. Today Valentino is a beautiful wonderland, in serene shades of mauve and pale pink and gold, with hand-painted floral borders done by a friend.

I believe strongly that this is an ongoing adventure—it is the travel, not the destination, that excites me. How could it not, given the way my life has gone so far? I have come a long way from that hardworking, confused young man whose goal was to earn his living with his head, as a professional. Ten years ago maybe ten percent of our customers would ignore the menu and ask us to design a special meal. Now it's up to about fifty percent. People come to Valentino for an experience they will not have anywhere else.

That is what keeps me going: the desire to give my customers a truly unforgettable evening. It requires constant effort. I send chefs back to Italy to learn new things, and I open my doors to artisans who want to offer me new food or wine. To stand still is to perish: I want to read more, to visit more places, to explore. The difference, after all these years, is that there is less worry than there was in those first days. We have a sense of security, we have a team. But we must continue to move forward.

Since 1986, Angelo Auriana has been our chef at Valentino, and he has taken the food one dramatic step further. Pino stuck to classic Italian cuisine, presented in a lighter, fresher style. Angelo has what he calls an Italian "intention," but he works with an international inventory of products—fish flown in almost daily from the Mediterranean, artisanal cheeses, locally grown produce. That is what this cookbook is all about: using high-quality products with which you can improvise on classic Italian themes. Make a recipe once to understand it, and then make it your own with whatever changes you think will work.

I do believe that you have to put your own *fantasia*—your own imagination, your sense of how a dish should taste—into your cooking. You have to put your own twist on it. If it doesn't work out exactly, you may have to try again, but I think you have to get your flavor the way you like it. These recipes are meant to guide you, but there has to be a personal touch.

Sometimes you change a dish because of certain restrictions—perhaps you are allergic to onion or pepper. Then you listen to logic and search for an alternative, and perhaps you make a dish with shallot instead of onion. Sometimes it's because you have a sense that lemon would work as nicely as vinegar, and you love the flavor of lemon. The food at Valentino and its younger siblings has always been a combination of spontaneity and discipline. You look at what you have available, and then you use sense, and logic, and your own memories to create a dish.

There is no reason to be intimidated by a recipe. Food has always been fusion. Think about it: The Americans brought corn and potatoes to Europe, the Arabs brought couscous and raisins and so much else to Italy, tomatoes came from South America and Mexico.

We have all been borrowing from each other forever. Look at me: I am the perfect fusion individual. The first seventeen years I was an Italian's Italian, but the rest? I still have an accent after thirty-whatever years. So what am I? I suppose an Italian American, a bit more American than Italian because I've been here longer. I run three Italian restaurants—where you can find caviar, or Belon oysters, or Luciano's famous barbecue sauce. We reinterpret memories, and if a dish works we add it to the portfolio. We like to challenge ourselves.

Is it authentic? There is a recipe in this book for a crab and potato pancake, which is a favorite of Luciano's. This is not an Italian dish, but we love it. We cannot get the classic Venetian *molleche*, their soft-shell crab, so we use crab from Louisiana, and we do our own preparation. It has the authenticity of our kitchen and our philosophy. It is an American dish with an Italian feeling.

This is where my journey has taken me, from my traditional Italian beginnings to a playfulness with food. When Valentino opened we were very Italian, and we insisted on Italian products—until we got burned by bad mozzarella, mediocre cheese, fish that took so long to get here I couldn't tell what it was when it arrived. Eventually I said, "Let's be logical here. Let's work with the best the market can offer and see where we go." Maybe I'll get cuttlefish from the Mediterranean, and I'll serve it the night it arrives. But perhaps another night we'll work with a Florida snapper or a Chilean sea bass instead. Santa Barbara spotted prawns are the best; why not use them? Strictly regional food, at this point, is a sentimental effort.

I'm not saying you break the rules entirely. We have never served hamburgers, no matter how much I love them, because our restaurants are not American restaurants. Until now, that is: We do have them at PS Italian Grill, the casual part of Valentino Las Vegas, because we want to be able to accommodate families with kids. But we do them our way, our interpretation. We revisit the hamburger. And I think we should call them *polpettine*—meatballs—instead.

## ON WINE

My first encounter with wine was enough to put me off it forever. Between fourth and fifth grades I got a reward for doing well in school: My father invited me to drive around the island with him in his truck. Midday he stopped to have a carafe of local wine with some of his friends, and I joined them.

*"Bevi, Pierino,"* my father said. I felt important, like one of the guys. So I drank—potent, unfiltered, unpasteurized wine. The hangover lasted for a week and made me hate wine. When my parents sent me to the *putia,* the local wine shop, Donna Santina would fill up my carafe with red wine directly from the barrel. I did the errand because I was a dutiful boy, but I was far more interested in the display of desserts and sodas than I was in the wine. Until I came to America, I always preferred a Coca-Cola or a *gassosa,* a 7UP, to a glass of wine.

When I came to live with my uncle John in California, I began gradually to understand that there was more to drinking than the raw liquid that came out of those barrels. As a young waiter at The Marquis, I learned first about the martini, because in the 1970s that was what people drank with a meal—three of them was the standard. Matching food with wine was not yet an art, and the few people who did order wine always took us by surprise. In fact, they often ended up waiting halfway through a meal for their wine, since there was such miscommunication about what they wanted and where we had stored it. Usually the waiters had to ask one of the managers to hunt for it. And we knew nothing about vintage or the importance of certain producers. During all my serving experience, mixed drinks were in style.

Can you imagine today a guy drinking a martini and smoking a cigarette while he eats his spaghetti? That's how completely things have changed. Like food, wine has improved dramatically over the last three decades. It has been a gradual awakening: The quality of wine began to improve with California's boutique wineries of the 1970s, which exploded in popularity in the 1980s. Now people turn to wine instead of hard liquor. And they realize that it is a far better accompaniment for a meal than a mixed drink. It enhances the flavors, while hard liquor actually dulls the palate and makes it more difficult to taste what's on your plate.

When I opened Valentino in 1972 we had only a short list of obvious wines. There was no passion on my part, it was just part of the job. But on the third day of business a customer asked me, "Is that all the wine you have?"

"Why?" I asked. "Don't you think we have enough?"

"No" was his blunt reply.

"Please be patient," I said. "We don't have enough money to buy wine." I was not about to confess that I had no idea what to buy, money or not.

I remember him fondly, because he forced me to think about what I was doing. I started buying books about wine. I talked more to the salesmen, and I went to seminars. I listened to my customers: If someone asked for a specific bottle that he liked, I'd order two, one for him, for the next time he came in, and one for me. I tasted everything. Slowly, our list began to grow.

The timing was perfect. We got caught up in the new curiosity about wine, and I began to develop personal relationships with various wine makers, whether they came from Tuscany or Napa Valley.

Eight years after we opened, I made my second pilgrimage to Italy. The first one had been to learn about food. This time, I was there to learn about wine. I had the same tutor, Pino Khail, and this time he took me around to the wineries. We went to Friuli to meet a great wine maker named Livio Felluga, whom I, in turn, helped make famous in this country. We met Orfeo Salvador, one of the fathers of Friuli wines, who explained big-production wine making to me. We also went to the Piedmont region. The wine makers didn't know who I was, but I was with a gentleman they respected, and I was eager. I kept saying, "I have to have this wine on my list." The genie was out of the bottle. I was enchanted.

I became a pioneer. Until that time, except for Chianti, Americans thought of France and California when they ordered wine. But I had to have what I found on that trip, I had to bring those wines back to California: For me, those wines carried memory and romance. The wine had brought me full circle, back to my childhood home, with a new appreciation of one of its most beautiful products. It inspired me to visit the wineries of my new home, California; I found a wine guru there, a man named Harry Weiss, and together we traveled through Napa Valley, visiting special wineries like Beaulieu Vineyard and Freemark Abbey.

I was moving fast. In 1981, *Wine Spectator* magazine gave Valentino its first Grand Award, and a decade later we had over 60,000 bottles of wine in our cellar. Then, in 1994, the Northridge earthquake struck. I arrived at the restaurant to see a river of red flowing under the front door, and 20,000 broken bottles upstairs. I was devastated—and very moved by the response from wine makers. Pino Khail wrote to the vintners whose wines I had introduced into this country, and one by one they helped me recover. They sent me wine as a gift, as a way of saying thank you for being their ambassador. They replaced many bottles, and inspired me to rebuild, with an even more varied inventory.

Today Valentino has over 100,000 bottles, 75,000 of them upstairs, with new shelving to protect them. Wine is no longer just part of doing business, as it was in 1972. For me now it is a passion, a great love. When I drink a glass of fine wine, it is the quintessential reward of life. I appreciate every single note, just like with music; the delicacy of the composition, the uniqueness of the flavors. It's a wonderful pleasure—and to be able to share it with my customers gives me a great satisfaction. I like to be able to take other people with me, to surprise them with a bottle from a small, artisanal supplier, or to serve friends who have been to Italy a bottle from the region he or she visited.

There is nothing mysterious about wine. Think about wine the way you think about food: You know the difference between a great apple and a mediocre apple—the taste and texture are different. It is no different with a great wine and a mediocre wine.

When I give seminars, I tell people to begin with the five S's: see, smell, swirl, sip, and swallow. Pour some wine into your glass and look at it. The color is very important—the color should be pure, not cloudy, because cloudiness means that air has gotten into the bottle, and an oxidized wine will not taste right.

Next, drink the wine with your nose. What I mean is, smell the wine and think about what you smell, whether it's certain fruit, greenery, tobacco, leather, vanilla, or lemon. You can identify the elements yourself.

The third step is to swirl the wine in the glass. The swirling breaks open the wine, so that it becomes like a blossoming flower.

Then, of course, you sip the wine, roll it around in your mouth, try to identify the complex flavors. And last, you swallow—though I always tell people, if you're at a wine tasting and there are several wines, what you really want to do is spit it out, like the pros. Otherwise you're going to have a lot of hangovers on your way to enlightenment.

The difference between a great wine and a good wine is one of degree. You consider the clarity of color, the fruit, the level of acidity, and the complexity of the various elements.

A quality low-yield wine is one where you gently press the grapes, get the best juice, and that's it. A bad wine? One that tastes harsh and is made carelessly. It is the opposite of a low-yield wine: Certain producers will overcraft their grapes, which means that they squeeze and squeeze to get more juice, even though it is not the best juice. It's easy for you to recognize: Take a sip and it tastes thin or sulfuric. And it leaves a burned aftertaste in your mouth. You can trust your own senses on that one.

Once you start to taste, and think about pleasant combinations of food and wine, you can enjoy pairing them. I like to play around with combinations. The wine recommendations that accompany the recipes in this book are meant as suggestions. They are my choices, but use them as a starting point for your own experimentation.

I have some general preferences, too, which will help you get started:

We are supposed to serve white wine with fish, but for meaty fish like tuna, salmon, or halibut I like a soft red wine that provides an excess of flavor: a fruitier, light red like a young Pinot Noir or a Valpolicella.

I like a dry, steely white wine with delicate seafood, because I'm afraid an overly oaky white will detract from the freshness of the product. I have a hard time matching a Chardonnay, like anyone who is serious about wine, because the terms most people use to describe Chardonnay are "fatty," or "tropical fruit," or "overly rich with vanilla." Those are all strong sensations that can overpower a dish. A glass of wine is supposed to cleanse the mouth, to finish the sensation, not to keep stretching into new sensations. It is not a meal on its own.

I like bigger white wines with rich sauces, a big white burgundy to accompany a shrimp or lobster dish with any kind of sauce.

And, of course, a long-aged red wine—a Cabernet, Merlot, Barolo, or red Rhone—is perfect with main courses like lamb, rabbit, or game. You have such a richness in the meat, such a fattiness in the taste, that you need a perfectly matured wine to mix in between the flavors.

There are rules about what not to do, too, though much of this is common sense. A light white wine with a steak doesn't make any sense, nor does a sweet wine with a grilled lamb chop. If you don't know a lot about wine, find someone to trust, like a local wine merchant, and tell them what you're serving. They should be able to keep you from making a bad mistake.

I also suggest that people who are not overly sophisticated about wine stay away from highly tannic wine like a young Bordeaux or Brunello. Eventually the tannin will develop into fruit, but if you do not have a trained palate you are tasting elements that are more chemical than pleasurable. It's like looking at a flower blossom that is still closed.

Beyond that, a handful of foods make trouble for wine—artichokes, which can make a wine taste sweeter than it is; chocolate, a strong, complicated food that defies many wines; and an excess of vinegar in a salad dressing, which will fight with whatever wine you serve. There are ways around artichokes and chocolate, which you will find in the recipes that include those ingredients. As for vinegar, our salads are dressed lightly, or drizzled with olive oil alone, and will not present a problem.

As you become confident, you will find yourself more willing to try new things. It's all a matter of tasting and thinking, and letting your imagination and experience guide you. When I started, I played by the rules because I didn't know anything, and those rules protected me from dreadful mistakes. Now I have knowledge, and a team of people at the restaurants who love to experiment with wine. Together we have become trendsetters in terms of what happens with Italian food and Italian wine. I see wine not as a winery tourist, not as a consumer, but as part of a developing group of people who are passionate about wine. The restaurant—or, as you try these combinations of food and wine, your dining room—is the last link in a chain that begins with Mother Earth and the grapes planted there, and ends when a wonderful wine is poured into a glass.

## THE ESSENTIALS

When I was a boy every kitchen had a *dispensa,* a big cupboard where everything was stored. In the old days there were more glass jars than canned goods, because most things were homemade—like tomato paste, which was a collaboration with the neighbors. In September, when tomato season was over, we would buy the leftovers at a discounted price, and everyone on the street would get together. The women squeezed the liquid and the flesh out of the tomatoes, pureed them, added a little olive oil, and put it into jars.

Then the tomato skins were dried in the sun, sprinkled with some salt—and magic, we had sun-dried tomatoes. We put them on wooden mats, covered them with nets against the flies, and when they were dry put them in glass jars, again with olive oil. That way we had tomatoes all winter. We used them to make sandwiches, sprinkled with some more oil and basil. We used them with pasta. We cut some salami and some of our homemade bread, served it with a dried tomato, and there was another tradition. And always some cheese, locally made.

Those were the staples of the dispensa: tomatoes, olive oil, salami, cheese, bread. And we had jars of peppers, green and black olives, dried beans and lentils, and *baccalà*—the salted, dried cod. Refrigeration was almost nonexistent—the iceman sold ice and that was it—so we depended on things that did not have to be kept cold. There was always something in the dispensa that could be turned into a meal.

The same is true today. On those nights when you don't feel like going out—not to a restaurant, not even to the market—you can make a meal out of what you have in the pantry. But you have much more to choose from than we did. Between your pantry, refrigerator, and freezer, you can have on hand a wonderful array of staples.

Starting with the pantry—always have some canned tomatoes and dried or canned beans, and of course some dry pasta. In ten minutes you can make a flavorful instant meal of pasta with tomatoes or pasta with lentils.

A bottle of extra-virgin olive oil is indispensable, along with white vinegar to make a vinaigrette. Balsamic vinegar is nice to have on hand, but it's really just for specialty dishes.

You have to have onions, because they are the start of any sauce. A little garlic is always welcome, but never powdered. Fresh garlic lasts for a long time, and there is nothing like peeling it at the last moment to get the juice and pungency. Powdered garlic has almost a chemical smell. I stay away from it.

But dried herbs are okay, since it's hard to find fresh ones all the time—at least dried oregano, thyme, rosemary, and bay leaves. Salt to give balance to your food—normal salt to spice up a dish and kosher salt for cooking and marinating. Fresh pepper to spark a salad, a bland pasta, a piece of fish. Salt is the balance; pepper is the kick.

And have some cans of good Italian tuna, in olive oil or water. Tuna should be in every pantry because it adds a lot of flavor to any salad or pasta. A couple of jars of artichokes and peppers, and you have everything you need for an antipasti and a nice first course.

Finally, there are a few basic items you have to have. You need flour and sugar in case you're going to be ambitious about pasta or dessert. You need either homemade or canned chicken broth and beef broth—no little cubes, they're as bad as powdered garlic—and a little bottle of clam juice. That's it. That's the pantry.

In the refrigerator, always have unsalted butter, olives, and an eggplant. Keep a couple of lemons and a head of lettuce, a good spicy *salame*, and two basic cheeses—a hard cheese like Parmesan or pecorino that you can grate fresh at the last moment, and a creamy cheese to put out whenever you feel like it.

In the freezer, keep a chicken, some pizza dough, and some bread dough, so you're close to my tradition of fresh bread with a meal.

For dessert, let's be honest: There is nothing like Häagen-Dazs. Beyond that I believe in doing things with fruit—something simple, like strawberries in balsamic vinegar. Keep eggs in the refrigerator and you can whip up a quick zabaglione with eggs, sugar, and a touch of marsala wine or sherry.

To make a pantry work, though, you have to use your imagination. It's all about improvising—you see what you have in cans, what's left over, what's fresh, and you come up with some ideas. You have a couple of tomatoes and some leftover bread? Warm the bread, cut it into small slices, top with chopped tomato and a drizzle of olive oil, and you have bruschetta for an antipasto.

YOU CAN STOCK YOUR HOME with a basic selection of wines, as well. Here are some guidelines:

Don't have expensive wines unless you have a proper cellar. Or buy them for a special occasion.

Stay with light, fresh wines, primarily whites. Two good basic whites are Pinot Grigio and Pinot Bianco. I like the Trebbiano grape, or Sauvignon or Chardonnay. Then have a French white that costs a little more but doesn't break the bank, one with an interesting flavor, a Sancerre or other Loire. That way you've covered a good range.

Serve the Pinot Grigio or Pinot Bianco to start, while you snack on some olives or a little piece of cheese or pâté. Then go to the Chardonnay if you're going to have a light seafood, a squid salad or carpaccio of tuna. If you have a spicier, more aggressive appetizer, go for the Sancerre or again, the Chardonnay. If you're going on to a pasta or second course, serve a red wine, but with moderation—something light, fresh, and crispy.

For red wines, look for value, don't look for the big name. Try a young Chianti or a French Beaujolais, or a wonderful Pinot Noir from the Sonoma Carneros area or from Oregon. Go to a wine store where they seem sincere about what they are doing, and be straight about what you're looking for: Spend six dollars on something from Chile, or southern Italy, or Australia, and educate yourself.

I would be very happy to keep a varietal called Barbera in my home, whether from California or Italy, or a Regaleali Rosso from Sicily, or a good Chilean Cabernet. You don't have to spend a lot of money.

As for storage, if you don't have a cellar, put the bottles underneath your bed. Or in your closet where it's dark. Don't store it in a wine rack on top of the refrigerator or just hanging around the kitchen. After a couple of days the sun and heat exposure will affect it.

So now you have everything you need to make a nice dinner without having to leave your house. The only question remaining is: What equipment do you need to make it?

EQUIPMENT

The idea behind these recipes is to spend your money on the ingredients, not on a lot of specialized kitchen equipment. We have standard ingredients in the pantry that serve as the basis for many dishes—and in the same way, we have a basic array of pots, pans, and utensils. If you want to buy a pasta maker, a reasonably priced manual machine is all you need; it is what we use in the restaurant. And if your life doesn't make time for fresh pasta, then buy it fresh. You can find it now at many grocery stores, and it works for all but the most elegant dishes. You can buy a ravioli cutter, or a mold that cuts a long sheet into dozens of ravioli at once—or you can use a kitchen knife. Remember, these are dishes that got their start long before we had fancy appliances, so don't be intimidated.

Here is what you need:

*Sauté pans or skillets:* These are the most useful pans in the Valentino kitchen; we have stacks of them at the restaurant. Look for ones that are ovenproof. For home use, you need several different sizes.

> three 7-inch, nonstick
> two 9-inch
> one 12-inch

*A stockpot, with a cover and a pasta insert:* for soups and pasta, 8–12-quart capacity.

*Saucepans:* again, an array of sizes, same as above. Also, one of each of the following:

> 2¼ quart
> 3¼ quart
> 5¼ quart

*A large colander or strainer.*

*Mixing bowls:* We like to have a lot of little bowls around, for chopped herbs or garlic, or to hold ingredients prepared in advance. And a set of graduated mixing bowls, from small to large.

*A roasting pan:* 10 × 13 inch, with a rack.

*A baking sheet and a jelly roll pan,* which is basically a baking sheet with sides.

*Utensils:*
Knives: from very small ones to a bread knife to a fish knife and a meat knife for deboning.

Wooden spoons: We insist on wooden spoons to stir risotto, because you can't feel the rice with a metal spoon. You can't have too many of these.

> Tongs
> Spatula
> Measuring spoons and cups

*A cheese grater.*

*A food processor:* essential for purees, and great for a fast batch of pasta or pizza dough.

Those are the essentials. If you want to go further and be able to tackle almost anything in this book, you'll need to add a few more items:

A pasta machine, if you're determined to make your own
4-ounce custard cups
A ravioli cutter
A pastry bag for piping fillings or decorative desserts

I have seen many different restaurant kitchens, and I have watched the Valentino kitchen grow from a little two-man operation to a beautifully efficient place where fifteen people turn out as many as 150 to 200 dinners in a single evening.

To keep a restaurant kitchen running, you have to do "prep" in advance; in fact, we have a prep staff, whose job it is to get ingredients ready for the chefs. If our chef is making the pheasant breast with pancetta, he has at his disposal chopped garlic, chopped onions, clean, fresh herbs, even the cleaned and trimmed pheasant breasts. Someone else did it for him.

Most home cooks are not that lucky, though you may be able to enlist a family member to help scrape carrots or dice onions. But there are always chores you can do in advance, to give yourself some breathing room. Whenever possible, we have divided the recipes in this book into two parts—"Preparation," which can be done early, and "The Dish," which is what you do right before a meal.

The idea is to make the cook part of the dining experience. You should not be scrambling in the kitchen while your guests enjoy a glass of wine and a good conversation. With a little bit of advance work, you can enjoy the meal you've made.

One note about ingredients: We have a handful of basic rules in our restaurant kitchens, and they apply when making these recipes in your homes, as well. When we call for olive oil, we mean extra-virgin olive oil. Butter is always unsalted and we never use margarine. Parmesan should be the best you can buy, and certainly, if it's a featured part of a recipe, ask for Parmigiano Reggiano. Garlic is always fresh, never powdered, and always chopped, never put through a garlic press, because it releases its flavors better that way. And stock never comes from a cube.

THE VALENTINO COOKBOOK

# Antipasti

✤

Toasted Garlic and Garlic-Infused Olive Oil
Herb-Infused Olive Oil
Frico (Parmesan Chips)
I Pomodorini (Little Tomatoes)
Le Arancine di Lina (Lina's Rice Croquettes)
Le Creme di Paola (Dips)
Triangoli di Mozzarella in Carrozza (Hot Mozzarella Triangles)
Sfogliantine di Asparagi (Asparagus in Puff Pastry)
Cappe di Funghi con Spinaci (Spinach-Filled Mushroom Caps)
I Carciofi Ripieni di Lina (Lina's Stuffed Artichokes)
Peperoni Imbottiti di Zia Santina
(Aunt Santina's Stuffed Peppers)
Grilled Pizza
Involtini di Melanzane (Wrapped Eggplant and Cheese)
Involtini di Pesce Spada con Couscous Trapanese
(Swordfish Involtini with Couscous)
Involtini di Pesce Spada con Salsa al Salmoriglio
(Stuffed Swordfish Rolls with Salmoriglio Sauce)
Involtini d'Anatra (Duck Involtini)
Gamberetti Avvolti in Zucchine con Sentori di
Senape ed Arancio
(Zucchini-Wrapped Shrimp with Orange Mustard Dressing)
Variation: Rotolo di Zucchine con Gamberi in Insalata
(Shrimp in Zucchini)
Gamberoni e Cannellini all'Olio Toscano
(Shrimp and White Beans in Tuscan Oil)
Crostata di Carciofi all'Aglio e Gamberi di Fiume in Brodo d'Aragosta
(Artichoke Tart with Crayfish and
Roasted Garlic in Lobster Broth)
Couscous con Gamberoni Piccanti
(Marinated Shrimp with Couscous)
Polpette di Astice e Gamberetti (Shrimp and Lobster Polpette)

※

*Tortino d'Astice allo Spumante*
*(Lobster Tortino with Champagne Sauce)*
*Frittelle di Granchio e Patate*
*(Crab and Potato Pancakes with Roasted Garlic Butter Sauce)*
*Capesante Avvolte in Piccole Melanzane con*
*Fagioli Cannellini*
*(Jumbo Scallops Wrapped in*
*Japanese Eggplant with Tuscan Beans)*
*Cozze al Basilico in Salsa di Agrumi*
*(Mussels with Basil in a Citrus Sauce)*
*Carpaccio di Salmone (Cured Salmon)*
*Carpaccio di Tonno ai Capperi*
*(Tuna Carpaccio with Caper Dressing)*
*Crostata di Funghi con Fontina e Crema di Tartufo*
*(Mushroom Tart with Fontina and Truffle Cream Sauce)*
*Polpettine di Carne*
*(Little Meatballs with Peppers)*

*Antipasti*

# ✤ *Antipasti*

EVERYTHING WE SERVE AT THE RESTAURANTS GOES THROUGH THE FUN-
nel of my food culture, which started in Sicily with the basics. How did we begin a big meal? My mother would put out colorful plates of tomatoes, peppers, eggplant, olives, and perhaps a little bit of cheese. And at boarding school, even though the nuns had to feed about a hundred kids, there was always the little starter. We believed in the ritual of the antipasti.

What I remember best were the *fritti* they served us: little fried fish, smelts and sardines—people's fish. Forty years later, that has become the grand *fritto misto,* with scallops and shrimp and all of those fine things. But when I look back, I sometimes think that those very basic fish had a wonderful depth of flavor—served fresh, lightly coated with a little breading and lemon and garlic. Or the nuns would serve little pieces of fish mixed with potatoes, and maybe some greens.

The beauty of growth and evolution is that you don't have to forget the essentials, what came before. So the antipasti recipes are all about taking simple ingredients and turning them into an inviting start to a meal.

For me, they can be a whole meal. One of the most memorable evenings I ever spent was at a little restaurant called L'Ambasciata, near Mantua, in late 1985. Valentino was very successful, and I was looking for new inspiration, a new challenge. I wanted to open a second restaurant, Primi, for people like me, who love an array of small tastes. So I came to this restaurant, in a little house in a microscopic village, Quistello, where Romano, his sister, and his niece, all impeccably dressed in white, presided over the fifteen tables. I asked them to send us only *primi,* first courses.

In no time, two plates were put in front of us: three tortelli for me, dished right out of the copper pan, and three for my friend Maurizio Zanella, owner of Ca'del Bosco, one of the foremost Italian wineries. Just as we bit through this melting pasta, a forkful of noodles in oxtail ragù arrived. And on, and on; a meal I will never forget. It convinced me that a restaurant like Primi could happen. It was my idea of the perfect meal—somebody stands behind your chair and keeps serving little portions of many different things.

In a formal meal, antipasti and primi are separate courses—the primi are usually pasta or risotto. But at Primi, anything could, and did, come first. The idea was to put a lot of plates on the table and try things. Antipasti could be a whole meal; many people never got around to the pastas. An assortment of salami and a beautiful plate of greens, or our famous crepes filled with a savory duck puree, were a standard light dinner for many of our customers.

We use that same idea at Valentino, though in a more ambitious way. A great deal of the time, people simply say, "Leave it up to Piero," and I am responsible for designing a meal and matching wines to the various dishes. When I compose a tasting menu, a *fantasia,* I like to start with a cold antipasto, then a hot one. Or maybe two of each, if everyone is having fun. After that, we move on to a pasta or risotto. If the customers start looking at me as if to say, "No more punishment," then we skip the *secondi* and think about cheese or dessert. A full Italian meal has been accomplished, though not in the traditional manner.

But concentrating on antipasti is the perfect way to have fun eating. You can play around with second courses and turn them into antipasti—or the other way around, if you like a first plate so much that you lose interest in whatever is supposed to come next. Really, you get to decide.

## TOASTED GARLIC AND GARLIC-INFUSED OLIVE OIL

1¼ cups olive oil

10–15 garlic cloves, thinly sliced

In a saucepan or skillet, warm ¼ cup of the olive oil over medium heat. Add the garlic slices and sauté until medium golden in color. Drain and reserve the oil for cooking something else. Place the garlic in a glass jar or bottle and add the remaining olive oil. Store in a cool, dark cabinet or in the refrigerator, for up to 10 days.

## HERB-INFUSED OLIVE OIL

2 cups olive oil

2 sprigs fresh rosemary

6 sprigs fresh thyme

6 sprigs fresh Italian parsley

3 sprigs fresh tarragon (or any fresh
    herbs you like)

In a glass jar, combine the olive oil and herbs. Allow to sit for 2–3 days, then remove the herbs and discard. The oil should be kept in a dark cabinet.

# FRICO / Parmesan Chips

*4–6 servings*

I had heard that some people were making a delicious snack with leftover cheese rind, and I was puzzled by the idea. I called Antonio Santini, owner of Dal Pescatore, one of three three-star restaurants in Italy, and he gave me his interpretation, where you practically grill the rind. Luciano Pellegrini, the chef at Posto, and I decided to experiment. We weren't satisfied, because the rind was kind of chewy. So we decided to try the cheese in a nonstick pan. The cheese is so oily and full of flavor, I thought, let's just stick it in the pan and see what happens. That turned out to be the key to success. The traditional *frico* is a Friulian dish made with Montasio, a creamier cheese that is very hard to find in America. That's fried cheese, almost like a pancake topped with meat or vegetables. This is flakier and softer. Serve it when people walk in the door.

---

*2 cups domestic Parmesan cheese, processed to a powder*

⚙ *Chef's Tip:* Domestic Parmesan cheese—the supermarket kind—is fine for this recipe. The imported Italian Parmesan cheese used for eating or adding to pasta is actually too dry. Buy a tub of already grated domestic Parmesan cheese and process in a food processor until it has a powdery consistency. And cook on medium heat; any higher and the oil in the Parmesan cheese comes out, making a gummy texture.

Heat a nonstick skillet over medium heat. Sprinkle enough Parmesan cheese to just cover the bottom of the pan (for a 9-inch pan, use about 3–4 tablespoons cheese). When it is golden brown—which can take less than 1 minute—use a pair of tongs to grab the edge and gently lift it out of the pan. Turn and cook the other side briefly.

Blot excess oil on a paper towel.

Working quickly, shape the frico on a rolling pin to form a cylinder, or around the base of a cup to form a basket.

Serve alone as an *assaggino*—the little morsel you offer guests when they arrive. Or use the frico as a container—for example, to hold the couscous in the marinated shrimp-and-couscous antipasto.

*Wine:* It is traditional to start with a glass of sparkling wine, which we Italians call the *aperitivo*. I'm particularly fond of Prosecco, which is made by the *methode charmat*, where they rack the whole barrel, shaking it back and forth to stabilize the pressure, rather than the *methode champenoise*, where individual bottles are turned by hand, so it's not so labor intensive. I suggest Prosecco di Valdobbiadene, and my favorite producer is Ruggeri. Or try a fresh Pinot Grigio or the Vin Gris de Cigare by Bonny Doon.

❈

*Making frico: "Working quickly, shape the frico on a rolling pin to form a cylinder."*

## I POMODORINI / Little Tomatoes

*4 servings*

A movie producer used to come in every night for two or three years, and his standard salad was greens with cherry tomatoes. He loved them. The classic Italian salad has Roma tomatoes instead, but he loved these so much we started playing with them. We were already stuffing mushrooms and zucchini. So we tried tomatoes, and then went to the next level of sophistication with three different fillings. The combination of seafood and tomatoes is a given in Italian cuisine, as is tomatoes and cheese. So we used several "poor" ingredients, leftovers, to come up with something flavorful. You can use your imagination. But color and presentation are important here—serve on a beautiful ceramic platter or a plain white dish with bunches of greens.

---

*24 cherry tomatoes*
*Fresh parsley for garnish*

FOR THE TUNA FILLING
*4 ounces imported canned tuna*
  *in oil, drained*
*2 select anchovy fillets*
*½ cup (4 ounces) cream cheese*
*6 imported black olives, pitted*
  *and chopped*
*2 chives, finely chopped*

FOR THE CHEESE FILLING
*8 ounces Gorgonzola cheese*
*½ cup (4 ounces) cream cheese*
*4 tablespoons Italian parsley,*
  *finely chopped*
*1 tablespoon capers, finely chopped*
*Salt and pepper, to taste*

*Preparation:* Scoop out the pulp and seeds of the tomatoes, and discard. Sprinkle the tomatoes with salt. Allow to drain upside down on a paper towel.

TO MAKE THE TUNA FILLING: In a small bowl, combine the tuna, anchovies, and cream cheese and mix well to blend. Stir in the olives and chives.

TO MAKE THE CHEESE FILLING: In a small bowl, mash the Gorgonzola cheese with a fork. Add the cream cheese, parsley, capers, and salt and pepper.

TO MAKE THE PESTO FILLING: In a blender or food processor fitted with the steel blade, combine the pine nuts, Parmesan cheese, garlic oil, cream cheese, parsley, basil, and salt and pepper.

Refrigerate the fillings until ready to serve.

*The Dish:* Using a small spoon, stuff 8 tomatoes with the tuna filling, 8 with the cheese filling, and 8 with the pesto filling.

Arrange them on a platter and garnish with sprigs of fresh parsley.

FOR THE PESTO FILLING

*1 tablespoon pine nuts*

*2 tablespoons Parmesan cheese,*
*grated*

*2 tablespoons Garlic-Infused*
*Olive Oil (see page 7)*

*¼ cup cream cheese*

*4 tablespoons Italian parsley*

*4 tablespoons fresh basil*

*Salt and pepper, to taste*

*Wine:* Again, pour a glass of Prosecco to start. Or serve a wine that is dry and light, but also elegant and fresh, such as a Soave Classico—Gini or Pieropan—or a crisp, refreshing wine from the central part of Italy, like a Grechetto from Umbria, or a Verdicchio di Matelica.

## LE ARANCINE DI LINA / Lina's Rice Croquettes

*6 servings*

2 cups Beef Stock (see page 73)
  or Chicken Stock (see page 74)
1 tablespoon onion, chopped
8 ounces arborio rice
2 tablespoons olive oil
1 teaspoon saffron, optional
2 tablespoons Parmesan cheese,
  grated
2 tablespoons pecorino cheese,
  grated
3 large eggs
1 small onion, chopped
¼ cup (2 ounces) butter
4 ounces ground veal or pork
1½ cups Tomato and Basil Sauce
  (see page 84)
3 tablespoons frozen peas
Salt and pepper, to taste

1 large egg, hard-boiled
4 ounces mozzarella cheese
⅔ cup flour
1 cup bread crumbs
1 gallon peanut oil

*Preparation:* Heat the broth.

In a heavy casserole dish, toast the tablespoon of onion and the rice over medium-high heat. When the rice begins to crackle, add the olive oil, a pinch of salt, and 1 cup of warm broth. Cook according to the basic risotto recipe (see page 128), adding broth until the rice is al dente. Add the saffron at the last minute. Remove from the heat and let cool.

*The Dish:* Combine the cooled rice with the grated cheeses and 1 egg.

In a small skillet over medium heat, sauté the remaining onion in the butter. Add the ground meat and cook until meat is browned. Add the tomato sauce, let simmer for 15 minutes, and add the peas. Salt and pepper to taste.

Chop the hard-boiled egg and the mozzarella cheese, and set each aside. Beat the remaining 2 eggs.

To assemble the arancine, dust your hands with flour and take a small amount of rice in the palm of your hand. Flatten the rice, and place 1 teaspoon of the meat ragù in the center, along with a little mozzarella cheese and hard-boiled egg.

Close your palm and form an oval shape, adding more rice if necessary. Shape the rice into a cone, making sure the filling is securely sealed in the center. Roll each rice cone in the flour, the beaten eggs, and then the bread crumbs. Continue until you have used up all the rice.

Heat the peanut oil to about 350 degrees and fry the arancine until golden brown on all sides. Drain on paper towels and serve immediately.

*Shaping arancine with Lina, Piero's mother.*

I have an adopted mother in my life, Paola Di Mauro, who lives outside of Rome. She is a woman of many skills, who in her later life has put to work all her great talents—gardening, making wine, preparing preserved items. But her biggest talent is her cooking. In her house, you find that embrace of the table that is so Italian and so important. The art of eating merges with the art of living.

Paola is the first person who made me understand the pleasure of elegant and creative food outside of restaurants. In a very small kitchen, with one little stove, she produces memorable dinners with a great variety of courses. I learned about foods that are brilliant, simple, uncamouflaged—a triumph of freshness. It all comes from the meticulous choice of great ingredients.

These *creme* are *assaggino*—little things to serve with little bruschette, toast, or special crackers while people are standing around waiting to eat.

---

FOR THE CREMA DI PROSCIUTTO
*8 ounces imported prosciutto cotto
    or cooked ham*
*½ cup ricotta cheese*
*½ cup (4 ounces) butter*
*1 cup mascarpone cheese*
*1 teaspoon pink peppercorns, crushed*

FOR THE CREMA DI TONNO
*8 ounces imported canned tuna
    in oil, drained*
*1 cup mascarpone cheese*
*1 teaspoon chives, chopped,
    for garnish*

FOR THE CREMA DI GORGONZOLA
*½ cup (4 ounces) Gorgonzola cheese*
*¾ cup mascarpone cheese*
*½ cup heavy cream*
*Dash of cognac*
*1 teaspoon Italian parsley, finely
    chopped, for garnish*

*Preparation:* Soak prosciutto or ham in cognac for 5 minutes.

*The Dish:* TO MAKE EACH CREMA: Combine the ingredients in a food processor and blend until smooth. Refrigerate until ready to eat, garnish with herbs, and serve with crusty bread.

*Wine:* Serve wines that are silky, clean, and have flowery tones, like a Marino Oro Bianco from Colle Picchione or a Regaleali Bianco from Sicily. Otherwise a very buttery Chardonnay like Kistler, Flowers, or Freemark Abbey.

# TRIANGOLI DI MOZZARELLA IN CARROZZA /
## Hot Mozzarella Triangles

*6 servings*

This was the first recipe the *Los Angeles Times* asked us to print back in the days of checkered tablecloths. We still serve it as a little knickknack, a finger food. It doesn't have to be the same as it used to be. You can make delicate *crostini,* and not emphasize the anchovy or cheese. But this is Italian-American food from day one.

FOR THE MARINARA SAUCE

*½ cup olive oil*

*1 large onion, chopped*

*3 garlic cloves, chopped*

*3 anchovy fillets, chopped*

*1¼ pounds fresh Italian plum*
*    tomatoes, peeled, seeded,*
*    and coarsely chopped*

*Salt and pepper, to taste*

*8 basil leaves, thinly sliced*

FOR THE FRIED CHEESE

*3 tablespoons all-purpose flour*

*12 slices fresh mozzarella cheese*
*    (in water), 2 inches square,*
*    ½ inch thick*

*3 large eggs, beaten*

*2 cups bread crumbs, finely ground*

*4 cups vegetable oil*

*Preparation:* FOR THE SAUCE: In a medium-size saucepan, warm the olive oil over medium heat and add the chopped onion, garlic, and anchovies. Sauté until the onions are a light golden color and add the tomatoes. Season with salt and pepper.

Bring to a boil, reduce heat, and simmer for 15 minutes. Add the basil. Strain the sauce, discard the solids, and return the liquid to the pan.

*The Dish:* Flour the slices of cheese on both sides and dip in the egg. Roll in the bread crumbs to coat on all sides.

In a large skillet, heat the oil until hot (350 degrees). Fry 3–4 slices of mozzarella cheese at a time, until browned on both sides. Remove from oil and drain on paper towels. Place on a serving dish and ladle the warm sauce over the cheese.

*Wine:* A very fresh Barbera, like Conterno-Fantino—rich in fruit, clean, and able to cleanse the anchovy, or a very dry, rich sparkling wine like Ca'del Bosco—a *blanc de noir,* well structured, fresh, and harmonious.

This is just a little appetizer for a special evening, when you want something conservative that everyone will like—and what's more conservative than asparagus and puff pastry? The ricotta makes it a little more flavorful—we hope it becomes addictive.

---

*2 bunches (1½ pounds) baby asparagus*

*2 cups fresh ricotta cheese, drained well*

*2 large eggs*

*1 pound puff pastry (if frozen, defrost according to directions on package)*

*Preparation:* In a pot of boiling salted water, blanch the asparagus stalks for 3 minutes. Rinse in cold water and dice into ¼-inch pieces.

In a medium bowl, mix together the asparagus, ricotta cheese, and 1 egg. Spoon mixture into a pastry bag with a large tip.

In a small bowl, whisk the remaining egg. Set aside for brushing the pastry.

*The Dish:* Divide the puff pastry in half and return half to the refrigerator. On a lightly floured surface, roll out the pastry into a rectangle, about ⅛ inch thick. Working with the longer side parallel to the edge of the counter, pipe a 1-inch-thick row of filling, 1 inch above the bottom edge of the dough. Brush the top edge of the dough with egg. Starting at the bottom, roll up the pastry to enclose the filling. Slice the log into small individual pieces, 1 inch wide. Place on a parchment-lined baking sheet and brush with egg. Refrigerate for 30 minutes.

Preheat the oven to 300 degrees. Bake for 10–15 minutes and serve at once.

*Wine:* Champagne to start. For a less expensive bottle, stick with California—Chandon Brut or Iron Horse, or try a Spanish or Italian brut. If this is the start of a fancier meal, I like Louis Roederer Premier.

*6 servings*

In the early days at Valentino we tried hard to come up with alternatives to old-fashioned Italian appetizers like shrimp scampi, and also have an option for vegetarian requests. This is a twist on the traditional mushrooms stuffed with bread crumbs and garlic. The spinach gives a light flavor and a healthy, creamy texture. Depending on the size of the serving, you can use it in many different ways. And though it's a dish from the past, we've now discovered better mushrooms—fresh portobellos, shiitakes, many other varieties—so it's worth revisiting.

---

*12 large mushrooms, uniform in size*
*6 tablespoons (3 ounces) butter*
*2 shallots, finely chopped*
*1 cup steamed or boiled spinach,*
*    finely chopped, water*
*    squeezed out*
*Salt and pepper, to taste*
*1 large egg*
*1 tablespoon Italian parsley,*
*    finely chopped*
*¼ cup plus 2 tablespoons fresh*
*    bread crumbs*
*½ cup dry white wine*

*Preparation:* Trim the stems off the mushrooms and finely chop stems. Melt half of the butter and set aside.

*The Dish:* Preheat the oven to 375 degrees.

In a large skillet over medium heat, brown the shallots in the remaining butter for about 5 minutes. Add mushroom stems to the shallots and cook about 3 more minutes. Stir in the spinach and salt and pepper and cook for 1 more minute. Remove from the heat and allow to cool.

Oil a shallow baking pan and place the mushroom caps in it. Sprinkle them with salt and pepper.

In a large bowl, combine the egg, parsley, and ¼ cup of the bread crumbs. Add the spinach mixture and mix to combine. Fill the mushroom caps with the mixture and sprinkle with the remaining bread crumbs. Drizzle the melted butter over the mushrooms.

Pour the wine into the baking pan and bake for about 20 minutes, until the mushrooms are soft and the bread crumbs are lightly browned.

*Wine:* A soft red: a rich, almost creamy Sangiovese, especially from Emilia-Romagna, or a flowery red from Verona, like a Valpolicella or a no-oak Cabernet—these will all provide a very friendly marriage. They are easy to sip and are clean in the mouth, tasting of blackberries and a little grass, with a smoky finish of herbs and violets.

I remember this dish from my childhood. The artichokes were placed in the center of the table and we all ate from the dish together. You can easily make this the day before, for the flavors will stay with it.

---

*6 large artichokes*

*1 lemon, cut into quarters*

*2 tablespoons bread crumbs,*
*finely ground*

*2 anchovy fillets, chopped*

*2 garlic cloves, finely chopped*

*1 tablespoon parsley,*
*finely chopped*

*¼ cup olive oil*

*1 cup dry white wine*

*Preparation:* Remove the outer leaves and slice off the top 1–2 inches of the artichokes. Scoop out the fuzzy inner choke. Squeeze the juice from the lemon into a large bowl of water, along with the lemon, and store the trimmed artichokes in the water until ready to use. The lemon prevents them from turning brown.

TO MAKE THE STUFFING: Combine the bread crumbs, anchovies, garlic, and parsley. Stuff the cavity of the artichoke, filling between the inner leaves with any extra stuffing.

*The Dish:* In a small saucepan, warm the oil over medium heat. Add the stuffed artichokes and pour the wine over them. Simmer gently for 1 hour, until the leaves pull off easily and their meat is tender. Serve hot.

*Wine:* For this dish, you'll want a neutral, light red wine to contrast with the harshness of the artichoke. I suggest a very basic table wine from the south of Italy: a Corvo Rosso from Sicily, or a Cirò from Calabria. Hopefully the rich stuffing will compensate for the metallic flavor of the simple artichoke.

## PEPERONI IMBOTTITI DI ZIA SANTINA /
## Aunt Santina's Stuffed Peppers

*6 servings*

Peppers are a way of life in southern Italy, and stuffed peppers were something I loved as a child. My mother made them for the holidays, and the nuns made them on special occasions for obvious reasons—peppers are a cheap vegetable you can stuff with crumbs, canned tuna, and whatever leftovers you have. As we learned later, you can use colorful peppers, smaller peppers, and you can lighten the stuffing. Since I am Sicilian, this recipe goes back to the Arab tradition, with raisins and pine nuts, eggs, cheese, and crumbs. Everything else is optional.

---

*3½ ounces (about 2 slices) white bread, without the crust*

*½–1 cup milk, for soaking the bread*

*6 large yellow bell peppers*

*¼ cup raisins*

*½ cup water or wine, for soaking the raisins*

*1 small bunch (1 cup) basil, finely chopped*

*1 small bunch (1 cup) parsley, finely chopped*

*8 anchovy fillets, finely chopped*

*3 tablespoons capers, finely chopped*

*3 tablespoons pine nuts*

*1¼ cups imported black olives, pitted and sliced*

*Salt and pepper, to taste*

*½ cup olive oil*

*1¼ cups canned tomato puree*

*Preparation:* Soak the bread in the milk until soft, about 10–15 minutes. Squeeze out excess milk and set aside.

On a grill or over an open flame on the stove, roast the peppers for about 10 minutes, turning frequently, until blackened. Place in a paper bag to steam for 10 minutes. Remove the blackened peel, cut off the tops, and without tearing the peppers scoop out the seeds and membranes and discard.

In a small bowl, cover the raisins in the water or wine and soak for 5–10 minutes, until softened.

*The Dish:* Preheat the oven to 350 degrees.

Crumble the bread into a bowl and add the raisins, basil, parsley, anchovies, capers, pine nuts, and olives. Season with a little salt and pepper and stir in 4 tablespoons of the olive oil. Stuff the peppers, evenly distributing the filling among them.

Place peppers close together in a shallow baking pan. Pour the tomato puree and remaining oil over them. Bake for 40 minutes and serve hot or cold.

*Wine:* I like a very robust southern Italian wine—Taurasi from Naples, or an Etna Rosso from Sicily—or something from Puglia: a Salice Salentino or a Primitivo, father of the California Zinfandel.

# GRILLED PIZZA

*6 servings*

Chefs George Germon and Johanne Killeen, who are good friends, were an inspiration for this dish because they make a similar pizza at Al Forno, their restaurant in Providence, Rhode Island. However, I've always said this is really a *piadina*, the traditional bread of Emilia-Romagna, which is served as a sandwich, or with toppings. It's very thin, without that thick edge of crust all around. But Americans know pizza, so that's what we call it.

---

FOR THE DOUGH

*1 cup water, room temperature*
*1 cup milk, room temperature*
*1½ teaspoons active dry yeast*
*4¼ cups high-gluten flour or bread flour*
*1 teaspoon salt*

FOR THE SAUCE

*3 cups canned tomato puree*
*3 tablespoons Garlic-Infused Olive Oil (see page 7)*
*2 tablespoons olive oil*
*Salt and pepper, to taste*

---

*1 cup (3–4 ounces) mozzarella cheese, grated*
*1 teaspoon dried oregano*
*6 paper-thin slices of imported prosciutto*

*Preparation:* In a large mixing bowl, combine the water and milk. Whisk the yeast into the liquid until it dissolves and the mixture bubbles. Let sit for 15 minutes.

In a food processor fitted with the steel blade, pulse to combine the flour and salt and add the yeast mixture. Process until the dough forms a ball and cleans the side of the processor. On a floured board, knead the dough for 5 minutes or until it pops back up when you press it with your finger.

Set aside in a warm place and let the dough rise until doubled in volume, about 40 minutes. Roll into a log and divide into 6 pieces. Flour your hands and shape each piece into a small ball. Cover the balls of dough with a towel and let sit in a warm place for 20 minutes.

TO MAKE THE SAUCE: In a medium bowl, combine the tomato puree, garlic oil, olive oil, and salt and pepper.

*The Dish:* Heat the grill to medium-high.

Preheat the oven to 450 degrees.

Dust the work surface with flour. Flatten 1 ball of dough into a 6-inch circle and roll it out very thin, about ⅛ inch thick.

Place the circle of dough on the medium-hot grill and flatten with a spatula if it starts to puff up. Grill for 1–2 minutes and flip it over to grill the other side for 1 minute. Remove from the grill.

Spread about ½ cup of the sauce over the pizza and cover with the mozzarella. Sprinkle on the oregano.

Bake for 3 minutes or until the cheese has melted.

Remove from the oven and place a thin slice of prosciutto on top before serving.

*Wine:* A wonderful everyday wine—a young Barbera from Italy, a rich Zinfandel from California, a Petit Chateau or Provencal Vin de Pays from France.

※

*A very thin crust and slices of prosciutto adorn the elegant grilled pizza, inspired by George Germon and Johanne Killeen at Al Forno in Providence, Rhode Island.*

*Involtini,* rolled dishes, are a great part of Sicilian tradition, much more so than in northern Italy. We start with turnovers having a pizzalike crust. Or there is the glorious involtino, the Fassu Magru di Lina (page 191), which is a stuffed flank steak. At Valentino we make little veal rolls, Rollatini di Vitello (page 196), no bigger than a fat cigar. I always enjoy the idea of food with a surprise inside.

Eggplant is such a big part of any Italian kitchen. This dish is very easy and practical, because you can prepare the involtini way ahead. It's a wonderful appetizer or little *assaggino.* And the discovery of caprino cheese, a soft goat cheese that is both tart and sweet, made my life much easier because we could combine the eggplant with the wonderful, creamy texture of the cheese. It works very well.

---

*2 medium eggplants, firm and*
*   glossy*
*2 tablespoons kosher salt*
*1 cup olive oil*
*1 cup (8 ounces) caprino cheese*

---

*2 tablespoons red wine vinegar*
*2 garlic cloves, thinly sliced*
*2 tablespoons basil, chopped*
*1½ cups Italian parsley, half of*
*   it finely chopped*

Slice eggplants vertically into ⅜-inch-thick slices. Salt each side and let slices sit in a strainer or on a towel for about 1 hour. Pat the slices dry with paper towels to remove the moisture and salt.

In a large skillet, heat ¼ cup of the olive oil over medium-high heat. Fry the slices in batches until golden brown, about 2–3 minutes on each side. Add more olive oil as necessary, allowing it to heat up before frying the next batch. Place the fried eggplant slices on paper towels and allow to cool for a few minutes. Spread 1 tablespoon of the caprino cheese across each slice and roll up tightly. Arrange the rolls seam-side down in a single layer in a shallow baking dish.

To make the marinade, combine 6 tablespoons of olive oil, the vinegar, garlic, basil, and chopped parsley. Pour the marinade over the eggplant rolls and refrigerate for at least 1 hour, occasionally spooning the liquid over the eggplant.

To serve, remove the rolls from the refrigerator and let them reach room temperature. Arrange on a platter and garnish with the remaining whole parsley leaves.

*Wine:* Start with a very light red: a Bardolino (Masi), a Cabernet Franc from California, or even a good Lambrusco to cut through the vinegar in a supple way.

## INVOLTINI DI PESCE SPADA CON COUSCOUS TRAPANESE /
## Swordfish Involtini with Couscous

*4 servings*

Here we have rediscovered ingredients that go back many centuries. Couscous is not just part of the Israeli or Arab tradition; with all the Arab influences on the Mediterranean, Sicily long ago incorporated couscous into its cooking. To me it is also Italian, part of our tradition. And swordfish—Trapani is the capital of swordfish in the Mediterranean. This is where they have the famous *tonnara,* where they catch tuna and swordfish. So we took a grain that has been ours for hundreds of years, and a fish we catch every day, and created a new dish.

---

*½ cup couscous*

*2 teaspoons garlic, finely chopped*

*2 tablespoons (1 ounce) butter*

*3 tablespoons olive oil*

*8 large prawns, shelled, deveined,
    and roughly chopped*

*¼ cup red bell pepper,
    finely chopped*

*¼ cup yellow bell pepper,
    finely chopped*

*¼ cup zucchini, finely chopped*

*¼ cup celery, finely chopped*

*¼ cup carrots, finely chopped*

*½ cup dry white wine*

*Salt and pepper, to taste*

---

*8 thin slices swordfish*

---

*Baby lettuce, for garnish*

*1 tablespoon white wine vinegar*

Preheat the oven to 500 degrees.

In a small saucepan, bring 1½ cups of salted water to a boil. Add the couscous, cover, and remove from heat. Let sit until all water has been absorbed, about 5–7 minutes. In a skillet over medium heat, sauté 1 teaspoon of the garlic in half of the butter and 1 tablespoon of olive oil. When the garlic is golden in color, add the prawns and vegetables. Add the wine and reduce. Stir in the couscous and season with salt and pepper.

Lay the swordfish slices on a clean surface, divide stuffing evenly on top of the slices, and roll them up. Put the swordfish rolls in a shallow roasting pan, add 1 tablespoon olive oil and the remaining butter and garlic, and season with salt and pepper. Put in the oven for 7–10 minutes, until the swordfish is lightly colored. Place the swordfish rolls on a bed of greens. Over high heat, reduce the leftover juices for a few minutes, add the remaining olive oil and white wine vinegar, and drizzle over the lettuce.

*Wine:* Choose a full-bodied white, rich in citrus, tartar, and dry fruits—a California Chardonnay that is not too oaky, like Littorai or Iron Horse, with just a touch of austerity. Champagne is a richer choice—a Blanc de Blanc or even a wonderful rosé.

*"We took a grain that has been ours for hundreds of years, and a fish we catch every day, and created a new dish."*

## INVOLTINI DI PESCE SPADA CON SALSA AL SALMORIGLIO / Stuffed Swordfish Rolls with Salmoriglio Sauce

*4 servings*

Here, instead of the usual grilled or baked swordfish, we have a new presentation. This is a traditional Sicilian recipe that we have revisited our own way, with our own stuffing. It can be served as a single item, wrapped in a leaf of Belgian endive, or as an appetizer, or can even be used as a whole course. A very flexible dish.

---

*2 pounds swordfish*

SALMORIGLIO SAUCE

*2 tablespoons lemon juice*
*2 tablespoons white wine vinegar*
*2 tablespoons olive oil*
*1 teaspoon fresh oregano, finely chopped*
*1 teaspoon Italian parsley, finely chopped*
*Salt and pepper, to taste*

---

*1 medium yellow onion, finely chopped*
*1 garlic clove, finely chopped*
*1 tablespoon olive oil*
*¼ cup Italian parsley, chopped*
*¼ cup fresh basil, chopped*
*2 tablespoons oil-packed anchovies*
*⅓ cup raisins or black currants*
*¾ cup bread crumbs*

(continued)

*Preparation:* Slice the fish into 24 paper-thin slices, 3–4 inches across, reserving 10 ounces of trimmings to use in the stuffing. Cut the swordfish trimmings into ¼-inch pieces.

> *Chef's Tip:* If possible, have your fishmonger slice the fish, but make sure to reserve the trimmings for the stuffing.

TO MAKE THE SALMORIGLIO SAUCE: In a small bowl, combine all the sauce ingredients. Whisk 1–2 minutes until the sauce thickens.

*The Dish:* In a large skillet, sauté the onion and garlic in olive oil until lightly colored. Add the swordfish trimmings and cook 3–4 more minutes.

Add the parsley, basil, anchovies, raisins, bread crumbs, capers, and orange juice, and cook over medium heat for about 2 minutes, until the mixture thickens and becomes pasty.

Remove from the heat and let cool. Add the provolone cheese, eggs, and salt and pepper to the mixture.

*1 tablespoon capers, Sicilian if*
*possible*
*½ cup fresh-squeezed orange juice*
*3 ounces sharp provolone cheese,*
*diced into ½-inch cubes*
*2 large eggs*
*Salt and pepper, to taste*

Flatten the swordfish slices slightly and place 1–2 table-spoons of the filling about ½ inch away from the bottom edge. Fold over the left and right edges about 1 inch and fold the bottom edge up over the filling to start the roll. Roll up completely and secure with a toothpick.

Grill for 2–3 minutes on each side. Spoon the sauce over the rolls.

*Wine:* Try an intense white—a good California Chardonnay or French Chablis. You need a wine with elegance and a nice floweriness to add gentleness to the strong flavors, to complement them, and to leave a clean mouth.

# INVOLTINI D'ANATRA / Duck Involtini

*4 servings*

I always like to serve contrasting flavors, and it is even more exciting when I have a great product. We are blessed with wonderful little game farms in Carpinteria, where we get great duck breasts. Since game is so popular in regional Italian cooking, and duck is so widely available in our markets, we decided to come up with a series of *involtini,* little wrapped and rolled *primi piatti.* This one is very original and easy to make. It is a "thinking" dish: Rather than using the traditional veal scaloppini, we wanted to do something new and creative. And it tastes great as a leftover, or in a picnic basket.

---

3 tablespoons olive oil, plus extra
    for garnish
1 pound duck breasts, fat removed,
    diced into ½-inch cubes
1 large carrot, peeled and diced into
    ¼-inch cubes
2 red bell peppers, 1 whole and
    1 diced into ¼-inch cubes
1 yellow bell pepper, diced into
    ¼-inch cubes
8–10 fresh shiitake mushrooms,
    cleaned with a damp towel,
    chopped into ½-inch pieces
Salt and pepper, to taste
2–3 sprigs fresh thyme
½ cup dry white wine

---

32 leaves flat-leaf spinach, about
    5 inches wide, washed well,
    dried, and stems removed
5 ounces ricotta salata cheese,
    coarsely grated

*Preparation:* Preheat the oven to 375 degrees.

In a large skillet, heat the olive oil over high heat and sear the duck breasts until nicely browned, 1–2 minutes on each side. Turn the heat to medium and add the carrot. After 2 minutes, add the diced red and yellow peppers and cook 1–2 minutes more. Add the mushrooms, a pinch of salt and pepper, and the thyme.

Pour in the wine and boil on high heat until the wine is evaporated, about 2 minutes.

Lower the heat, cover the pan, and simmer until tender, about 15 minutes.

On a grill or over an open flame on the stove, roast the whole red pepper for about 10 minutes, turning frequently, until blackened. Place in a paper bag to steam for 10 minutes. Remove the blackened peel, cut off the top without tearing the pepper, and scoop out the seeds and membranes to discard. Slice the pepper into thin strips and set aside for garnish.

Let the duck mixture cool, and process in a food processor fitted with the steel blade. Add half the ricotta salata cheese, and pulse a few times. The duck should not be a smooth puree, but a slightly coarse and sticky mixture.

*The Dish:* Place 2 tablespoons of the filling at the tip end of a spinach leaf and roll it up. Arrange the involtini on a plate, garnish with the slices of roasted pepper, and sprinkle with the remaining ricotta salata cheese. Drizzle with olive oil.

*Chef's Tip:* The filling will keep in the refrigerator for 2–3 days. The involtini can be served as an appetizer, as part of a buffet, or over a frisee or radicchio salad as a first course.

*Wine:* A Pinot Noir or a Burgundy, with an intense flavor of berries and various fruits. This dish calls for a wine that is more supple than powerful, that has more finesse than strength.

## GAMBERETTI AVVOLTI IN ZUCCHINE CON SENTORI DI SENAPE ED ARANCIO /
### Zucchini-Wrapped Shrimp with Orange Mustard Dressing

*4 servings*

---

20 medium shrimp, shelled and
    deveined
Salt and pepper, to taste
1 teaspoon fresh thyme, chopped
4 zucchini, cut lengthwise into
    20 paper-thin slices
½ cup mayonnaise
1 tablespoon Toasted Garlic
    (see page 7)
1 tablespoon whole-grain mustard
1 tablespoon orange zest,
    finely chopped
¼ cup fresh-squeezed orange juice
12 ounces mixed baby greens

Season the shrimp with the salt, pepper, and thyme. Wrap each shrimp with a slice of zucchini, place them in a steamer pan, and steam for 3–5 minutes. In a small bowl, combine the mayonnaise, garlic, mustard, and half of the zest. Gradually whisk in the orange juice. Spread the dressing on individual plates, reserving some to dress the greens. Place the shrimp on the outer edge of the plate and mound the dressed salad in the center. Sprinkle with the remaining orange zest.

*Wine:* You will want to cleanse the palate, after the slightly bitter taste of the zucchini and the sharp aftertaste of the mustard, with a wine of delicacy rather than intensity. Something fresh and spicy: Semillon by Signorello, or Semillon blended with Sauvignon Blanc from Bordeaux or California.

*"Wrapping is about the marriage of different flavors."*

## ROTOLO DI ZUCCHINE CON GAMBERI IN INSALATA /
### Shrimp in Zucchini
*4 servings*

---

5 tablespoons (2½ ounces) butter

20 medium shrimp, shelled and
    deveined

4 medium zucchini, cut lengthwise
    into 20 paper-thin slices

2 teaspoons Toasted Garlic
    (see page 7)

4 tablespoons whole-grain mustard

1 cup fresh-squeezed orange juice

12 ounces salad greens

In a large skillet, heat the butter over medium-high heat until brown, about 3 minutes.

Wrap 1 slice of zucchini around each shrimp. Cook the shrimp in the brown butter for 2 minutes on each side. Remove from the pan. Add the toasted garlic, mustard, and orange juice and reduce for a few minutes. Remove from heat.

Mound mixed salad greens on individual plates and arrange 5 shrimp on top of each. Taste the sauce and correct the seasoning. Spoon over the shrimp and greens and serve.

*Wine:* A Pinot Bianco or Tocai, from Schiopetto or Villa Russiz—these are flowery, aromatic wines of elegance, which blend easily with the scent of fruit essence in the seafood sauce. Or you might try a California Sauvignon Blanc.

# GAMBERONI E CANNELLINI ALL'OLIO TOSCANO /
## Shrimp and White Beans in Tuscan Oil
### *6 servings*

This dish came to the United States with the Tuscan rage, about ten years ago. Suddenly, shrimp and beans made it big-time. It was a combination of the rich and the poor—the richness of the shrimp and the extreme modesty of the beans. But the fun thing about this dish is its flexibility. Use great shrimp, like fresh tiger or Mexican, and try beans of different flavors. Add some good olive oil, the flavors of different vegetables, and you come up with something you can serve hot, cold, as a first course, or in the middle of a meal. Personally, I like it as a refreshing first course—especially if the shrimp are beautiful, al dente, and very crunchy. The creaminess of the beans is like a *contorno,* an accompaniment.

---

*1 stalk celery, coarsely chopped*
*4–5 garlic cloves, cut in half*
*1 bay leaf*
*½ carrot, peeled and coarsely chopped*
*3 cups dried cannellini beans, soaked overnight*
*3 tablespoons kosher salt*
*Pepper, to taste*
*4–6 tablespoons olive oil*
*1 tablespoon red wine vinegar*

---

*1 tablespoon salt*
*Juice of 1 lemon*
*1 cup dry white wine*
*18 fresh large tiger or Mexican shrimp, shelled and deveined*
*1 cup Citrus Vinaigrette (see page 53)*
*Baby arugula, for garnish*

*Preparation:* In a large stockpot, bring 6 quarts of water to a boil. Add the celery, garlic, bay leaf, and carrot. Return to a boil. Add the beans. Return to a boil again, then turn the heat down and simmer 45 minutes to 1 hour, or until the beans are tender.

Remove from the heat and allow the beans to cool in the cooking liquid.

*The Dish:* When the beans are cool, drain well. Add the kosher salt, pepper, oil, and vinegar, and set aside.

In a medium-size saucepan, bring 3 quarts of water to a boil. Add the salt, lemon juice, and wine and return to a boil. Add the shrimp and boil for about 5 minutes. Drain and immediately plunge into ice water or rinse under cold running water to stop the cooking process.

To assemble, mound the drained beans in the center of each plate and top with 3 shrimp per serving, fanning them out over the beans. Spoon citrus vinaigrette over the shrimp and garnish with baby arugula.

*Wine:* A dry white Tuscan wine, such as a fresh, clean Vernaccia di San Gimignano—straw, very crispy, with a hint of vanilla, a nice flavor that clings to the palate, and beautiful aromatics of lemon zest and apple. Or try a wonderful Fumé Blanc from California, a wine that has a bouquet, floweriness, a touch of grassiness that cuts the sweetness of the shrimp and gives you fresh herbal sensations.

## CROSTATA DI CARCIOFI ALL'AGLIO E GAMBERI
## DI FIUME IN BRODO D'ARAGOSTA /
### Artichoke Tart with Crayfish and Roasted Garlic in Lobster Broth

*6 servings*

12 ounces puff pastry (if frozen,
  defrost according to directions
  on package)

6 baby artichokes

¾ cup artichoke paste (available at
  specialty stores)

3 tablespoons (1½ ounces) butter

8 ounces crayfish tails

2 tablespoons Toasted Garlic
  (see page 7)

1 teaspoon fresh dill, chopped,
  plus 4 sprigs for garnishing

Salt and pepper, to taste

¼ cup sparkling wine

1 cup Lobster Broth (see page 75)
  (if you buy whole crayfish,
  substitute with Crayfish Broth
  [see page 75])

*Preparation:* On a lightly floured work surface, roll the puff pastry to ⅛ inch thick, flouring the pastry as necessary. Cut out six 5-inch circles, place on a parchment-lined baking sheet, and chill for 30 minutes.

Remove the tough outer leaves and slice off about 1 inch from the top of each artichoke. Cut each one into 6 wedges and steam until tender, about 5 minutes. Set aside.

*The Dish:* Preheat the oven to 400 degrees.

Using an offset spatula or the back of a spoon, spread the artichoke paste evenly on each circle and bake for 10–15 minutes, until the crust is lightly browned and crisp. Meanwhile, melt 2 tablespoons of the butter in a sauté pan over high heat for 1–2 minutes, until golden brown. Add the artichokes, crayfish, garlic, and chopped dill. Season with salt and pepper. Continue to cook on high until all of the ingredients are slightly crisp. Remove the crayfish mixture from the pan and keep warm. Add the wine to the pan, and return it to high heat. Reduce by half and add the lobster broth or crayfish broth. Reduce again by half, add the remaining butter, and cook until the sauce thickens a bit.

Place each puff pastry on a plate, top with the crayfish mixture, and spoon the sauce over it. Garnish with a dill sprig.

*Wine:* Artichokes and wine have a little disagreement—the artichokes are so acidic, with so pungent an aftertaste, that they fight the wine and make it taste almost metallic. But here we have the crayfish, and the lobster broth or crayfish broth, and roasted garlic. When I think of something that will stand up to all those flavors together, I turn directly to champagne. A good solid brut. Or a fresh Prosecco, a sparkling wine from the Veneto. To be safe, avoid still white wines. They just won't work well.

## COUSCOUS CON GAMBERONI PICCANTI /
### Marinated Shrimp with Couscous

*4 servings*

With a lot of the food at Primi, we started with the basics and livened them up. This is a very Mediterranean dish, done in a fusion style: strong, bold flavors with an elegant presentation. Couscous is a popular porridge with its own flavor, but it's like mashed potatoes—it needs a kick; it's too quiet on its own. The tomatoes and the couscous are a southern Italian influence, but the reason I love this dish has nothing to do with my childhood. I just bless it because I like the way it tastes, and because you can eat it cold. It's the perfect starter.

*16–20 medium uncooked shrimp, shelled and deveined*

*1 tablespoon olive oil, plus extra for garnish*

*2 tablespoons red wine vinegar*

*2 tomatoes, diced to equal 1½ cups*

*1–2 serrano chilies, finely chopped*

*¼ medium yellow onion, cut in thin slivers*

*1½ cups couscous, prepared according to package instructions, with 1 teaspoon butter added*

*Salt and pepper, to taste*

*Curly leaf lettuce, for garnish*

*Preparation:* Bring a medium-size pot of water to a boil. Boil the shrimp for 4–5 minutes. Drain and immediately plunge into ice water or rinse under cold running water to stop the cooking process, and set aside.

*The Dish:* In a medium-size bowl, whisk the olive oil and vinegar to combine. Add the tomatoes, chilies, onion, and couscous and mix well. Season with salt and pepper to taste.

Mound the couscous mixture into a lightly oiled pastry mold or cup, pack firmly, and turn out onto a plate. Arrange a leaf of lettuce alongside and stand the shrimp so that they lean against the molded couscous.

Drizzle olive oil on the shrimp.

*Wine:* I would start sipping right away on a supple white wine with personality—a Soave from Gini or Pieropan, or a Vermentino from Liguria, which is refreshing with a wonderful structure. From California, Tocai Friulano by Podere dell'Olivos is fresh and clean, and it perfectly complements the strong flavors of the dish.

*4 servings*

Mamma made small, soft little meatballs with ground pork or red veal meat every Sunday night, served with chicken broth. It was a special meal for *la festa,* the holiday. She still makes them for me and my sons when she visits. Long after those childhood dinners, I realized *polpette* could be done in many variations, which is how we created this popular appetizer.

Luciano Pellegrini says that lobster lovers can make these little seafood cakes from equal portions of shrimp and lobster, "depending on how expensive they want their appetizer to be." He offers one economical hint: Buy small shrimp, since they taste as good as the big ones and are going to be diced.

---

FOR THE POLPETTE

*8 ounces uncooked shrimp, shelled*
  *and deveined*
*4 ounces lobster (or the meat from a*
  *1-pound lobster)*
*½ teaspoon Garlic-Infused Olive*
  *Oil (see page 7)*
*1 teaspoon fresh dill, finely chopped*
*Salt and pepper, to taste*

FOR THE SAUCE

*1 large leek, root and dark green top*
  *cut off*
*3 tablespoons (1½ ounces) butter*
*1 tablespoon olive oil*
*½ teaspoon garlic, finely chopped*
*1 tablespoon tomato, chopped*
*Salt and pepper, to taste*
*1 tablespoon balsamic vinegar*
*1 tablespoon brandy*
*¼ cup plus 2 tablespoons Lobster*
  *Broth (see page 75), clam juice,*
  *or Fish Stock (see page 74)*

*Preparation:* Bring a large pot of water to a boil.

Cut the leek into quarters lengthwise, discard the outer leaf, and wash thoroughly in cold water. Cut into ½-inch cubes and set aside for the sauce.

Blanch the leek in boiling water for 1 minute. Remove with a slotted spoon and drain.

Steam the lobster above the boiling water for 5 minutes. Coarsely chop the shrimp and lobster meat, or pulse a few times in a food processor.

*The Dish:* In medium-size mixing bowl, combine the shrimp, lobster, garlic oil, dill, and salt and pepper, and mix well.

Wet your hands or coat them with olive oil and measure 1 heaping teaspoon of the mixture for each polpetta. Shape the balls in the palms of your hands and then flatten each to ½-inch thickness and set aside.

TO MAKE THE SAUCE: In a 9-inch skillet, heat 1 tablespoon of the butter, the olive oil, and the garlic over medium-high heat. When the garlic is golden, add the leek, cook for 2 more minutes, and add the tomato. Season lightly with salt and pepper. Stir in the balsamic vinegar and reduce.

In another skillet, melt 1 tablespoon of the butter over

*¼ teaspoon pink peppercorns, crushed*
*1 tablespoon heavy cream (if needed)*
*Several fresh dill tops, for garnishing*

medium heat and then fry the polpette. Cook 1–2 minutes on each side, until cakes are firm to the touch. Transfer the polpette to a plate, and remove the skillet from the heat.

> *Chef's Tip:* Always use butter, not olive oil, when cooking seafood or meat—it sticks to the pan less that way.

Add the brandy to the skillet you used to fry the polpette, and return to high heat. Add the lobster broth, clam juice, or fish stock. Turn the heat to low and add the remaining butter and pink peppercorns. To make additional sauce, add 1 tablespoon cream, bring to a boil, and immediately remove from the heat. Combine with the tomato leek sauce.

Serve 2 polpette per serving, and top with approximately 1 tablespoon of sauce. Garnish with dill tops.

Note: Remove the pan from the heat before adding alcohol, and then return the pan to the heat. You don't need it to flame; alcohol is the first thing to evaporate, so it only needs to cook briefly.

*Wine:* Definitely a white. There is a great deal of texture to the seafood, and this is an intense sauce, so you have to clean the palate with something fresh. Also, the wine's flavors can act like additional ingredients in the sauce—you're taking into your mouth an extra sensation. I like a Pinot Bianco, a fresh young Chablis with a little oak, or a crisp, fresh wine from the Trebbiano grape. Or a twist with Viognier, where the intensity of the fruits will be a welcome addition, like adding fruit to the recipe. Viognier is more aggressive, but that's part of the fun. The others don't interfere with the taste sensations.

# TORTINO D'ASTICE ALLO SPUMANTE /
## Lobster Tortino with Champagne Sauce
*4 servings*

My philosophy is variety and exciting flavors, not quantity. You can have a great meal with a big green salad and a 15-ounce steak, but thank you very much, I'd rather have the same amount of food in an assortment of flavors. Try a cold and a hot appetizer, or two hot ones of different textures: this tortino and then the Lobster Crespelle, and a pasta, and that's it.

---

FOR THE CHAMPAGNE SAUCE
*1 shallot, finely chopped*
*2 tablespoons (1 ounce) butter*
*1 cup champagne*
*½ cup clam juice*
*½ cup heavy cream*
*Salt and pepper, to taste*

FOR THE TORTINO
*1–2 Maine lobsters, steamed,*
*    or ½ pound lobster meat*
*½ cup heavy cream*
*4 large eggs, separated*
*Salt and pepper, to taste*

*Preparation:* FOR THE SAUCE: In a small pan over medium heat, sauté the shallot in the butter until translucent. Add the champagne and clam juice and reduce by half. Add the cream, turn down the heat, and simmer until the sauce has thickened and coats the spoon. Add salt and pepper to taste. Strain the sauce and set aside. Reheat on low when ready to serve.

*The Dish:* Preheat the oven to 350 degrees.

Remove the lobster meat from the shells and roughly chop. Place in a food processor with the cream and pulse a few times for a chunky texture. Remove to a large mixing bowl and stir in the egg yolks. Using an electric mixer fitted with the whisk attachment, beat the egg whites until stiff peaks form, and gently fold into the lobster mixture with a spatula. Season with salt and pepper to taste.

Butter four 4-ounce soufflé cups and divide the lobster mixture evenly among them. Place them in a baking pan with high sides and fill the pan with warm water, halfway up the sides of the cups. Bake for 40 minutes. Run a sharp knife around the edge of each cup and invert onto an individual serving plate. Spoon the sauce over the tortino.

*Wine:* I am tempted to serve champagne, for this is a festive dish that demands elegance. The yeasty structure and the cleanliness of champagne enrich anything salty, like caviar and smoked salmon, or creamy and delicate, like this tortino. Stay away from acidic or vinegary dishes with champagne— but for this soufflé it is perfect. A brut, California or French, or a demi-sec for an extra sensation of fruit in the mouth.

# FRITTELLE DI GRANCHIO E PATATE /

## Crab and Potato Pancakes with Roasted Garlic Butter Sauce

*4 servings*

This is not Italian, but it is one of Posto's most popular dishes. Sometimes I trust the chefs to take advantage of fabulous ingredients, like all the crabmeat we get. We have learned that a restaurant has to have a dependable selection of signature dishes, but it also has to be flexible. In this case, we came up with a dish that was hardly authentic Italian, but everyone who tries it at Posto loves it, so it stays on the menu. Would I serve it at Valentino? Maybe not, because we try to maintain more of a traditional Italian feeling there.

---

FOR THE FRITTELLE

*¾ pound Yukon Gold potatoes,*
    *peeled and cut into quarters*
*1 tablespoon all-purpose flour*
*2 tablespoons milk*
*2 large egg yolks*
*Salt and pepper, to taste*
*1 tablespoon fresh dill, chopped*
*2 tablespoons (1 ounce) butter*
*6 ounces fresh crabmeat, cooked*
*1 tablespoon capers*

FOR THE SAUCE

*6 tablespoons (3 ounces) butter*
*2 tablespoons garlic, sliced*
*¼ cup white wine*
*2 tablespoons heavy cream*
*Mixed greens and chopped tomato*
    *to garnish*

TO MAKE THE FRITTELLE: In a medium-size pot of boiling water, cook the potatoes until tender. Mash and set aside. In a medium-size mixing bowl, whisk together the flour, milk, and egg yolks. Add the warm potatoes and season with salt and pepper and half the dill.

Preheat the oven to 300 degrees and warm an ovenproof serving platter.

Melt the butter in a nonstick pan over medium-high heat. Spoon an eighth of the potato mixture into the pan in a circle, place a few tablespoons of crabmeat on top of it, and push down lightly. Repeat the procedure, frying 3–4 cakes at a time. Sprinkle some capers on top and put in the oven for about 5 minutes, or until golden and crusty. Turn them over and return to the oven until ready to serve. Repeat with remaining potato mixture, adding more butter as necessary to prevent the potato from sticking to the pan.

TO MAKE THE SAUCE: In a sauté pan, sauté the garlic with 3 tablespoons of the butter over medium heat, until the garlic is a light golden color. Turn the heat to medium-high, add the wine, and boil to evaporate. Add the cream and turn the heat down very low. Slowly whisk in 3 more tablespoons of butter. When all of it has melted, remove the pan from the heat, and season the sauce with salt and pepper, and remaining dill. Continue whisking for a few more minutes to stabilize the sauce.

Spoon some sauce onto the serving dish and place the cakes over the sauce, crab-side up. Garnish with mixed greens and a little chopped tomato, and spoon the remaining sauce over the cakes.

*Wine:* A very soft, very fruity red wine, a Gamay or a good Beaujolais, or, from Italy, a Dolcetto or a very young Barbera. Though this is seafood, the pancake solidifies the dish, and the garlic and butter sauce needs a wine with fruit and a little spiciness. Or if you want a white, try one that's fresh and crispy, like Vermentino from Liguria, Lugana from Veneto, or a lightly oaked Pinot Blanc from California: Chalone or Etude.

## CAPESANTE AVVOLTE IN PICCOLE MELANZANE
## CON FAGIOLI CANNELLINI /
Jumbo Scallops Wrapped in Japanese Eggplant with Tuscan Beans

*4 servings*

Wrapping is about the marriage of different flavors. You can do it in so many ways: veal wrapped in pancetta, pork in spinach, shrimp in swordfish, and, in this case, seafood and a vegetable. It gives an extra dimension, and makes the basic ingredients more intriguing. And it's a sealing process—the vegetable wrap acts like a blanket to preserve the moistness of the seafood.

FOR THE BEANS

*1 cup dry cannellini beans,*
  *soaked overnight*
*Bouquet garni: fresh sage,*
  *rosemary, 2 bay leaves,*
  *4–5 sprigs thyme, and parsley,*
  *wrapped in cheesecloth and*
  *tied with twine*
*3 whole garlic cloves*
*1 teaspoon cracked black pepper*
*1 tablespoon kosher salt*

*8 large scallops*
*2 Japanese eggplant, sliced*
  *lengthwise into thin slices*
*12 chives*
*2 tablespoons (1 ounce) butter*
*2 tablespoons olive oil, plus*
  *extra for garnish*
*Salt and pepper, to taste*
*½ teaspoon garlic, finely chopped*
*½ cup fresh tomato, chopped*
*½ teaspoon fresh thyme,*
  *finely chopped*

*Preparation:* Rinse the beans and place them in a large pot with abundant cold water, the bouquet garni, garlic, and pepper. Bring to a boil and simmer for 1½ hours, or until tender. Drain, reserving ½ cup of the liquid, add the salt, and set aside.

*The Dish:* Wrap each scallop with a slice of eggplant and tie with a chive string. In a sauté pan over high heat, sear the scallops in the butter and olive oil, lightly browning them on all sides. Season with salt and pepper. Remove the scallops and keep them warm in the oven. Add the garlic, tomato, and thyme to the pan, sauté for 1 minute or so, then add the beans and measured liquid. Reduce liquid by half and divide evenly into 4 bowls. Finely chop the remaining chives. Place the scallops on the beans, garnish with chives, and drizzle olive oil over everything.

*Wine:* Something elegant and well balanced, like Cloudy Bay Sauvignon Blanc from New Zealand, or Michele Chiarlo's Countac, a lovely blend of Gavi and Cortese from Piedmont. Or since I consider jumbo scallops a meat, I think a Pinot Noir would work well here, with the robust beans and the slight bitterness of the eggplant. Try a good one from Oregon, from Domaine Drouhin or Beaux Frères, or a very spicy and elegant wine, like a Sanford Pinot Noir from the Santa Ynez Valley.

## COZZE AL BASILICO IN SALSA DI AGRUMI /
## Mussels with Basil in a Citrus Sauce

*6 servings*

FOR THE SAUCE

*1 bunch (about 2 cups) fresh basil*
*3 blood oranges*
*Salt and pepper, to taste*
*1 cup olive oil*

*36 large mussels, cleaned and rinsed*
*⅔ cup dry white wine*

*Preparation:* Reserve 12 basil leaves for garnish and chop the rest. In a large bowl, combine the chopped basil, the juice of 2 of the oranges, and salt and pepper. Slowly pour in the olive oil, whisking constantly until the dressing thickens.

*The Dish:* In a large skillet over high heat, cook the mussels in the wine, covered, until they open. Remove them immediately and discard the upper shells or any unopened mussels.

Arrange the mussels on 6 individual plates and pour the dressing generously over them. Peel the remaining orange and cut it into 6 slices. Garnish each plate with 1 orange segment and 2 basil leaves.

*Wine:* A crispy French Chablis, a Vermentino from Liguria, or a Viognier from the central coast of California. All are wines that add dimension to the citrus flavors and the fresh seafood taste.

## CARPACCIO DI SALMONE / Cured Salmon

*6 servings*

½ *Norwegian salmon (about*
   *4 pounds), trimmed and cleaned*
   *but skin still intact*
½ *cup coarse salt*
¼ *cup sugar*

FOR THE MARINADE AND DRESSING
*1 cup olive oil*
*Juice and zest of 3 oranges*
*Juice and zest of 3 lemons*
*Salt and white pepper, to taste*
*12 ounces mixed baby greens*

*Preparation:* Place the salmon skin-side down in a large nonreactive pan (glass or stainless steel). Coat the fish with the salt and sugar and put in a cool place to cure for 2 days. Scrape off the seasonings.

In a small bowl combine ¾ cup of the olive oil with the juice and zests of 2 of the oranges and all the lemons. Pour over the salmon and marinate for 1 day.

TO MAKE THE DRESSING: In a small bowl combine the remaining olive oil, orange juice, and salt and pepper.

*The Dish:* Remove the salmon from the marinade, slice thinly, and serve on a bed of greens. Drizzle the dressing over the salmon and greens.

*Wine:* A wonderful Chardonnay from Kistler, Peter Michael, or Joseph Phelps—all are wines of great elegance, good depth, and intense structure, which can stand next to the intense flavors of the fish and the marinade.

## CARPACCIO DI TONNO AI CAPPERI /
## Tuna Carpaccio with Caper Dressing

*4 servings*

*4 teaspoons capers*
*2 tablespoons white wine*
*2 bunches (8 ounces) arugula*
*2 teaspoons lemon juice*
*½ cup olive oil*
*8 ounces ahi tuna, sliced as thinly as possible*
*Balsamic vinegar, to taste*
*1 handful (2 ounces) radish sprouts*
*Chopped shallot, to taste*
*1 medium tomato, sliced*

*Chef's Tip:* Arugula wilts easily. Estimate the right amount; don't crush the leaves in a measuring cup.

*Preparation:* Rinse the capers with cold water and soak them overnight in the wine. Tear the arugula into large pieces.

*The Dish:* If the slices of tuna are still a bit thick, place them between 2 plastic sheets and pound gently. Drain and finely chop the capers and, in a small bowl, combine them with the lemon juice and ¼ cup of the olive oil. Combine the remaining olive oil with the vinegar and toss with the arugula. Place a portion of the arugula in the middle of each plate. Arrange the tuna over the greens and garnish with radish sprouts, chopped shallot, and tomatoes. Spoon on the caper dressing and serve.

*Wine:* A Viognier by Joseph Phelps or Calera—the apple sensation and the crispness will harmonize with the spicy ingredients and cut into the fattiness of the fish.

12 ounces puff pastry (if frozen,
    defrost according to package
    directions)
12 ounces mixed mushrooms
    (chanterelle, porcini, shiitake,
    and morel), cleaned and sliced
4 fresh sage leaves
1 teaspoon Toasted Garlic
    (see page 7)
2 tablespoons (1 ounce) butter
1 tablespoon olive oil
¼ cup white wine
1 cup heavy cream
Salt and pepper, to taste
4 slices imported fontina cheese,
    about ⅛ inch thick and
    3–4 inches in diameter
1½ ounces black truffle, finely
    chopped
Whole parsley leaves, for garnish

*Preparation:* On a lightly floured work surface, roll the puff pastry to ⅛ inch thick, flouring the pastry as necessary. Cut out four 5- to 6-inch circles, place on a parchment-lined baking sheet, and chill for 30 minutes.

*The Dish:* Preheat the oven to 375 degrees. In a large skillet over medium-high heat, sauté the mushrooms, 2 sage leaves, and garlic in 1 tablespoon of butter and the olive oil. When the mushrooms are tender, add 1 tablespoon of the wine and 1 tablespoon of the cream, and season with salt and pepper. Cook another minute, remove from the heat, and discard the sage leaves.

Divide the mushrooms evenly over the 4 circles of puff pastry. Bake for 8 minutes, until the pastry puffs and is lightly colored. Remove from the oven and top with the slices of fontina cheese, making sure that the cheese does not hang over the edges of the tarts. Return to the oven until the cheese melts, about 3 minutes.

In a small skillet over medium heat, melt the remaining butter. Add the chopped truffle and remaining sage leaves. When the butter is golden in color, add the remaining wine and cook until it evaporates. Add the remaining cream, reduce by half, and season with salt and pepper. Remove the sage, spoon the sauce into the middle of each plate, and place the tarts on top of the sauce. Garnish with whole parsley leaves.

*Wine:* Red wine and mushrooms are a beautiful marriage. And the truffle cream and fontina make the dish creamier, softer—you need a lighter, fruity, supple red wine, like a Valpolicella from a small producer like Masi, Allegrini, or Quintarelli. Or from California, a Cabernet Franc from Francis Coppola with all the cherry character coming forward.

## POLPETTINE DI CARNE / Little Meatballs with Peppers

*4 servings*

I always remember the little meatballs Mamma served with *pasta asciutta*. When it was time for Valentino to come up with something recognizable, tasty, and versatile, we chose to make our little meatballs, but with an original twist. The sharpness and sweetness of different peppers spice up the meat, making you want to keep popping them into your mouth. If you have some leftover pasta, you can also just pour these meatballs on top.

---

**FOR THE SAUCE**

*2 tablespoons olive oil*

*1 large white onion, finely chopped*

*½ cup warm Vegetable Stock
   (see page 76)*

*3 bell peppers, 1 yellow, 1 green,
   1 red, seeds removed and cut
   into thin strips*

*2 small sprigs fresh thyme*

*Salt and pepper, to taste*

**FOR THE MEATBALLS**

*2–3 tablespoons stale bread, crust
   removed*

*2 tablespoons milk*

*8 ounces lean ground beef*

*4 ounces imported prosciutto, diced*

*3–4 tablespoons Parmesan cheese,
   grated*

*1 large egg*

*1 tablespoon fresh marjoram,
   finely chopped*

*1 tablespoon fresh basil,
   finely chopped*

(continued)

*Preparation:* TO PREPARE THE SAUCE: In a large saucepan heat the olive oil over medium heat. Add the onion and 1 tablespoon of the stock and cook for 5 minutes.

Add the peppers, thyme, and remaining stock. Cut a piece of parchment paper into a circle ½ inch larger than the lid of the pan. Place the paper over the opening and place the lid over it. Cook over low heat for 15 minutes.

Soak the bread in the milk until soft, about 10–15 minutes. Squeeze out excess milk and set aside.

*The Dish:* TO PREPARE THE MEATBALLS: Place the ground beef and prosciutto in a food processor and process to a paste. Transfer to a large bowl and add the bread, Parmesan cheese, egg, marjoram, basil, chives, and salt and pepper. Mix well and form into small 1-inch balls. Roll the meatballs in flour until lightly coated.

In a large skillet, heat the olive oil over medium heat and brown the meatballs on all sides. Cook for about 10 minutes and transfer them to a paper towel to drain.

Mix the meatballs with the sauce and adjust seasonings.

1 tablespoon chives, finely chopped
Salt and pepper, to taste
2–3 tablespoons all-purpose flour,
    for dredging
5 tablespoons olive oil

*Wine:* You'll want a red wine to match the intense, robust flavor of this dish—a Chianti Riserva, a Cerasuolo from Sicily, or, closer to home, a lush Zinfandel. These big wines have the hearty flavors of ripe fruit with a wonderful lingering taste of chocolate and *frutti di bosco,* berries of the woods.

Insalate e Contorni

*Insalate e*

# Insalate e Contorni

I SOMETIMES ATE SALAD WHEN I WAS A KID. IT WASN'T A BIG THING, just the basic *insalata mista,* the mixed green salad. Mamma always liked to put cucumbers and tomatoes in it, and sometimes olives, but nothing more than that.

The elegant composed salad came later. It evolved in restaurants, when some customers wanted a large salad for their whole meal. The lunch salad is an American invention: the Caesar salad, which is still popular; the great wilted spinach salad; and the Chinese chicken salad, which I think is a brilliant salad. I respect a good salad with grilled items on top, which has appeared in the last few years. But with all the wonderful greens that are available, there are so many more things you can do.

At Primi we made a superb salad with mozzarella and string beans. And the chicken and Gorgonzola cheese salad was very popular. We still make those dishes by request at the other restaurants, because people are sentimental about food, and you have to respect that. At Valentino we are not big on salad, because we are open for lunch only on Fridays. What we call "salad" there is usually a seafood dish; something with crabmeat, lobster, or shrimp, presented with greens. It's part of the antipasto or is one of the first courses. The salads we offer in these recipes are intended to be a smaller course, where greens are the background, not big bowls of lettuce with things heaped on top.

Vegetables are also used differently in Italy than they are in America. Here, vegetables are greens, things that you eat raw or marinate. When I was growing up, vegetables were something you cooked—you roasted the peppers, fried the eggplant, turned tomatoes into sauce. So the vegetables we serve at Valentino are little cooked accompaniments, like the vegetable timballo we make with an assortment of seasonal vegetables.

But regardless of the style of salad, what's most important is a wonderful variety of produce. Vegetables were central to the cuisine of my childhood, because they were plentiful and fresh, and because meat was simply too expensive to play a big role in my mother's kitchen. I would go to the vegetable market with my mother and see all these beautiful vegetables just picked up from the farmers a few hours before—squash, fennel, tomatoes, eggplant, lettuce, cabbage, and chard. And a bounty of fruit as well: watermelon, figs, peaches, and sometimes foreign fruits like bananas.

Today, American farmers' markets offer the same excitement. We see what is in season, we see what is new, and then we figure out how to reinterpret our memories. I may not have a jar of Mamma's tomato puree in the *dispensa* at Valentino, but when we can get little yellow tomatoes, we cook them into a delicate sauce, an old recipe with a new style of preparation, fancy tomatoes thrown in at the last moment.

## BASIC VINAIGRETTE

*2½ cups—can be stored in the refrigerator*

---

*½ cup plus 1 tablespoon fine wine*
  *vinegar (red or white)*
*1½ teaspoons Dijon mustard*
*Salt and pepper, to taste*
*1½ teaspoons pink peppercorns,*
  *freshly ground*
*2 cups olive oil*

In a medium-size bowl, whisk together the vinegar, mustard, salt and pepper, and pink peppercorns. Slowly pour in the olive oil, whisking to combine. Allow to rest 1–2 hours. Stir well before serving.

## CITRUS VINAIGRETTE

*2½ cups—can be stored in the refrigerator*

---

*½ cup fresh-squeezed lemon, lime,*
  *or orange juice*
*1 shallot, finely chopped*
*1 garlic clove, finely chopped*
*1 bay leaf*
*Salt and pepper, to taste*
*2 cups olive oil*

In a medium-size bowl combine the citrus juice and shallot and allow to sit for about 10–15 minutes. Whisk in the garlic, bay leaf, salt and pepper, and olive oil. Refrigerate until ready to use.

## CAESAR SALAD

*6 servings*

This American institution was invented in 1924 by Caesar Cardini in Tijuana, Mexico. In the old days, at The Marquis, I was the mixologist of the Caesar salad—standing at the table in my black tuxedo, with an empty salad bowl and a bigger bowl full of romaine. I performed the ceremony, chopping the anchovy, adding the garlic, oil, and other ingredients, spinning and whisking. There is no time today for such theater at the table, but it is still a popular item. It's always on the menu without being on the menu; it's like asking, "Do you have spaghetti?"

If I were creating a menu, I'd serve this as part of an American motif: a shrimp cocktail, a Caesar, a simple grilled meat, and corn or vegetables on the side. Apple pie to finish.

---

FOR THE CROUTONS

*¾ cup olive oil*

*1 medium clove garlic*

*8 half-inch slices of slightly stale bread, crust removed, cut into ½-inch cubes*

---

*1 large egg*

*1 medium clove garlic, minced*

*1 anchovy fillet, chopped*

*Juice of ½ lemon*

*1–2 tablespoons Worchestershire sauce*

*Salt and black pepper, freshly ground, to taste*

*3 medium heads romaine lettuce, outer leaves removed, torn into bite-size pieces*

*½ cup Parmesan cheese, grated*

FOR THE CROUTONS: In a medium-size sauté pan over medium heat, warm ¼ cup of the olive oil. Add the garlic clove, sauté for 1 minute, and discard the garlic. Turn up the heat to medium-high, add the bread, and, turning frequently, cook until crisp and golden on all sides. Drain on paper towels and set aside.

In a small saucepan full of boiling water, cook the egg for 1 minute and remove immediately. Rinse under cold running water to stop the cooking.

In a wooden bowl, combine the minced garlic, anchovy, lemon juice, Worchestershire sauce, and salt and pepper. Add the egg and whisk until combined. Slowly add the remaining ½ cup of olive oil, whisking constantly.

Add the lettuce, Parmesan cheese, and croutons to the wooden bowl and toss well. Serve immediately.

*Wine:* I find that Chardonnay works well with the Parmesan cheese and the eggy dressing. Think of a rich but slightly austere Chardonnay like Chateau Montelena, or a cleansing one like Sonoma-Cutrer.

*4 servings*

*4 medium vine-ripened tomatoes*

*6 ounces small uncooked shrimp,*
*shelled and deveined*

*1 tablespoon fresh dill, chopped*

*2 teaspoons shallot, finely chopped*

*2 tablespoons balsamic vinegar*

*¼ cup olive oil*

*Salt and pepper, to taste*

*8 ounces arugula*

*Preparation:* Cut off the tops of the tomatoes, scoop out the pulp, and set aside. Discard the seeds. Cut the shrimp into ½-inch chunks.

*The Dish:* Preheat the oven to 450 degrees.

In a small mixing bowl, combine the tomato pulp, shrimp, dill, 1 teaspoon of the shallot, 1 teaspoon of the vinegar, and 1 tablespoon of the olive oil. Season with salt and pepper. Stuff the tomato shells with the shrimp mixture, cover with the tops, and bake in a baking dish for 10 minutes.

TO MAKE THE DRESSING: In a small bowl, combine the remaining shallot, vinegar, and olive oil. Arrange the arugula on the outer edges of each plate, placing the leaves neatly one against the other. Place the baked tomato in the center and dress the arugula with the vinaigrette.

*Wine:* A smooth and dry Italian white like a Lugana by Zenato or a Soave Classico by Anselmi or Bertani.

## Tuna and Olive Salad with Roasted Peppers

*4 – 6 servings*

We used to have divine cans of tuna in the *dispensa*—an easy way to give ourselves a treat while Mamma was figuring out what to make for supper. She would improvise quickly—a little tuna, olives, maybe some fennel if we had it that day, or onion.

This recipe calls for good quality canned tuna, but as an alternative for a dinner party, use fresh tuna, grill it, and then slice it. You can coat the tuna in black pepper for an extra dimension—dress it up as you wish. There is nothing like a beautiful pink slab of sashimi-grade tuna, cooked just until it is medium-rare. The color will be part of the medley here: Between the pink tuna, the greens, and the olives, the dish becomes a little painting.

This is an improvised recipe. You need 8–10 ounces of fresh or canned tuna, but beyond that? Your taste buds will tell you what proportions are best.

---

*Romaine or iceberg lettuce*
*Chopped Kalamata olives*
*Capers*
*Diced roasted peppers*
*Tuna fish*
*Hard-boiled eggs, crispy bacon,
    and pickled hot pepper,
    optional*
*Basic Vinaigrette (page 53)
    with balsamic vinegar substituted
    for red wine vinegar*

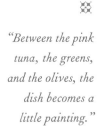

*"Between the pink
tuna, the greens,
and the olives, the
dish becomes a
little painting."*

Mix all ingredients and dress with vinaigrette.

*Wine:* Try a Soave, a Pinot Bianco, or a Pinot Grigio; or a simple Pinot Blanc or Chenin Blanc from California. These are wines of freshness, suppleness, and nice low acidity that cleanse the tuna and the saltiness of the olive. This is noshing food, and should be served with a light sipping wine.

# INSALATA DI POLLETTO GRIGLIATO CON SALSA AL GORGONZOLA /
## Warm Chicken Salad with Gorgonzola Dressing

*4 servings*

1 whole chicken breast
(about 1 pound), deboned

4 ounces Gorgonzola cheese

2 tablespoons Chicken Stock
(see page 74)

½ recipe Basic Vinaigrette
(see page 53)

12 ounces mixed baby lettuce

*Preparation:* Preheat the oven to 375 degrees.

Roast or grill the chicken breast until cooked all the way through, 12–15 minutes, and set aside to cool.

*The Dish:* Remove the skin from the chicken breast and cut the breast into thin slices on the diagonal. Divide the chicken into 4 mounds, and place in a baking dish. Cover the mounds of chicken with a third of the Gorgonzola cheese and bake for a few minutes, until the cheese is melted.

In a saucepan, combine the remaining Gorgonzola cheese with the chicken stock. Add the vinaigrette and simmer over low heat until the cheese melts. Reserve a small amount of the dressing and toss the rest with the lettuce. Arrange the lettuce on 4 plates and place the chicken and melted cheese on top. Pour the reserved dressing over the finished salad.

*Wine:* This dish seems simple, but it's actually tricky to match, because you have to worry about the Gorgonzola overpowering the wine. The chicken, with its crunchiness, enriched by the dressing, deserves a wine with elegance and structure. I suggest a pleasant but fairly robust red wine to stand up to the cheese and the vinaigrette: a good glass of Merlot from Ferrari-Carano, Silverado, or Duckhorn. Or a nice Burgundy, a Nuits-Saint-Georges, a Sauvigny les Beaune—wines that are almost flinty.

## INSALATA DI PERE E GRANCHIO /
### Romaine, Crab, and Shaved Pear Salad

*4 servings*

---

*1 whole cooked Dungeness crab, or*
    *6–8 ounces cooked crabmeat*
*2 Bartlett or Bosc pears*
*½ lemon*
*14 ounces romaine lettuce, cut into*
    *2-inch-wide pieces*

FOR THE DRESSING

*4 tablespoons olive oil*
*2 tablespoons white wine vinegar*
*1 teaspoon Dijon mustard*
*½ teaspoon pink peppercorns,*
    *crushed*
*½ teaspoon black pepper, crushed*

*Preparation:* Pull the meat off the crab, and set aside.

Peel and core the pears, slice them very thin, and place them in a bowl of ice water. Squeeze the juice from the lemon into the water and add the lemon, to keep the pears from turning brown.

In a blender, combine the oil, vinegar, mustard, pink peppercorns, and black pepper and blend until smooth.

*The Dish:* Drain the pears and pat dry. Mound the lettuce on individual plates, pile on the crabmeat and pear slices, and pour the dressing on top.

*Wine:* This wine suggestion depends on when you serve the dish. If you serve it as an appetizer, definitely use a very dry, steely, and fresh white wine that shows natural acidity and crispness, such as a Vermentino. The first ones that come to mind, and the most famous, are Pigato and Cinqueterre, from Liguria. If you want a California wine, try a nice Sauvignon Blanc like Selene or Duckhorn—ones that have earthiness but not an excess of vegetable flavor.

And if this is a main dish at lunch, try a robust Chardonnay with all the essence of vanilla and oak. I'm also never against having fruity red wine with seafood—a Pinot Noir from the Carneros region, such as an Etude or an Acacia.

## PERE, RUCOLA, E FETTINE DI PARMIGIANO /
### Arugula, Pears, and Shaved Parmesan

*4 servings*

4 Bosc pears
½ lemon
¼ cup olive oil
2 tablespoons balsamic vinegar
12 ounces arugula, rinsed well
    and dried
4 ounces Parmesan cheese, shaved

Peel and core the pears, slice them very thin, and place them in a bowl of ice water. Squeeze the juice from the lemon into the water and add the lemon, to keep the pears from turning brown.

In a blender or food processor, combine the olive oil, vinegar, and about 4 slices of pear and blend until smooth. Drain the remaining pear slices and dress with some of the vinaigrette. Toss the arugula with the remaining dressing and arrange a mound in the center of each plate. Top with shaved Parmesan cheese and place the pear slices around the lettuce.

## TIMBALLO DI PICCOLE VERDURE / Vegetable Timballo

*Six 4-ounce timballos*

Sometimes people don't consider vegetables to be elegant, so they don't take them seriously. In Sicily, vegetables are straightforward; a great deal of our cooking starts in the same way, with garlic, tomato paste, and then whatever vegetable you're using. But this dish is more sophisticated—rich in flavors and beautiful to look at, it's perfect as an imaginative antipasto or an accompaniment to an entrée.

---

*3 large yellow onions, thinly sliced*
*1 tablespoon olive oil*
*¼ cup white wine*
*½ teaspoon salt*
*½ teaspoon white pepper*
*¼–½ cup heavy cream*
*Vegetable oil to coat dishes*
*3 large eggs*
*½ cup Parmesan cheese, grated*

*Chef's Tip:* Other vegetables, such as carrots, broccoli, cauliflower, and mushrooms, are delicious in a timballo. Coarsely chop about 2 cups of one of the vegetables and half of an onion. Sauté and puree them according to directions.

Preheat the oven to 300 degrees.

In a skillet, sauté the onions in the olive oil over medium heat until tender and translucent. Pour the wine over the onions and cook slowly over low heat for 20 minutes. Add the salt and pepper.

Puree the onions in a food processor fitted with the steel blade and pour in the cream, processing until you have a thick, pasty puree.

Lightly coat six 4-ounce custard cups with vegetable oil.

In a large bowl, whisk together the eggs and Parmesan cheese. Add the onion mixture and mix well.

Fill the cups to the top with the custard. Place the cups in a jelly roll pan or roasting pan and pour about ¾ inch of water into the pan. Bake for 30 minutes, until the custard is slightly firm.

Run a sharp knife around the edge of the timballo and unmold.

## PURÈ DI PATATE AL FORNO / Baked Mashed Potatoes

*4 servings*

*4 small to medium baking potatoes*
*6 tablespoons (3 ounces) butter*
*2 fresh sage leaves, finely chopped*
*2 garlic cloves, thinly sliced*
*¼ cup plus 2 tablespoons Parmesan*
*   cheese, grated*
*⅓ – ½ cup whole milk*
*1 large egg*
*Kosher salt, to taste*
*A few gratings fresh whole nutmeg*

Preheat the oven to 400 degrees.

Bake the potatoes with the skins on, about 45 minutes to 1 hour, until well done. Meanwhile, in a small skillet, melt the butter over medium heat. Add the sage and garlic and sauté a few minutes.

Allow the potatoes to cool slightly. Cut off the top section of each potato and scoop out the inside into a medium-size bowl, keeping the skin intact. Mash the inside of the potatoes with the melted butter mixture, 4 tablespoons of the Parmesan cheese, and ⅓ cup of milk. Mix well and add more milk if necessary for a smooth and creamy filling.

In a small bowl, whisk the egg. Brush the potato skins with egg and sprinkle with kosher salt. Using a pastry bag or a spoon, stuff the potato skins. Sprinkle with the remaining Parmesan cheese and a few gratings of nutmeg and bake until lightly colored, about 10 minutes.

*Zuppe*
*Zuppe*

# *Zuppe*

# ✿ *Zuppe*

SOUP MAKES ME THINK ABOUT COLD WINTER NIGHTS, EITHER AT HOME or at boarding school, when the whole supper was a soup: a broth with beans or lentils, or a little pasta or rice—or maybe beans and pasta, a rustic version of *pasta e fagioli*. Supper was the light evening meal, and when it was soup, it had a soothing, spiritual feeling to it.

But people don't serve soup like that today. My favorite way to serve soup at Valentino is as the very first thing, in a little espresso cup. This is a wonderful way to refresh your palate, with a cold soup, or warm it up, with a hot soup. One of our specialties, included here, is a capon broth served with a bit of fresh truffle, an elegant introduction to a meal.

A heavier soup is best as part of a robust wintry dinner. I would put it after a cold appetizer, but again, only a small portion. It's the nicest way to ready your palate for the next experience.

All that is in the context of a larger meal. But I still like to eat soup the way I did as a boy, as the whole meal. Like minestrone. The word is magic. All it means is a mix, a blend, a potpourri of flavors and colors and proteins—whatever you want. Everybody should have minestrone in their refrigerator. And if you want something a little different, try the recipe for *passato*, which is simply a pureed minestrone.

Soup works as a light supper or a light lunch, or when you feel you want something with substance. Keep broth in the freezer, and if you have some left over, use it the next day. Rewarmed soup sometimes tastes better than the original. And it always tastes wonderfully like the past.

*8 – 10  s e r v i n g s*

Soup is part of everybody's memory. For me, it's memories of large batches for lots of people over many days, and having something in the refrigerator at all times. Mamma used to whip *passato* up in no time, using vegetables, potatoes, and the kitchen sink. It's a big minestrone, pureed.

---

*½ cup onion, diced*

*½ cup peeled carrot, diced*

*½ cup celery, diced*

*¼ cup olive oil*

*1 medium peeled potato, diced*

*½ cup cranberry beans, soaked*
  *overnight*

*½ cup cannellini beans, soaked*
  *overnight*

*3–4 cups (1 bunch) spinach, thinly*
  *sliced*

*2 cups (½ bunch) green chard,*
  *thinly sliced*

*1 zucchini, diced*

*1 cup cabbage, thinly sliced*

*½ cup corn*

*½ cup green peas*

*12 cups Vegetable Stock*
  *(see page 76)*

*Salt and pepper, to taste*

In a stockpot, sauté the onion, carrot, and celery in the olive oil until crispy. Add the potato, beans, spinach, chard, zucchini, cabbage, corn, and peas and braise for 10 minutes. Add the vegetable stock and bring to a boil. Turn the heat to low and simmer for 1–2 hours, until all the vegetables are tender.

Let the soup cool a little, and puree small quantities (1–2 cups at a time) in a blender or food processor. Adjust flavor with salt and pepper. Bring back to a simmer if soup is to be served right away, or cool further and refrigerate or freeze.

## ZUPPA D'ORZO CON RADICCHIO TREVISANO /
### Barley Soup with Radicchio Trevisano
*6 servings*

This has a little bit of the Venetian influence. Pino Pasqualato, the chef who worked so hard to improve Valentino's menu, came from that area, and one of the things we liked to do was show people that radicchio is more than just a red cabbage. In this dish, its strong, slightly bitter taste complements the nutty, crunchy taste of the barley, which is so widely used in Italy. Trevisano has long, thin leaves, and is crunchier and less bitter than regular radicchio.

---

*½ cup onion, finely chopped*
*½ cup peeled carrot, finely chopped*
*1 tablespoon garlic, finely chopped*
*1 teaspoon rosemary, finely chopped*
*1 teaspoon sage, finely chopped*
*½ cup olive oil, plus extra for*
*garnish*
*3 cups pearl barley, soaked*
*overnight*
*1 cup red wine*
*8 cups Vegetable Stock*
*(see page 76)*
*3 heads radicchio trevisano or*
*1 head regular radicchio*
*Salt and pepper, to taste*

In a stockpot, over medium heat, sauté the onion, carrot, garlic, and herbs in half the olive oil. When the onions are translucent, add the barley and stir well. Pour in the wine, turn up the heat, and boil until the wine evaporates. Add the vegetable stock and bring it to a boil. Turn down the heat and simmer for about 2 hours, or until the barley is tender.

Meanwhile, slice 2 heads of the radicchio trevisano or ¾ head of the regular radicchio into thin slices. In a skillet, sauté with the remaining olive oil until wilted. Add the cooked radicchio to the soup before serving and adjust the flavor with salt and pepper. Slice the uncooked radicchio into very fine strands. Serve the soup in heated bowls and garnish with the uncooked radicchio. Drizzle some olive oil over the soup.

*1 tablespoon onion, chopped*

*1 tablespoon shallot, chopped*

*2 tablespoons carrot, chopped*

*¼ cup olive oil*

*2 slices imported prosciutto,*
*chopped, optional*

*2 cups French lentils*

*1 cup red wine*

*2 quarts Chicken Stock*
*(see page 74)*

*8 ounces mixed wild mushrooms,*
*sliced*

*1 teaspoon garlic, chopped*

*1 teaspoon fresh rosemary, chopped*

*Salt and pepper, to taste*

In a stockpot, sauté the onion, shallot, and carrot in 2 tablespoons of the olive oil for about 5 minutes, until the onions are golden brown. Add the prosciutto and lentils and cook on low heat for a few minutes. Add the red wine, turn up the heat, and let evaporate. Add the chicken stock, bring to a boil, then reduce the heat to low to simmer for 90 minutes, uncovered.

In a large skillet over medium heat, sauté the wild mushrooms in the garlic, rosemary, and remaining olive oil. Season them with salt and pepper, and cook for a few minutes. Add to the soup.

For additional flavor, add a drizzle of good olive oil when serving.

## PURÉE DI GRANOTURCO CON PISELLI SECCHI SGUSCIATI /
### "Creamed" Corn and Split Pea Soup

*6 servings*

Twenty or thirty years ago in Italy, corn was something that was fed only to chickens. Now good sweet corn is beginning to find its place. When Italians come to America on vacation in the summer, they love the taste of sweet corn. So we developed this recipe, and the risotto with corn and peppers, as a way of introducing my new life to the old.

---

*4 ounces pancetta, finely chopped*
*½ cup olive oil*
*1 teaspoon sage, finely chopped*
*½ cup shallot, finely chopped*
*1 tablespoon garlic, finely chopped*
*5–7 ears fresh corn, kernels cut off
    the cob to equal 2¼ cups*
*2 cups split peas, soaked overnight*
*1 cup white wine*
*6 cups Chicken Stock (see page 74)*

In a stockpot over medium heat, sauté the pancetta in a few tablespoons of the olive oil until crispy. Add the sage, shallot, and garlic and cook a few more minutes. Add 2 cups of the corn and split peas and continue to cook for about 10 more minutes. Add the wine and boil until it evaporates. Add the chicken stock, bring to a boil, and lower the heat to simmer for 30 minutes, or until the peas are very tender.

When cool, puree the mixture in small quantities (1–2 cups at a time) in a food processor or blender. Return it to the pot and bring it back to a boil. Garnish with the remaining ¼ cup of corn.

## CREMA DI CAVOLO CON PANNA ACIDA /
### Cream of Cabbage with Sour Cream

*8 servings*

---

1½ *medium heads savoy cabbage*

1 *cup shallot, chopped*

¼ *cup olive oil*

8 *cups Vegetable Stock*

   *(see page 76)*

6 *tablespoons sour cream*

2 *tablespoons chives, finely chopped*

Julienne the cabbage and wash thoroughly. Drain well. In a stockpot, fry the shallot in the olive oil. When golden in color, add the cabbage and vegetable stock. Bring to a boil and allow to simmer for 20–30 minutes or until the cabbage is tender. Let cool a little, then puree in a blender.

If serving right away, return it to the pot and bring it to a boil again. Dissolve half the sour cream in the soup, and ladle into bowls. Garnish with remaining sour cream and chives. If not serving right away, refrigerate or freeze it after pureeing, then resume the recipe when reheating the soup.

# RAVIOLINI DI CAPPONE / Small Capon Ravioli in Broth

*6 servings*

This soup is a must at Christmas and New Year's. It's going to set up your whole life, your whole new year. The richness of a capon broth or a chicken broth with these ravioli and truffles is the perfect way to start a festive dinner. For me and my family—my wife, Stacy, and our three boys, Giorgio, Giampiero, and Tancredi—it's a tradition: We have this every year at holiday time.

FOR THE DOUGH

*3¼ cups all-purpose flour*

*5 large eggs*

*Pinch of saffron powder dissolved*
    *in ½ teaspoon water*

FOR THE STUFFING

*8 ounces capon meat (or substitute*
    *dark chicken meat), without*
    *bones and cut into 1-inch pieces*

*1 garlic clove, chopped*

*2 leaves fresh sage, finely chopped*

*1 tablespoon (½ ounce) butter*

*½ cup dry white wine*

*3 tablespoons Parmesan cheese,*
    *grated*

*2 large egg yolks*

*Salt and pepper, to taste*

*3–4 gratings fresh whole nutmeg*

*(continued)*

*Preparation:* TO MAKE THE DOUGH: In a food processor fitted with the steel blade, combine the flour, eggs, and saffron and process for 1 minute. On a floured work surface, knead the dough for a few minutes by hand and set aside to rest for 15–20 minutes.

TO MAKE THE STUFFING: Preheat the oven to 350 degrees.

In a large ovenproof skillet, sauté the capon, garlic, and sage in the butter, until the meat is lightly browned. Add the white wine and bake in the oven until the meat is well done, about 25–30 minutes. Remove from the oven and puree in a food processor with the Parmesan cheese and egg yolks. Flavor with the salt and pepper and nutmeg.

TO ASSEMBLE THE RAVIOLI: Run some dough through a pasta machine until it is as thin as possible. Cover a ravioli mold with a sheet of the pasta, fill the holes with stuffing, cover with more pasta (it may be necessary to brush the pasta with some water to seal the 2 layers together), and flatten with a rolling pin. Seal each ravioli with your fingers. Repeat until all of the stuffing has been used.

*2 quarts Chicken Stock*
  *(see page 74)*
*1 tablespoon truffle oil or paste*
*Fresh white truffle (optional)*

*The Dish:* In a medium-size saucepan, bring the chicken stock to a boil. Drop the ravioli into the liquid and cook until they rise to the top. Drain, put in serving bowls, and add the broth. Flavor with truffle oil, or in the winter, when they are in season, shave fresh truffle over the ravioli.

*"The richness of a capon broth . . . with these ravioli and truffles is the perfect way to start a festive dinner."*

# BRODO DI MANZO / Beef Stock

*2 – 3 quarts*

---

*5 pounds beef bones*
*3 carrots, coarsely chopped*
*1 large onion, coarsely chopped*
*2 stalks celery, coarsely chopped*
*2 tomatoes*
*1 head garlic*
*1 teaspoon fresh thyme*
*3 bay leaves*
*1 teaspoon whole black peppercorns*
*1 bunch Italian parsley*

Preheat the oven to 375 degrees.

Place the beef bones in a large roasting pan and brown in the oven for 1 hour. Transfer to a large stockpot and add water to cover. Add the remaining ingredients and bring to a boil over high heat. Reduce heat to low and simmer for about 5 hours. Strain into a clean pot, refrigerate, and then remove the fat that has risen to the top. If you don't plan to use the stock within a few days, freeze in airtight containers.

VARIATION

FOR BRODO DI AGNELLO (LAMB STOCK): To make lamb stock, just substitute lamb bones for beef bones and follow the recipe above.

## BRODO DI POLLO / Chicken Stock

*2 – 3 quarts*

---

*10 pounds chicken bones, including
wings, backs, feet, and necks*
*1 large onion, roughly chopped*
*1 carrot, roughly chopped*
*1 celery stalk, roughly chopped*
*1 head garlic, cut horizontally
in half*
*1–2 bay leaves*
*6 sprigs Italian parsley*
*4 sprigs fresh thyme*
*4 whole white peppercorns*

Place the bones and chicken parts in a large stockpot and cover with 1½ gallons of water. Bring the water to a boil over high heat and skim off the foam that accumulates on the surface. Add the remaining ingredients. Turn the heat down to medium-low and simmer gently, uncovered, for about 3½ hours, skimming off any foam that rises to the surface. Using a large colander, strain the bones and vegetables, pressing the liquid out of the solid matter. Strain 1 more time through cheesecloth. Refrigerate and skim off the fat that rises to the top. If you don't plan to use the stock within a few days, freeze in airtight containers.

### VARIATION

FOR BRODO DI PESCE (FISH STOCK): To turn chicken stock into fish stock, Angelo Auriana substitutes 2 pounds of fish bones for the chicken, and proceeds with the recipe. The only rule is to stay away from oily fish like salmon—he uses white fish like sole, snapper, bass, or turbot.

# BRODO DI ASTICE / Lobster Broth

*1 large onion*

*2 carrots, coarsely chopped*

*1 stalk celery*

*10–12 whole black peppercorns*

*5 garlic cloves, roughly chopped*

*4 tablespoons olive oil*

*2 bay leaves*

*2 tablespoons tomato paste*

*4 cooked lobster shells (use meat
   for another recipe)*

*1 teaspoon salt*

*Pepper*

*Bouquet garni: 6–8 sprigs of
   rosemary, thyme, and parsley
   tied together with twine*

*14 cups water*

In a large stockpot over medium heat, sauté the onion, carrots, celery, peppercorns, and garlic in the olive oil. Cook about 5 minutes, stirring frequently. Add the bay leaves, tomato paste, lobster shells, salt and pepper, and bouquet garni and sauté another 2–3 minutes. Add the water and bring to a boil over high heat. Reduce to a simmer and cook about 1 hour, skimming off the foam that accumulates on the top. Strain the broth, discarding the shells, vegetables, and herbs. Refrigerate or freeze in airtight containers.

VARIATION

FOR BRODO DI GAMBERO (CRAYFISH BROTH): In a medium-size pot of boiling water, blanch 2½ pounds whole crayfish for a few minutes. Cool and remove the meat from the tails to eat or use in another recipe. Scrape off any dark matter on the body of the crayfish and use the shells in the same way you would for lobster broth.

## BRODO DI VERDURE / Vegetable Stock

*2 – 3   q u a r t s*

Angelo Auriana says the best way to make vegetable stock is to "clean out your refrigerator," and put the vegetables in a pot. You can emphasize a flavor simply by adding more of a particular vegetable.

---

*2 stalks celery*

*2 yellow onions*

*1 large or 2 small carrots*

*1 leek, white part only*

*2 Roma tomatoes, sliced*

*¼–½ pound mushrooms*

*5 quarts water*

Roughly chop the celery, onion, carrots, and leek. Put all the ingredients in a large pot and bring to a boil. Reduce heat and let the stock simmer for 45 minutes. When cool, filter the stock and discard the solids.

# Pasta
Pasta

❖

Pasta Fresca *(Fresh Pasta)*
Salsa di Pomodoro e Basilico *(Tomato and Basil Sauce)*
Rigatoni con Melanzane, Pomodoro, e Rapini
*(Rigatoni with Eggplant, Tomato, and Rapini)*
Spaghetti al Tonno con Tanti Pomodorini
*(Spaghetti with Tomatoes and Tuna)*
Lasagnette di Verdure *(Vegetable Lasagne)*
Fusilli con Verdure Forti e Pancetta
*(Fusilli with Bitter Greens and Pancetta)*
Orecchiette con Broccoletti e Ricotta Salata
*(Little Ears with Broccoli and Dry Ricotta)*
Rotolini di Prosciutto e Spinaci
*(Little Spinach and Prosciutto Cannelloni)*
Fusilli con Olive, Piselli, e Pecorino
*(Fusilli with Olives, Peas, and Pecorino)*
Fusilli del Collegio con Lenticchie e Salsicce
*(Fusilli from Boarding School with Lentils and Sausage)*
Tagliolini con Cernia e Favette
*(Pasta with Grouper and Fava Beans)*
Pici alla Toscana *(Tuscan Pici with Ragù)*
Variation: Pici alla Senese *(Pici Sienese Style)*
Ravioli di Zucca al Burro e Parmigiano *(Pumpkin Ravioli)*
Lasagne di Zucca *(Pumpkin Lasagne)*
Uovo al Tartufo Dedicato a Nino Bergese
*(Pasta Stuffed with Eggs, Spinach, and Ricotta,
with Shaved Truffles)*
Timpano di Paola *(Paola's Holiday Pie)*
Timballo di Natale *(Christmas Pie)*

*Pasta*

*Crespelle (Crepes)*
*Crespelline d'Anatra con Mostarda di Cremona*
**(Duck Crepes with Cremona Mustard in**
**Red Wine Cream Sauce)**
*Crespelline di Porcini al Peperone Dolce*
**(Crepes with Porcini in a Sweet Pepper Sauce)**
*Crespelle d'Asparagi e Porcini*
**(Crepes with Asparagus and Porcini)**
*Crespelline ai Quattro Formaggi con Prosciutto*
*d'Oca e Salsa allo Zafferano*
**(Four-Cheese Crepes with Smoked Duck Prosciutto**
**in Saffron Sauce)**
*Gnocchi (Gnocchi, Done the Traditional Way)*
*Gnocchi Ripieni (Stuffed Gnocchi)*
*Tomato, Pesto, and Gorgonzola Sauce*
*Pesto Gnocchetti di Porcini in Fonduta Tartufata*
**(Porcini-Infused Gnocchi with Truffled Fonduta Sauce)**
*Polenta*

# Pasta

HERE IS MY MOST VIVID MEMORY OF CHILDHOOD: A BIG, STEAMING bowl of spaghetti, placed at the center of our table and tossed by my mamma or papá. Then, one by one, everybody offers their plate and gets their portion—me, my sister, my brother. It is like a dream to me, that simple daily ritual. It is what I think of when I think about how food brings people together.

When I was little, I ate pastina with broth and a little ricotta, and some lentils or beans. When I started school, I vividly remember coming home, saying, *"Cosa mangiamo?"*—what do we eat? Our big meal was lunch, and Mamma would always reply, *"Pasta asciutta,"* the Sicilian term for dry pasta. And we would sit down together to pasta with ricotta, pasta with *broccoletti,* pasta with tomato and anchovy, pasta with little capers and olives.

There was a tasty, inventive conglomerate of dishes, the colorful *fantasia* that is expected from Italians. Improvisation is so much a part of the Mediterranean culture. My mamma never worked from a cookbook. Recipes were *tramandate,* handed down from one generation to the next. When I asked my mother, "Who taught you how to do that?" she would answer that her mother had taught her, or the *antichi,* the ancient. People didn't put recipes into their computers or fax them to friends. A recipe was dictated at the stove. It was demonstrated and told.

Historically, Sicily is where the pasta tradition started. It seems to have been an Arab discovery. The Italians' main sustenance before the Arabs arrived was porridge—wheat, millet, barley, legumes, and cereals like oats. The Arabs discovered that if the wheat was pounded very hard and mixed with a little water, it could be stretched. They were the first ones to dry this stretched wheat in the sun, so they would have food that wouldn't spoil through long rides in the desert.

They left behind the method for making pasta, but at first pasta was only a dish for the rich—the flour was shaped and stuffed with meat. It was only when larger producers began to dry the pasta that they could make a great deal of it, and suddenly you had a dish that was very affordable.

It was in Naples that pasta became a staple of Italian cuisine. And in the eighteenth century, tomatoes were brought to Naples by American travelers. The ashes of Vesuvius make some of the most fertile soil for the juiciest and sweetest tomatoes, the San Marzano. And the dry climate of areas like Sicily, Sardinia, Calabria, and Campania, where Naples is, is the most suitable for pasta, because the secret of pasta is in the drying process, called the *essiccazione.*

For commercial dried pasta, the semolina flour is granular, like sugar, and the dough has to be kneaded for a long time. My three favorite brands are Martelli, Latini, and Rustichella, because they are very small, artisanal producers. They are compulsive about their product, almost to exasperation.

For example, at the wheat farms of Carlo Latini and his wife, as soon as the stalks of ripe wheat start to bend over, they're no good anymore. They won't use them unless they are perfect. They even number individual boxes of pasta—as though they were works of art, like a numbered silk screen print. The Martellis have a little mill where two brothers and their wives do everything themselves, but the true secret is their drying chamber. The best pasta requires three or four days to dry, and the Martellis have built a chamber with ideal conditions to dry their pasta in that amount of time. They don't feel comfortable making too many different shapes, so they only make four. And at Rustichella, they concentrate on the smaller shapes, like the orecchiette. In each case, you taste the little extra touch, the attention, when you bite into it. The pasta tastes more yeasty, and the flavors come across more intensely.

For me, pasta is an awakening, a refreshment, and I like to have small bites throughout the day. I am kind of a food snob on many other dishes, and if they are not properly prepared I get annoyed or I reject them. Yet with pasta, I am more accepting. And I still get excited when my mother comes from Modica for a visit and I get to taste flavors from my childhood again—olive oil, a little garlic, capers, olives. It's in my blood, and that of my three sons, too. Now, when Mamma comes, she cooks for them.

There are rules for pasta preparation:

- Cooking pasta is like swimming. There has to be room for the pasta to move as it cooks, lots of breathing room so it doesn't stick together. Add salt when the water boils, 1 tablespoon for each gallon. Or if you want to avoid salt, add lemon juice. A drop of olive oil doesn't interfere with taste at all, and will prevent sticking.
- Stir with a wooden spoon, because a metal one can break the pasta.
- Add long pasta all at once. Don't ever break it to fit into the pot. Pasta is holy. If it's long, just let it softly bend into the water.
- Absolutely no lid when cooking pasta. The pasta has to breathe.
- Pasta has to be al dente. You have to feel the grain as you taste it, feel a bite in your mouth. If it's cooked right, it tastes almost sweet. If it's gummy, it's over-

cooked. And the only way to tell is to sample it as you cook. Don't depend on the clock.

- Keep the pasta wet when it's done. Strain it, but don't shake it. The hot water is an insulation so the pasta will be steaming when it comes to the table for the moment of grace.

- If you have a seafood sauce, undercook the pasta and finish it in the pan. And no cheese with seafood. Use cheese in tomato sauces, but in very small quantities so you don't overpower the other flavors. If Americans have made mistakes with pasta, they are overcooking and oversaucing.

- For any pasta, warm the serving platter and the individual plates.

## PASTA FRESCA / Fresh Pasta

---

*3 cups plus 2 tablespoons all-purpose
    flour*
*5 large eggs*
*1 tablespoon olive oil*
*Salt and pepper, to taste*

VARIATIONS
*Pinch of saffron dissolved
    in ½ teaspoon water
    (for yellow pasta)*
*8 ounces raw spinach to equal
    5 tablespoons steamed spinach,
    chopped (for green pasta)*
*1 cooked beet, pureed to equal
    5 tablespoons (for purple pasta)*
*3 teaspoons squid ink (for black
    pasta), available at fish markets*

Place the flour on a wooden board, and make a well in the center. Pour the eggs into the well and add the oil, salt and pepper, and any additional flavorings or coloring. Using a fork, mix the liquids well. Slowly begin to draw in the dry ingredients with your fingers. Knead the dough until it is very elastic, about 5–8 minutes. Cover it with a damp cloth or plastic and let it rest for 15 minutes.

Cut the dough into small pieces, depending upon the size of your pasta machine, and flatten them with your hand or a rolling pin. Lightly dust the dough with flour and roll it through the machine, starting with the highest setting and gradually decreasing the thickness until the pasta is thin enough for the specific recipe you're preparing.

## SALSA DI POMODORO E BASILICO / Tomato and Basil Sauce

*2 cups*

---

*4 tablespoons olive oil*
*2 large garlic cloves, sliced*
*2 tablespoons onion, chopped*
*6 large Roma tomatoes, peeled,
    seeded, and diced*
*Salt and pepper, to taste*
*½ cup tomato puree*
*Fresh basil, chopped, to taste*

In a medium-size saucepan heat the olive oil over medium heat and sauté the garlic and onion until golden. Add the diced tomato and season with salt and pepper. Sauté a few more minutes. Add the tomato puree and simmer the sauce for 5–10 minutes for a fresh-tasting sauce, or up to 1 hour if you want a heartier, more complex sauce. Add the chopped basil.

## RIGATONI CON MELANZANE, POMODORO, E RAPINI / Rigatoni with Eggplant, Tomato, and Rapini

*4 servings*

This recipe is efficient, effective, and eternal. While recipe trends come and go, you can always enjoy the combination of tomato and eggplant and a green. Rapini is a very versatile vegetable—easy to cook, lots of flavor, with that bitter bite that adds so much to the sugar of the tomato. In my childhood, we had broccoli florets or cauliflower, whatever Mamma could find to give more substance and fill up our stomachs. She made a big cauldron of pasta and we had a *piatto unico*. Then if we were still hungry, we had more pasta for the second helping. And it tastes wonderful the next day: Fry it with just a little more tomato until the pasta is very crusty.

---

*6 Japanese eggplant*
*1 bunch rapini*
*1 garlic clove*
*½ cup olive oil, plus extra for garnish*
*2 tablespoons (1 ounce) butter*
*1 large shallot, minced*
*Red chili pepper flakes, optional*
*¼ cup dry white wine*
*20 small to medium fresh Roma tomatoes, peeled, seeded, and chopped*
*Fresh rosemary*
*Fresh thyme*
*1 bay leaf*
*Salt and pepper, to taste*
*12 ounces rigatoni*
*½ cup ricotta salata cheese, grated*

*Preparation:* Cut the tips off the eggplant and peel them partially by vertically cutting off a strip of skin with a vegetable peeler, leaving a strip as wide, and cutting off the next strip. Dice into ½-inch cubes.

Discard the rapini stems and coarsely chop the tops. Blanch for 2 minutes in boiling water and plunge into ice water to stop the cooking process. Drain and set aside.

*Chef's Tip:* If you use regular eggplant you must salt it for 1 hour and then drain, but it's not necessary with Japanese eggplant. The "hit and miss" partial peel is because too much eggplant skin gives a bitter taste—but you need some of it for color and texture. The eggplant can be prepared in advance and set aside.

A trick for keeping vegetables green is to add a pinch of baking soda to the boiling water before you cook the vegetables. Always scoop the vegetables out with a slotted spoon so that any tiny bits of sand, dirt, or stem will sink to the bottom of the pot.

In a nonstick sauté pan, over medium-high heat, brown the garlic in 5 tablespoons of the olive oil. Discard the garlic after 2–3 minutes, and cook the eggplant in the oil until golden, about 4 minutes. Put it in a strainer to drain off the excess oil, and set aside.

*The Dish:* Bring a pot of water to a boil and add salt.

In a sauté pan combine the butter and remaining olive oil and cook the shallot over medium heat until translucent. Add the chili flakes and sauté another minute. Add the white wine and boil until evaporated. Stir in the tomatoes, herbs, and salt and pepper. Add the eggplant and rapini and simmer over medium-low heat, uncovered, about 5 minutes.

*Chef's Tip:* Canned Roma tomatoes are all right for long-simmered sauces, but a quick sauce with fresh vegetables requires fresh tomatoes.

Cook the pasta until just al dente and add to the sauce in the sauté pan, tossing to combine. Drizzle with olive oil to taste, and top with grated ricotta salata cheese.

*Wine:* I would drink a red, medium-bodied wine with this dish. The first that comes to mind is always a Barbera, but a wine from southern Italy—a Cerasuolo di Vittoria or a Cirò from Calabria—will also work well. If you want something from California, I recommend a good Cabernet Franc, a wine with a lot of fruit.

## SPAGHETTI AL TONNO CON TANTI POMODORINI /
### Spaghetti with Tomatoes and Tuna
*4 servings*

This is Mamma's traditional dish, and I ate a great deal of it in my childhood. It requires very little work, but is nutritious and tasty. Tuna packed in water or olive oil is better for a quick dish than fresh tuna, which you would have to cook and flavor. But if you want to do this in an elegant way, you can grill the tuna and make the sauce with fresh tomatoes. There's the long road and the shortcut. It is a summer dish, made to be eaten at room temperature.

*2–3 garlic cloves, thinly sliced*

*3 tablespoons olive oil*

*1¼ pounds fresh tomatoes, preferably Romas, peeled, seeded, and diced, or 20 ounces canned Italian tomatoes, drained well (reserve ¼ cup tomatoes for garnish)*

*Two 5½-ounce cans imported Italian tuna in water or olive oil, drained*

*1 pound spaghetti*

*Salt and pepper, to taste*

*6 large basil leaves, julienned, for garnish*

> ⊠ *Chef's Tip:* The easiest way to peel tomatoes is to score the stem end with an X and plunge them into a pot of boiling water for 1 minute. Rinse under cold water until cool enough to touch and the peels will slip right off.

In a skillet over medium-high heat, sauté the garlic in 2 tablespoons of the olive oil for 1 minute.

Stir in the tomatoes and tuna and cook 2–3 minutes on medium-high heat.

Bring a large pot of water to a boil, add salt, and cook the pasta until just al dente. Drain and add to the sauce.

When cool, add the remaining olive oil and season with salt and pepper. Garnish with reserved chopped tomatoes and shredded basil.

*Wine:* The starch of the pasta, the rich tuna, and the acidity and texture of the tomatoes make a bold challenge, so I go for a big red, even though it's fish. I would try a rich Sangiovese or velvety Merlot, where the character of the wine and the richness of the grape will enlarge the texture and marriage of flavors even more.

## LASAGNETTE DI VERDURE / Vegetable Lasagne

*6 servings as a main course, or*
*12 servings as a first course*

Everybody loves a lasagne. We cooked up this one because everybody also loves fresh vegetables. And there are a lot of people who are at least quasivegetarian. We like to make a dish where they are included, and don't feel that they have to have a salad while they watch their friends eat a beautiful venison medallion or a bass just flown in from Italy. And there has been an evolution—almost an explosion—of farmers' markets across the country. It is wonderful to hear of people who religiously do their shopping European style, going from stall to stall, vendor to vendor, to pick the right ingredients, to choose, smell, interact—which we do not get to do in the supermarket.

---

*6 baby artichokes, outer leaves and*
*choke removed*
*1 pound asparagus, diced into*
*¼-inch cubes*
*¼ pound carrots, peeled and diced*
*into ¼-inch cubes*
*¼ pound baby zucchini, peeled and*
*diced into ¼-inch cubes*
*¼ pound fresh peas*
*1 pound fresh mushrooms, chopped*
*7 tablespoons olive oil*
*6 garlic cloves, chopped*
*6 tablespoons shallot, finely chopped*
*¾ cup dry white wine*
*Salt and pepper, to taste*
*1 recipe Fresh Pasta (see page 84)*
*¼ cup Parmesan cheese, grated,*
*for sprinkling on top*

FOR THE BÉCHAMEL SAUCE
*8 cups whole milk*
*14 tablespoons (7 ounces) butter*

*Preparation:* Slice each artichoke into about 6 wedges.

Sauté each vegetable separately with 1 tablespoon olive oil, 1 clove garlic, 1 tablespoon of the shallot, 2 tablespoons of the white wine, and salt and pepper, until tender. Set aside in separate bowls.

TO MAKE THE BÉCHAMEL: In a large saucepan, warm the milk over medium heat. In a separate saucepan, melt the butter over medium heat and slowly add the flour, stirring constantly. Add the heated milk a little at a time, stirring constantly. Add the Parmesan cheese, salt and pepper, and nutmeg. Divide the sauce into 7 equal portions and combine 6 of the portions with the separate bowls of vegetables, reserving the last portion for the top layer. Set aside.

*The Dish:* Preheat the oven to 400 degrees.

Bring a large pot of water to a boil, add salt, and add 1 tablespoon of the olive oil.

Prepare the pasta dough and work it through the pasta machine until it is very thin, about ¹⁄₁₆ inch. Cut it into 6-inch-wide strips. Blanch the strips in boiling water for 3 minutes, dip in an ice water bath to stop the cooking, strain each one, and pat dry with a cloth towel.

*1¼ cups plus 1 tablespoon*
   *all-purpose flour*
*¾ cup Parmesan cheese, grated*
*Salt and pepper, to taste*
*4–5 gratings fresh whole nutmeg*

Butter a large (10 × 18-inch) baking dish. Line the dish with 1 layer of pasta and evenly spread 1 of the vegetable/béchamel mixtures over it. Cover with 1 layer of pasta and then add the next vegetable mixture. Repeat this procedure until you have used all of the vegetables. Finish with a layer of pasta.

Spread the remaining béchamel over the top layer of pasta, sprinkle with the ¼ cup Parmesan cheese, and bake for 15–20 minutes.

*Wine:* A medium, balanced red wine—a nice Nero d'Avola, or a Sagrantino Rosso—elegant and clean, robust but not too aggressive, a wine that complements rather than one that overpowers. Or you can try a lighter, younger wine: a very fresh, young Chianti, a Cabernet Franc from California, a very fresh Pinot Noir from Oregon.

## FUSILLI CON VERDURE FORTI E PANCETTA /
### Fusilli with Bitter Greens and Pancetta

*4 servings*

Always finish pasta in the pan. It's a restaurant habit and also an important tradition. The last thirty seconds is the amalgamation—the still-moist pasta meets the sauce, the flavors; the sauce doesn't sit on top of the pasta. Besides, this way you're only pulling up what sauce you need. Anything else is left in the bottom of the pan. You can always serve your dish in a beautiful bowl when you're done.

Pancetta is Italian bacon, available at most gourmet delis. Buy it in one piece, not sliced.

---

*1 pound dried fusilli*

*4 tablespoons yellow onion, finely chopped*

*¼ pound pancetta, diced*

*3 tablespoons olive oil*

*1 garlic clove, thinly sliced*

*4 ounces Belgian endive, roughly chopped*

*3 ounces arugula, roughly chopped*

*1 small head radicchio, roughly chopped*

*Black pepper, freshly ground*

You can make this dish in the time it takes the pasta to cook, as long as you chop all the vegetables and garlic in advance. Bring a large pot of water to a boil and add salt. Cook the dried fusilli, until just al dente.

While the pasta cooks, sauté the onion and pancetta in the olive oil in a large skillet, on medium-high heat for 3–4 minutes.

Add the garlic and sauté another 1–2 minutes, stirring so it doesn't stick or burn.

Add the endive, arugula, and radicchio and sauté 5 minutes, until the onions are slightly browned and the greens have wilted. Drain the pasta and toss in the pan with the greens.

※ *Chef's Tip:* Don't add extra salt, because the pancetta is salty. You can add a pinch of pepper at the end.

*Wine:* A lively red—something clean on the palate and rich with fruit, such as a young Chianti, Montepulciano, or Pinot Noir.

※ *Quick and delicious: "You can make this dish in the time it takes the pasta to cook."*

## ORECCHIETTE CON BROCCOLETTI E RICOTTA SALATA /
### Little Ears with Broccoli and Dry Ricotta
*4 servings*

Orecchiette, which means "little ears," have recently gained in popularity. A few years ago people didn't know the word, but now there is a certain familiarity. Here, rapini complements the traditional dish from the Apulian region called *orecchiette alla barese*. This is our version—anchovies are optional, because a lot of people are a little turned off by the salt or fishiness of the anchovy. I also like to add little chunks of tomato.

---

*2 bunches rapini or broccoli,*
*tops only*
*½ cup olive oil*
*3 garlic cloves*
*3 anchovy fillets*
*Salt and pepper, to taste*
*12 ounces orecchiette*
*3 tablespoons ricotta salata cheese,*
*crumbled*

Bring a large pot of water to a boil and add salt. Coarsely chop the rapini tops and cook until very tender, 5–10 minutes. Remove with a slotted spoon (reserving the hot water for the pasta), drain well, and put in a large bowl. Mash the rapini with a fork into a rough puree.

In a skillet over medium heat, brown the garlic in the olive oil. Add the anchovies and mash them. Add this mixture to the rapini and season with salt and pepper.

Cook the pasta in the same water you used for the rapini, and toss the pasta with the sauce. Sprinkle the ricotta salata cheese on top and serve.

&#10074;&#10074; *Chef's Tip:* For stronger flavor, chop the rapini and sauté directly, without boiling first. After sautéing, cover the pan briefly to steam the rapini in its own juices, and then add it along with the anchovies, as above.

*Wine:* I like a medium-bodied wine with a good concentration of fruit, because the dish is quite robust. Something from the Apulian region that would match is a Salice Salentino; a good soft red from Friuli or the Veneto, or a Merlot d'Aprilia from Rome, would also work. These are wines of fruit and some elegance—good structure against the different sensations of the bitter greens and the chewy pasta.

# ROTOLINI DI PROSCIUTTO E SPINACI /
## Little Spinach and Prosciutto Cannelloni

*8 servings*

1 recipe Fresh Pasta (page 84)

**FOR THE FILLING**
¾ pound spinach, stems removed
¾ pound chard, stems removed
8 ounces prosciutto cotto, or
    cooked ham
1 cup Parmesan cheese, grated

**FOR THE SAUCE**
1 shallot, finely chopped
2 tablespoons (1 ounce) butter
1 cup heavy cream
Salt and pepper, to taste
2 tablespoons Parmesan cheese,
    grated

> ❈ *Chef's Tip:* You can use store-bought fresh lasagne if you don't have time to make the pasta yourself.

*Preparation:* Prepare the pasta dough according to the basic recipe and work it through the pasta machine until it is very thin, about 1/16 inch. Cut the dough into 6-inch squares. Cook the squares a few at a time in boiling salted water for 2–3 minutes until just al dente. Remove with a slotted spoon or strainer and dip in an ice water bath to stop the cooking. Pat dry with a cloth towel and keep the pasta covered.

Steam the spinach and chard for a few minutes until tender, and drain well. Chop coarsely and set aside.

*The Dish:* Preheat the oven to 375 degrees.

Place 1 pasta square partially on top of another, overlapping about 1½ inches, to form a rectangle. Sprinkle some of the greens, a piece of ham, and about 2 tablespoons of the Parmesan cheese on the longer edge. Carefully roll up and cut in half to make 2 rolls. Place in the prepared baking dish and repeat with the remaining pasta. Bake the rolls for 6–8 minutes.

TO MAKE THE SAUCE: In a small skillet, sauté the shallot in the butter over medium heat. When lightly browned, add the cream and season with salt and pepper. Reduce the sauce for a few minutes, until slightly thickened. Sprinkle in the Parmesan cheese.

Pour the sauce over the cannelloni and cover with foil. Bake another 8–10 minutes and remove the foil. Turn the oven to broil and return the pan to the oven briefly, until a golden crust forms.

## FUSILLI CON OLIVE, PISELLI, E PECORINO /
### Fusilli with Olives, Peas, and Pecorino
*6—8 servings*

This dish is the marriage of three wonderful flavors: the salty chunks of olive, the delicate taste of sweet pea, the finish of sharp pecorino. Pecorino is a sheep's milk cheese, not as creamy and sweet as Parmesan, but saltier, more masculine. This recipe is typical of southern Italy—strong flavors but intriguing in the mouth, especially if you match it to a nice robust wine. It's a very intense and satisfying dish. Serve it as a whole lunch or as a second or third course at dinner. To dress it up, garnish with *frico* (page 8).

---

*1 pound fusilli*
*½ cup olive oil*
*1 cup fresh peas, steamed until*
*tender*
*1 pound raw spinach, steamed and*
*chopped to equal ½ cup*
*Salt and pepper, to taste*
*2 whole garlic cloves*
*Red crushed chili peppers, optional*
*¼ cup dry white wine*
*5 fresh basil leaves, finely chopped*
*½ cup imported black olives,*
*chopped*
*½ cup aged pecorino cheese, grated*
*Frico (see page 8) for garnish*
*(optional)*

*Preparation:* In a large pot of boiling salted water, cook the fusilli until just al dente. Drain and toss with 1 tablespoon of the olive oil to keep the pasta from sticking. Set aside to cool.

In a food processor combine half of the peas and half of the spinach with 5 tablespoons of the olive oil. Puree until smooth. Salt and pepper to taste, and set aside.

*The Dish:* In a large skillet over medium heat, brown the garlic with the remaining olive oil. Discard the garlic. Add the chili flakes and sauté. Add the wine and let evaporate. Add the remaining peas and spinach, and the basil, and sauté another minute. Season to taste and set aside to cool.

In a large bowl, combine the pasta, sautéed vegetables, olives, three-fourths of the pureed vegetables, and the pecorino cheese, and toss well. Add more vegetable puree if needed. Serve within 3—4 hours at room temperature.

*Wine:* For this dish, we need a complex wine of rich fruit to cut through the saltiness of the ingredients and cleanse the palate with renewed sensations. I would try a robust Merlot (Matanzas Creek, Lewis Cellars, or St. Francis) or a Chianti Riserva (Antinori, Fonterutoli, or Castello di Ama).

# FUSILLI DEL COLLEGIO CON LENTICCHIE E SALSICCE /
## Fusilli from Boarding School with Lentils and Sausage

*6 servings*

It is an Italian custom to serve this dish on New Year's Eve; I always ate it when I was a little boy. The lentils gave me dreams of wealth. Mamma was big on pasta and vegetables, rice and vegetables, but the addition of the sausage increases the flavor and makes it heartier. I like the shape of the fusilli, those twisty things that, as you lift them from the plate, you can see stuck with all the little lentils.

---

*10 ounces spicy Italian sausage,
   casings removed*

*1 medium yellow onion, finely
   chopped*

*3 garlic cloves, finely chopped*

*1 large tomato, peeled, seeded,
   and chopped*

*1 carrot, peeled and finely chopped*

*1 stalk celery, finely chopped*

*1½ teaspoons dried rosemary*

*7½ cups water*

*1 cup lentils*

*8 ounces fusilli*

*Salt and pepper, to taste*

*1–2 tablespoons olive oil*

In a large saucepan, over medium-high heat, brown the sausage for about 3 minutes. Add the onion, garlic, tomato, carrot, celery, and rosemary and sauté for 6 minutes. Add the water and lentils and bring to a boil. Reduce the heat to low and simmer, stirring frequently, until the lentils are tender and the mixture thickens, about 35–40 minutes.

Bring a large pot of water to a boil. When the lentils are nearly done, salt the water and cook the fusilli until just al dente. Add the pasta to the lentil mixture and simmer for 2 minutes.

Season with salt and pepper and drizzle with olive oil.

## TAGLIOLINI CON CERNIA E FAVETTE /
### Pasta with Grouper and Fava Beans
*4 servings*

In northern Italy, they like to marry fish or seafood with rice—a mullet risotto, a sand dabs risotto. In the south, we combine fish and pasta. Not fish with pasta on the side, but a true marriage of flavors. Usually in these dishes, the pasta is soupy, with nice extra liquid. The ingredients here are traditional, but the dish is our own invention. And if you can't find fava beans at the farmers' market, soak some dried beans. Substitute sea bass, poached salmon, or tuna for the grouper. Just keep the basic idea: the crunchiness of a bean, and a fish with structure.

---

*½ pound fresh fava beans*

*1 whole 2½-pound grouper or a similar large, flavorful fish, like sea bass or red snapper, cleaned and scaled*

*1 pound fresh tomatoes, peeled, seeded, and diced*

*Bouquet garni: fresh rosemary, thyme, sage, parsley, and a bay leaf tied together with twine*

*¼ cup onion, finely chopped*

*2 tablespoons parsley, finely chopped, plus extra for garnish*

*½ cup olive oil*

*1 cup dry white wine*

*2 tablespoons Tomato and Basil Sauce (see page 84)*

*12 ounces dried tagliolini, fettuccine, or lasagnette*

*Preparation:* Remove the fava beans from the pod. Bring a medium-size pot of water to a boil and blanch the beans for 1–2 minutes. Strain and remove the outer skin, squeezing the beans out with your fingers. Set aside.

In a large sauté pan over medium heat, slowly cook the fish, tomatoes, and bouquet garni in 2 quarts of salted water for about 30 minutes. Remove the fish to a work surface and strain the broth well through a fine mesh strainer. Discard all but 3 cups of the broth. Pull the meat off the bone and add it to the broth.

*The Dish:* In a large saucepan or skillet over medium-high heat, sauté the onion, fava beans, and 2 tablespoons of the parsley in the olive oil for a few minutes, until the onion is translucent. Add the wine and allow it to evaporate. Add the tomato sauce and the broth with the fish shreds, and simmer on low heat for 20 minutes. Meanwhile, cook the pasta, drain, and add to the sauce. Garnish with the remaining chopped parsley.

*Wine:* I recommend a robust white wine, like the Vernaccia from the husband-and-wife wine makers Teruzzi & Puthod, from San Gimignano in Tuscany, or a Greco di Tufo or Fiano di Avellino from Campania. These are wines with depth of color, body, rich aroma, and flavor that can sustain a very intense dish such as this.

*The crunchiness of fava beans, the firmness of grouper, and ribbons of taglioni combine in this perfect wedding of flavor and texture.*

## PICI ALLA TOSCANA / Tuscan Pici with Ragù

*6 servings*

*Pici,* or *pinci,* an ancient specialty of Tuscany, are hand-rolled strands of fresh pasta made with only flour, water, and a little salt. Because eggs were considered too precious to waste, originally none were used in making this pasta. Now that they are easier to come by, we have added them to our recipe. Because each pici strand must be rolled individually, the process is time-consuming. You can substitute a round, somewhat thick, dried pasta such as perciatelli if you are in a hurry.

FOR THE PICI
*6 cups all-purpose flour*
*3 tablespoons olive oil*
*2 cups water*
*2 large eggs*

FOR THE MEAT SAUCE
*½ cup olive oil*
*¼ cup onion, finely chopped*
*1 tablespoon celery, finely chopped*
*1 tablespoon carrot, finely chopped*
*1 tablespoon sage, finely chopped*
*1 tablespoon rosemary,*
*    finely chopped*
*1 tablespoon thyme, finely chopped*
*¼ pound ground beef*
*4 ounces rabbit meat or chicken*
*    liver, chopped*
*½ cup red wine*
*1 tablespoon canned tomato puree*
*1 cup Vegetable Stock*
*    (see page 76)*

*Preparation:* TO MAKE THE PASTA: Place the flour in a mound on a work surface and make a well in the center. Pour the eggs into the well and add 2 tablespoons of the oil, and the water. Using a fork, mix the liquids well. Slowly begin to draw in the dry ingredients, mixing with your fingers. Knead the dough until very elastic, about 5–8 minutes. Cover it with a damp cloth or plastic and let it rest for 15 minutes.

Form round balls, about 2 inches in diameter. Flour your hands and roll the balls into logs. Using both hands, begin to stretch the rope, holding 1 end steady with 1 hand as the other hand rolls and pulls the other end to lengthen it. Dust with flour as necessary until the rope is about 16 inches long and the thickness of a pencil. Store them on a wet kitchen cloth, lightly dusted with flour to prevent sticking.

TO MAKE THE SAUCE: In a large saucepan, sauté the onion in the olive oil over medium heat, until translucent. Add the vegetables, herbs, beef, and rabbit meat or liver, and sauté for a few more minutes. Add the wine and let it evaporate for a few minutes. Stir in the tomato puree and broth and simmer for another 20 minutes.

*The Dish:* Cut the ropes in half to make 8-inch-long pieces. Add the remaining tablespoon of olive oil to salted boiling water and cook the pici for 4–5 minutes. Drain and toss with the sauce.

## PICI ALLA SENESE / Pici Sienese Style

*6 servings*

---

1 recipe Pici (see page 98)

FOR THE SAUCE
½ cup olive oil
8 large garlic cloves, lightly crushed
1 cup (5 ounces) large dried
   bread crumbs
8 anchovy fillets, rinsed, dried,
   and chopped
1 tablespoon fresh tarragon,
   finely chopped
Salt and black pepper, coarsely
   ground, to taste
Fresh basil, chopped, to garnish

*Preparation:* Make *pici* according to the recipe (see page 98).

*The Dish:* Bring a large pot of water to a boil, add salt, and begin to cook the pasta. In the meantime, in a medium-size sauté pan, warm the olive oil and garlic over low heat so the garlic flavors the olive oil without browning. Turn heat to medium-high, add the bread crumbs, and fry for 1–2 minutes until golden and crunchy. Remove the garlic before it browns and becomes bitter. Add the anchovies and ¼ cup pasta water taken directly from the boiling pasta pot. Remove from the heat. The topping will look like moist sand at this point.

When the pasta is just al dente, reserve 1 cup of the cooking water. Drain the pasta, leaving a little water clinging to the strands, then immediately add to the topping. Add the tarragon and toss. Pour in the reserved pasta water as needed to make a little sauce, so the pici don't dry out. Season with salt and pepper to taste. Transfer to individual plates, sprinkle with basil, and serve immediately.

*Wine:* A great Chianti, of course, full of Tuscan flavors, supple and yet rich and full-bodied to sustain the robust flavors of the dish. Ruffino, Antinori, and Castello dei Rampolla are some of my favorite producers. Even a "Super Tuscan" blend from any good Tuscan producer will do.

## RAVIOLI DI ZUCCA AL BURRO E PARMIGIANO / Pumpkin Ravioli

*4 – 6 servings*

For many centuries, Italians, especially in Mantua, have done wonderful things with pumpkin. Serve it as a stuffing mixed with macaroons, or with extra cheese, depending on how sweet or delicate you want the flavor to be.

---

FOR THE PASTA

*2 large eggs*

*4 large egg yolks*

*1 tablespoon olive oil*

*1 teaspoon saffron*

*1 cup plus 2 tablespoons*
*all-purpose flour*

FOR THE FILLING

*1 sugar pumpkin or butternut*
*squash, seeds and fibers removed*

*Salt and pepper, to taste*

*2 tablespoons mostarda di Cremona*
*or fruit chutney, chopped*

*1 dozen Traditional Amaretti*
*(see page 252), crushed*

*½ cup Parmesan cheese, grated*

*6 tablespoons (3 ounces) butter*

*6 fresh sage leaves*

*Preparation:* TO MAKE THE PASTA DOUGH: In a large bowl combine the whole eggs with the yolks and olive oil. Dissolve the saffron in the mixture. Place the flour in a mound on a work surface and make a well in the center. Pour the egg mixture into the well and, using your fingers, slowly draw in the flour. Mix thoroughly, and knead the dough for 5–10 minutes, until very firm and elastic. Cover with a towel and let rest for 30 minutes.

Preheat the oven to 400 degrees.

Cut the pumpkin into 4 pieces and bake in a baking dish covered with foil, 30 minutes or until soft. Let cool.

*The Dish:* Pass the cooked pumpkin pulp through a sieve to eliminate all fiber. Season with salt and pepper, and add the mostarda, crushed cookies, and half of the Parmesan cheese. In a small saucepan, cook the butter with the sage leaves until the butter is browned, about 5 minutes. Discard the sage leaves and add half of the browned butter to the pumpkin mixture. Mix well and taste to adjust seasoning. Set aside the remaining butter for serving.

Flour the dough and roll it through a pasta machine until it is very thin, about 1/16 inch thick. Put half aside and cover with a damp cloth to keep it from drying out. Spoon 1 teaspoon of stuffing (for each raviolo) in rows on the sheet of pasta, leaving about a 3-inch space in between and about a 1½-inch space on each side. Brush water along the edges of the pasta and place the second sheet of pasta on top.

Gently press down around the stuffing to squeeze out all the air. Using a fluted pasta wheel or ravioli cutter, cut in between the mounds of stuffing to make approximately 3-inch-square ravioli. Press the edges together with your fingers to seal the stuffing inside.

Cook the ravioli in abundant salted boiling water. When they rise to the top, drain them and place on a platter. Pour hot browned butter over them and sprinkle the remaining Parmesan cheese on top. Serve while hot.

## LASAGNE DI ZUCCA / Pumpkin Lasagne

*4–6 servings as a main course, or*

*6–8 servings as a first course*

---

*1 medium sugar pumpkin or*
*butternut squash, seeds and*
*fibers removed*

*2 cups heavy cream*

*3 tablespoons (1½ ounces) butter*

*3–4 fresh sage leaves*

*1 recipe Fresh Pasta (see page 84)*

*1 cup Traditional Amaretti*
*(see page 252), crushed*

*1 cup Parmesan cheese, grated*

*Salt and pepper, to taste*

*A few gratings fresh whole nutmeg*

*Preparation:* Preheat the oven to 400 degrees.

Cut the pumpkin into 8 pieces, place on a baking sheet, and cover with aluminum foil. Bake until tender, about 30 minutes. Pass the cooked pumpkin pulp through a sieve to puree and eliminate all fibers.

In a small saucepan, bring 1 cup of the cream to a boil.

In a small skillet, cook the butter with the sage leaves until the butter is browned, about 3–4 minutes. Discard the sage leaves and set the butter aside.

Prepare fresh lasagne pasta (see page 88).

*The Dish:* In a large bowl, combine the pumpkin puree, the browned butter, half of the crushed cookies, and ½ cup of the Parmesan cheese and mix well. Season with salt and pepper and ground nutmeg. Add the warm cream.

Butter a baking dish and cut a layer of pasta to fit. Follow with a layer of pumpkin mixture over the pasta, and another sheet of pasta. Spread another layer of pumpkin, and sprinkle with Parmesan cheese and cookies. Continue until you have a 6-layer lasagne. Bake for 20–30 minutes. When done, let set for 5 minutes. Cut portions from baking dish.

Meanwhile, in a small saucepan, reduce the remaining cream by a third, flavor with salt and pepper and nutmeg, and pour over the lasagne just before serving. Garnish each plate with a sprinkle of Parmesan cheese.

*Wine:* Pumpkin lasagne is part of the tradition of southern Lombardy, so I turn there for a wine and suggest a Lambrusco or Albana di Romagna, a typical local varietal. This is a dry white, but not totally so—there is a little bit of a sweet aftertaste, a complexity to the flavor, that makes it the perfect accompaniment to the pumpkin.

## UOVO AL TARTUFO DEDICATO A NINO BERGESE /
Pasta Stuffed with Eggs, Spinach, and Ricotta, with Shaved Truffles

*4 servings*

We dedicate this dish to Nino Bergese, who cooked for the royal family of Italy before World War II, and remained with them after they abdicated and left the country. Many years later he offered his expertise as a consultant at the restaurant San Domenico in Imola, a temple of gastronomy in Italy. It was at that restaurant that I had a revelation, learning about Italian dishes I had never experienced as a child.

In this dish, you cut through the raviolo and the sensation is mainly truffles—the jewel of the earth, such an expensive rarity—and then the nice mixture of ricotta, spinach, a whole poached egg, and cheese with the truffle, an incredible symphony of flavor. My first reaction was, of course, "Wow." My second reaction was "How did he do it?" How could a perfectly cooked egg be encased in the dough? I figured they cooked the egg and then prepared the dough, put it together, and put these other things on top, but then how did they keep it from being hard-boiled?

Of course there is a secret to everything. Later on I was blessed with this recipe, which has become, especially at truffle time, one of our signature dishes. The secret is to cook the raviolo with a raw egg inside for 3 minutes. That will poach the egg to a soft, warm texture, and the very thin dough will be cooked enough. I am afraid on this one that store-bought fresh pasta is too thick, and often has been frozen. The dough has to be soft enough to close the raviolo, and I don't think that's possible with commercial dough. This is the quintessential "I want to do something out of the ordinary" dish. You fill each circle of pasta with ricotta and spinach and make a well, place the egg very gently in the middle, and then close it into a full-moon raviolo. Then you cook it and finish it with grated Parmesan cheese and truffles.

---

*¼ cup steamed spinach, chopped*
*¼ cup fresh ricotta cheese*
*1⅓ cups Parmesan cheese, grated*
*1 large egg*
*A few gratings fresh whole nutmeg*
*Salt and pepper, to taste*
*8 sheets of Fresh Pasta dough*
    *(see page 84), rolled thin*
    *and cut into four 4-inch circles*
    *and four 5-inch circles*

(continued)

Combine the spinach, ricotta cheese, half the Parmesan cheese, the whole egg, nutmeg, and salt and pepper, and mix well.

Place the smaller circles of pasta on a baking sheet. Divide the spinach mixture evenly among them. Make an indentation in the center of the spinach mixture and pour in 1 egg yolk. Brush the edges of the pasta with cold water and place a larger circle of pasta on top. Press down gently with your fingertips around the filling, to seal the edges well.

TO MAKE THE SAUCE: In a small saucepan, melt the butter until lightly browned. Meanwhile, bring a large pot of water to a boil and add salt. Cook the pasta for 2½ minutes.

*4 large egg yolks*
*½ cup (4 ounces) butter*
*2 ounces shaved truffles*

Carefully remove the ravioli with a spatula and drain well. Place them in a deep pasta dish. Pour the butter over them, sprinkle on the remaining Parmesan cheese, and shave truffles over the pasta.

*Wine:* You can drink marvelous things with this. Go with an expensive wine: a great "Super Tuscan" like Ornellaia or Tignanello; a rich Piedmontese wine, like a Monprà by Conterno-Fantino or Pin by Rivetti, which are a blend of Barbera and Nebbiolo; or a spicy, rich, and elegant Cabernet like Silverado. Wine that is piquant, spicy, with a lot of cassis, one that will be able to support all the different sensations you get from this dish.

❖

*Making Uovo al Tartufo: "Make an indentation in the center of the spinach mixture and pour in 1 egg yolk."*

*"Brush the edges of the pasta with cold water and place a larger circle of pasta on top. Press down gently with your fingertips around the filling, to seal the edges well."*

# TIMPANO DI PAOLA / Paola's Holiday Pie

*6 servings*

Paola came to Los Angeles for a social visit in 1996, and we convinced her to cook a dinner with Angelo Auriana at Valentino. This was one of the dishes we served, Paola's interpretation of a typical ancient Roman dish, combining both sweet and savory flavors.

---

### FOR THE CRUST

*1½ cups all-purpose flour*

*¼ cup plus 1 tablespoon
granulated sugar*

*10 tablespoons (5 ounces) butter,
chilled and cut into small pieces*

*3 large egg yolks*

*¼ teaspoon ground nutmeg*

### FOR THE MARINARA SAUCE

*¼ cup olive oil*

*4 whole garlic cloves*

*½ small onion, finely chopped*

*¼ cup white wine, optional*

*One 28-ounce can Italian peeled
tomatoes, seeded and chopped*

*Pinch of dried chili flakes, crushed*

*Salt and pepper, to taste*

### FOR THE MEATBALLS

*¾ pound ground veal*

*½ cup bread crumbs*

*Salt and pepper, to taste*

*1 tablespoon fresh rosemary,
finely chopped*

*1 tablespoon fresh sage,
finely chopped*

(continued)

*Preparation:* TO MAKE THE CRUST: In a food processor fitted with the steel blade, combine the flour and sugar. Add the butter and process until just combined. Add the egg yolks and nutmeg and pulse a few more times to incorporate. Wrap in wax paper and chill at least 2 hours.

Divide the dough into 2 pieces, one slightly larger than the other. Roll each piece into a ¼-inch-thick circle. Fit the larger circle into a buttered 9-inch deep-sided pie pan, and reserve the smaller circle on a baking sheet to use as the top crust. Chill both until ready to use.

TO MAKE THE SAUCE: In a sauté pan, lightly brown the garlic in the olive oil over medium heat. Discard the garlic. Lower the heat, add the onion, and cook until it's translucent. If the onion begins to brown, add the wine to take the temperature down. Add the tomatoes and chili flakes and simmer about 25–35 minutes. Season with salt and pepper to taste. Set the sauce aside.

TO MAKE THE MEATBALLS: Combine the ground veal with the bread crumbs, salt and pepper, and herbs. Coat your hands in olive oil and form small balls about ½ inch in diameter. In a sauté pan, cook them in the olive oil and butter, until slightly browned, about 10 minutes. Add them to the sauce.

In a large pot of boiling salted water, cook the pasta until al dente. Mix with a little of the sauce, and set aside to cool.

*1 tablespoon fresh thyme,
    finely chopped*
*2 tablespoons olive oil*
*2 tablespoons (1 ounce) butter*

FOR THE STUFFING
*10 ounces dried ziti*
*2 large eggs, hard-boiled*
*6 ounces smoked mozzarella cheese,
    diced*
*4 tablespoons Parmesan cheese,
    grated*
*2 tablespoons (1 ounce) butter*

*The Dish:*  Preheat the oven to 350 degrees.

To assemble the torta, begin layering the ingredients in the pasta shell—first the ziti, followed by the meatballs, the hard-boiled egg, the mozzarella cheese, and the Parmesan cheese. Continue layering until the ingredients are gone, reserving some sauce for serving. Top with a layer of Parmesan cheese and dot with butter.

Cover the torta with the top crust and seal the edges with a fork.

Bake the torta for 40 minutes. Serve the remaining marinara sauce on the side.

*Wine:*  You could try a very fresh and fruity Viognier from Alban or Calera, but with the combination of sweet and sour flavors, you could go with a very rich, powerful Zinfandel or Syrah from the Rhone region, Hermitage or Côte Rôtie.

This is the kind of dish we serve at a holiday meal, where the family sits together for hours, sharing a celebration. It is Angelo's interpretation of an elegant baked pasta.

*½ pound ground veal*

*2 tablespoons fresh rosemary,*
   *finely chopped*

*2 tablespoons fresh sage,*
   *finely chopped*

*2 tablespoons fresh thyme,*
   *finely chopped*

*Salt and pepper, to taste*

*¾ cup bread, finely cubed*

*½ cup Parmesan cheese, grated*

*1 recipe Fresh Pasta (see page 84),*
   *cut into lasagne noodles*

*1 recipe Béchamel Sauce, kept warm*
   *(see Vegetable Lasagne,*
   *page 88)*

*5 cups marinara sauce (see Paola's*
   *Holiday Pie, page 105)*

*¾ pound fontina cheese, cut into*
   *⅛-inch-thick slices*

*¼ pound prosciutto cotto,*
   *thinly sliced*

*2 tablespoons (1 ounce) butter*

*Preparation:* In a bowl, combine the veal, herbs, and salt and pepper. Add the bread and ¼ cup of the Parmesan cheese. Coat your hands with olive oil so that the meat mixture will not stick, and form small meatballs, about ½ inch in diameter. Refrigerate until ready to use.

In a large pot of boiling salted water, cook the pasta, a few strips at a time, until al dente. Carefully place the lasagne on a nonstick baking sheet and set aside.

*The Dish:* Preheat the oven to 325 degrees.

TO ASSEMBLE THE TORTA: Spoon about 1 cup of the béchamel sauce onto the bottom of a nonstick 9-inch cake pan. Follow with a layer of pasta, marinara sauce, meatballs, fontina cheese, and prosciutto. Combine the next layer in the same order and keep layering until the pan is three-fourths full. You will have 5 or 6 layers. Finish the final layer with pasta, béchamel, and a drizzle of marinara sauce. Dot with butter and bake for 40 minutes. The torta will rise slightly as it cooks. Remove from the oven when the top is crusty, and set aside for 1–2 hours.

A half hour before serving, preheat the oven to 375 degrees. Rewarm the torta for 10 minutes and serve with about ¼–½ cup of béchamel drizzled over each serving.

> ✖ *Chef's Tip:* You can assemble the torta the day before, cook for about 25 minutes, cool, and refrigerate. When ready to serve, preheat the oven to 375 degrees and reheat the torta for 25 more minutes.

*Wine:* I would serve a special-occasion wine—an elegant Burgundy, like Chambertin, or a "Super Tuscan" like Ornellaia. Or the wine of your birth year, if it's a good one. You'll want a red wine of character and finesse that is still robust enough for a dish that is rich.

## CRESPELLE / Crepes

*8 crepes*

When we opened Primi, it was full of *bergamaschi,* young chefs from Bergamo whom we brought in to make a menu of appetizers only, small portions, "cute things," as I call them. Everyone made cannelloni with crepes, and stuffed desserts, so what else could we do? It was easy to think of ricotta or vegetables, but we went a step further and created several original dishes. The best-known is with duck, cooked for a long time to incorporate other flavors, pureed and folded into the crepe and topped with Italian mostarda di Cremona. In the sixteen years I owned Primi, the menu changed enormously, with one exception—we always had the crepes. Now we serve them at Valentino.

---

*1 large egg*
*¾ cup milk*
*¼ cup all-purpose flour*
*1 tablespoon (½ ounce) butter*

In a medium-size bowl, beat the egg with 1 tablespoon of the milk. Add the flour and mix well. Incorporate the rest of the milk little by little, and strain mixture through a fine mesh sieve. Melt the butter in an 8-inch nonstick skillet over medium-low heat. Let the butter cool and add it to the crepe batter. Heat the same pan again and ladle a few tablespoons of the batter into the pan, tilting it so that the bottom is evenly coated. When the edge of the crepe begins to color, turn it over and cook the other side for a few seconds. Repeat the procedure with the rest of the batter and let the crepes cool.

# CRESPELLINE D'ANATRA CON MOSTARDA DI CREMONA /
## Duck Crepes with Cremona Mustard in Red Wine Cream Sauce

*4 servings (8 crepes)*

---

*1 recipe Crepes (see page 109)*

**FOR THE FILLING**

*3 tablespoons (1½ ounces) butter*

*6 ounces lean duck meat, cut into*
    *½-inch cubes*

*1 tablespoon onion, finely chopped*

*¼ teaspoon juniper berries*

*1 teaspoon fresh sage, finely chopped*

*1 teaspoon fresh rosemary,*
    *finely chopped*

*1 tablespoon Toasted Garlic*
    *(see page 7)*

*1 cup red wine*

*½ cup Chicken Stock (see page 74)*

*1 cup heavy cream*

*2 tablespoons mostarda di Cremona*
    *or fruit chutney (chopped)*

*2 tablespoons Parmesan cheese,*
    *grated*

*¼ cup Italian parsley, chopped,*
    *for garnish*

*Preparation:*  Make the crepes according the recipe on page 109.

*The Dish:*  Preheat the oven to 375 degrees.

In a sauté pan, melt 2 tablespoons of the butter over high heat and brown the duck. Turn the heat down to medium and add the onion, juniper berries, sage, and rosemary, stirring frequently. When the onion is caramelized, add the garlic and red wine, and cook until the wine evaporates. Add the chicken stock and cream and reduce by a third. Drain off half of the liquid and set it aside to finish the dish. In a food processor, puree the duck mixture until smooth.

Divide the filling among the 8 crepes. Fold the crepe in half to form a half-moon shape and fold in half again to form a triangle. Place the crepes in a single layer in a heavily buttered baking dish, and top with the mostarda and Parmesan cheese. Bake for 10 minutes or until the top of the crepe is nicely colored. Spoon the sauce onto individual plates and arrange 2 crepes on top of the sauce. Garnish with chopped parsley.

*Wine:*  Champagne, because of the sweet spiciness of the chutney or the Cremona mustard and the very soft duck filling. The crepe is thin and also soft, so with that kind of harmony, I don't see anything overpowering. A champagne will be very cleansing, almost elegant, as a finishing touch. I would go with a brut, Schramsberg or Iron Horse; or if you want to go to something Italian, a Prosecco. Fresh and clean, it nicely absorbs all the different sensations.

## CRESPELLINE DI PORCINI AL PEPERONE DOLCE /
### Crepes with Porcini in a Sweet Pepper Sauce

*4 servings (8 crepes)*

---

*1 recipe Crepes (see page 109)*

FOR THE FILLING

*2 tablespoons (1 ounce) butter*

*2 teaspoons Toasted Garlic
   (see page 7)*

*6 ounces porcini mushrooms
   (sliced fresh or frozen)*

*¼ cup fresh ricotta cheese, drained
   well*

*2 large egg yolks*

*¼ cup Parmesan cheese, grated*

*Salt and pepper, to taste*

*A few gratings fresh whole nutmeg*

*1 shallot, finely chopped*

*2 tablespoons olive oil*

*2 medium red bell peppers, sliced
   into thin strips*

*2 tablespoons heavy cream*

*2 tablespoons whole Italian parsley
   leaves*

*Preparation:* Make the crepes according to the recipe on page 109.

*The Dish:* Preheat the oven to 500 degrees.

In a skillet, brown 1 tablespoon of the butter. Add half of the garlic and all of the mushrooms and sauté over medium-high heat for a few minutes. Turn the heat down and cook for 5 more minutes. Transfer to a large bowl and allow to cool. Stir in the ricotta cheese, egg yolks, and 2 tablespoons of the Parmesan cheese. Season with salt and pepper and a little nutmeg to taste.

In the skillet, sauté the shallot in olive oil over medium heat. Add the remaining garlic and the peppers and reduce to a simmer. Cover and cook until tender, about 10–12 minutes. In a food processor, combine the peppers, cream, and remaining butter and pulse until smooth. Season with salt and pepper.

Place about 2 tablespoons of the porcini filling on each of the 8 crepes. Fold them in half to form a half-moon shape and fold in half again to form a triangle. Place the crepes in a single layer in a lightly buttered baking dish. Spread the remaining porcini stuffing on top of each crepe, sprinkle with the remaining Parmesan cheese, and bake for 5–10 minutes, or until the crepes are crispy and light brown in color. Spread the red pepper sauce on 4 plates and place 2 crepes on each plate. Garnish with whole parsley leaves.

## CRESPELLE D'ASPARAGI E PORCINI /
Crepes with Asparagus and Porcini

I grew up on Mamma's lasagne, but when I came to this country, I found that the chefs made crepe lasagne. Every day I saw crepes being made for many purposes—crepes suzette, pancakes, crepe cannelloni. So we invented this recipe at Primi, and it has been on the menu since the restaurant opened in 1986.

This isn't a quick recipe, but the ultimate result is always satisfying because asparagus and porcini are both vegetables of tremendous personality. I find this dish irresistible. Serve it as an *assaggino* before you sit down to dinner, or place it on the table as a first course. Everybody will be surprised and delighted.

---

*1 recipe Crepes (see page 109)*

FOR THE FILLING
*1 bunch thin asparagus*
*¼ cup (2 ounces) butter*
*8 ounces porcini mushrooms, fresh or*
*    dried (if dried, soak in warm*
*    water for 10–15 minutes to*
*    soften), diced*
*1 tablespoon shallot, chopped*
*Salt and pepper, to taste*
*1 recipe Béchamel Sauce*
*    (see Vegetable Lasagne,*
*    page 88)*
*¼ cup Parmesan cheese, grated*

*Preparation:* Make the crepes according to the recipe on page 109.

In a medium-size pot of salted water, blanch the asparagus for 2–3 minutes. Drain and slice into ½-inch diagonal slices.

TO CLARIFY THE BUTTER: Melt the butter over low heat. Allow to stand, and then remove the white solids. Spoon off 2 tablespoons of the clarified butter.

*The Dish:* Preheat the oven to 500 degrees.

In a skillet, sauté the asparagus, mushrooms, shallot, and clarified butter. Season with salt and pepper. Add this to the béchamel sauce, and stir in about 1 tablespoon of Parmesan cheese. Divide the stuffing among the crepes, fold them to form a half-moon shape, and then fold again to form a triangle. Place the crepes in a single layer in a buttered baking dish. Sprinkle with Parmesan cheese and bake for 5–10 minutes.

*Wine:* A fresh red or white with a little age but lots of fruit character. A young Nebbiolo like Favot from Aldo Conterno. Or a Rosso Conero from Umani Ronchi, or a Sangiovese from Romagna. If you'd like a traditional French wine, a good Gamay Villages or Fleury from Beaujolais. You want a sense of freshness, of strawberries and cherries—fruit without an excess of astringency—to liven the delicacy of the dish.

## CRESPELLINE AI QUATTRO FORMAGGI CON PROSCIUTTO D'OCA E SALSA ALLO ZAFFERANO / Four-Cheese Crepes with Smoked Duck Prosciutto in Saffron Sauce

*4 servings (8 crepes)*

*1 recipe Crepes (see page 109)*

FOR THE FILLING

*6 ounces mixed cheeses (1–2 ounces each of 4 different cheeses, for example: taleggio, Gorgonzola, fontina, caprino)*

*12 chives*

*16 thin slices duck prosciutto*

FOR THE SAUCE

*1 tablespoon (½ ounce) butter*

*1 tablespoon shallot, chopped*

*Pinch of saffron, dissolved in ½ teaspoon water*

*¼ cup white wine*

*1 cup heavy cream*

*Salt and pepper, to taste*

*Preparation:* Make the crepes according to the basic recipe on page 109.

*The Dish:* Preheat the oven to 375 degrees.

In a food processor fitted with the steel blade, combine the cheeses and process to blend. In a small pot of salted boiling water, blanch 8 of the chives for a couple of minutes and rinse immediately in cold water. Finely chop the unblanched chives and set aside for garnish. Divide the cheese stuffing equally onto the center of each crepe. Place 1 slice of duck prosciutto over the cheese. Fold crepe in half and gather outer edge toward the center to form a string purse. Tie with 1 blanched chive stalk and place in a lightly buttered baking dish. Repeat with remaining crepes. Bake 6–8 minutes, or until edges of the crepes are slightly crispy and colored.

In a skillet over medium-high heat, sauté the shallot in butter while the crepes are cooking. When the shallot is golden in color, add the saffron and wine. Cook to evaporate the wine, and add the cream. Simmer on low heat until reduced by half. Season with salt and pepper. Spoon the sauce onto plates and place 2 slices of prosciutto on each plate. Transfer crepes from the baking dish and place on top of the duck. Sprinkle with chopped chives.

There are different versions of gnocchi in different areas of Italy. You have Cavatelli, where you take the dough and you flip it against a fork with your finger, like Grandma told us to do in the old days, or you can make a little rope, or stuff them, or infuse them. We have seafood gnocchi, porcini gnocchi, squash, beef, spinach—the colors change, the flavors change, the shape and size change. What doesn't change is that this is a nourishing food, very robust. Past, present, contemporary, eternal. Serve it with a roast, from an osso buco to a veal knuckle—a *stinco*—or some grilled meat or sausage.

---

*4 tablespoons (2 ounces) butter*

*3 fresh sage leaves*

*2 pounds potatoes, preferably Yukon Gold, peeled and cut in half*

*½ cup Parmesan cheese, grated*

*4 large egg yolks*

*Salt and pepper, to taste*

*A few gratings fresh whole nutmeg*

*3 cups plus 2 tablespoons all-purpose flour, plus a little more to work with*

⚙ *Chef's Tip:* The key to gnocchi is to work fast. The potatoes go right from the pot into the ricer, and then right into a bowl with the other ingredients. Roll out the dough, cut it, shape the gnocchi, and cook them. If you want to work in advance, plunge them into ice water after cooking and set aside. But once you start the process you have to finish. Otherwise, says Luciano Pellegrini, "You just get little rubber things." The longer the potatoes or dough are allowed to sit, the softer and wetter they get. Pellegrini prefers steaming the potatoes to boiling them, because they absorb less moisture that way.

In a small saucepan over high heat, melt the butter with the sage leaves. Cook for 4–5 minutes until browned, and discard the sage.

Steam the potatoes until very tender. Immediately put through a ricer and into a large bowl. Add the Parmesan cheese, 3 tablespoons of the browned butter, the egg yolks, salt and pepper, and the nutmeg.

Flour the work surface liberally and turn out the potato mixture. Sprinkle over the flour, and using your hands, work the mixture together. Knead briefly to bring into a ball.

Flour your hands, and on a lightly floured work surface, shape the dough into a loaf. Slice the loaf into about 6 sections. Roll each section of dough into a rope, about ½ inch in diameter, and slice into 1½-inch pieces. Working with 1 piece at a time, roll the ends with your fingers to round off the edges. Hold a fork in 1 hand, and with the thumb of the other hand, press each gnocchi against the fork. Roll it down and forward, off the tines of the fork. The gnocchi should be slightly curled with ridges on the outer edge. This dough does not absorb sauce—but the ridges will.

Bring a large pot of water to a boil, add salt, and add the gnocchi. Stir along the bottom of the pot with a wooden spoon to make sure they don't stick. The gnocchi are done as soon as they float to the top. Remove with a slotted spoon.

If you are serving them immediately, toss with sauce. Otherwise, plunge the gnocchi into ice water to stop the cooking. Drain and place in a single layer on an oiled baking sheet. Cover with plastic wrap and

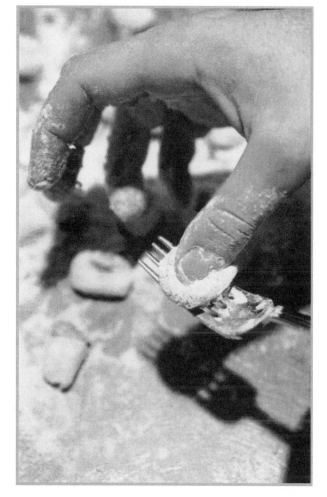

*Traditional gnocchi: "This is nourishing food, very robust. Past, present, contemporary, eternal."*

FOR THE SAUCE

*2 tablespoons (1 ounce) butter*
*2 tablespoons Toasted Garlic*
  *(see page 7)*
*4–6 fresh sage leaves*
*1 cup fresh asparagus, chopped*
*2–3 tomatoes, chopped,*
  *to equal 1 cup*
*Salt and pepper, to taste*

refrigerate. When ready to serve, plunge into hot water for about 30 seconds and combine with sauce.

TO MAKE THE SAUCE: In a small saucepan over high heat, melt the butter and add the toasted garlic. Cook for 1–2 minutes, add the sage leaves, and continue cooking for 2 more minutes. Add the asparagus and tomatoes and season with salt and pepper. Cook over medium heat for 3–4 minutes, until the asparagus is tender.

*Wine:* A young Sangiovese, fruity and fairly supple, medium-bodied with lots of cherry fruit, from California, or a nonoaky, mellow Friulian Cabernet, because you can taste the fruit without the overpowering smoky oak.

# GNOCCHI RIPIENI / Stuffed Gnocchi

*6–8 servings*

1 recipe Gnocchi (see page 114)

FOR THE STUFFING
¼ cup (2 ounces) butter
6 whole fresh sage leaves
1 cup fresh ricotta cheese
2 tablespoons Parmesan cheese,
    grated
1 tablespoon all-purpose flour
Salt and pepper, to taste
A few gratings fresh whole nutmeg
2 large egg yolks
Tomato, Pesto, and Gorgonzola
    Sauce (see p. 119)
2 ounces Parmesan cheese, shaved,
    for garnish
Fresh basil, for garnish
¼ cup fresh tomatoes, chopped,
    for garnish

Prepare the gnocchi dough according to the recipe on page 114.

In a small saucepan over medium-high heat, melt the butter with the sage leaves. Cook 4–5 minutes, until browned, and discard the sage.

TO MAKE THE STUFFING: In a large bowl combine the ricotta cheese, Parmesan cheese, flour, salt and pepper, and nutmeg. Add 1 egg yolk and 1 tablespoon of the browned butter, and mix well.

Flour your hands well, and on a lightly floured work surface, shape the dough into a loaf. Cut it into 6 sections and roll the sections into ropes of about 1-inch diameter. Flatten the ropes until they're ¼ inch thick and about 2 inches wide. Pipe or spoon a ½-inch row of filling just above the bottom edge of each strip. Brush the top edge of the strip with egg yolk. Gently lift up the bottom edge and fold it over, rolling the strip upward. Brush off any excess flour and cut the ropes into 1½-inch pieces. As you cut, the gnocchi will seal itself.

Flour the gnocchi lightly and place in a strainer when ready to cook. Cook according to the instructions for gnocchi (see page 115).

Toss the sauce with the gnocchi. Sprinkle with the Parmesan cheese, basil, and fresh tomatoes, or pour the gnocchi and sauce into individual 6-inch shallow ovenproof bowls, top with shaved Parmesan cheese, and put under a broiler until cheese is melted and lightly colored, about 30 seconds. Garnish with basil leaves and fresh tomato.

*Wine:* My first inclination, a big wine, might overwhelm such a rich dish. So let's think of a wine with delicacy in fruit and structure that will not overpower the food. A Merlot from Umbria, or a nonoaky, light, fresh Cabernet from the Triveneto. Or a red Corvo from Sicily. In California, a Pinot Noir from Monterey, or one from Oregon. The common denominator is a supple, distinctive fruit flavor, a continuation of the richness of the sauce.

*"Brush off any excess flour and cut the ropes into 1½-inch pieces."*

*Making Gnocchi Ripieni: "Pipe or spoon a ½-inch row of filling just above the bottom edge of each strip. Brush the top edge of the strip with egg yolk."*

*"Gently lift up the bottom edge and fold it over, rolling the strip upward."*

## TOMATO, PESTO, AND GORGONZOLA SAUCE

*¼ cup tomato sauce or tomato puree*
*¼ cup heavy cream*
*¼ cup Pesto (see below)*
*2 ounces Gorgonzola cheese, cubed*

In a small saucepan, heat the tomato sauce, cream, and pesto over medium heat, until bubbling. Stir in the Gorgonzola cheese.

## PESTO

*3 cups*

The word "pesto" is a contraction of *pestato* (to crush) and was traditionally made by using a mortar and pestle. We use a blender or a food processor.

*3 cups basil leaves*
*3 tablespoons pine nuts*
*1 teaspoon salt*
*1 cup olive oil*
*½ cup Parmesan cheese, grated*
*½ cup pecorino Romano cheese*
*2 garlic cloves, chopped*

In a blender at a low speed, combine basil, pine nuts, and salt, and slowly add olive oil. When combined, add the cheeses. When the paste is grainy add the garlic, and blend until everything is well mixed. If the paste seems too thick, add more olive oil until it is the proper consistency.

# GNOCCHETTI DI PORCINI IN FONDUTA TARTUFATA /
## Porcini-Infused Gnocchi with Truffled Fonduta Sauce
*6 servings*

This is the next level of cooking: developing a dish with Italian flavors, following the basic ingredients for something as traditional as gnocchi, but using the finest ingredients, like porcini and truffles, for a dish of new sensations and elegance. The sweetness of the potato versus the strength of the dried porcini make a wonderful dish. Don't waste fresh porcini in this recipe—they don't work as well, and more important, they don't show. Our rule is, if it's on the inside, use dry porcini. If it's on the outside of a dish—if it shows—then use fresh.

---

### FOR THE GNOCCHI
*6 ounces dried porcini mushrooms*
*4 large russet potatoes*
*2–3 cups unbleached white flour*
*2 large eggs*
*1 cup Parmesan cheese, grated*
*Salt and pepper, to taste*

### FOR THE SAUCE
*1 cup heavy cream*
*1 cup fontina cheese, diced*
*1 tablespoon truffle oil*
*1 teaspoon white truffle shavings*

In a medium-size bowl, submerge the dried porcini in enough hot water to cover, until softened, about 30 minutes.

Bring a medium-size pot of salted water to a boil and cook whole potatoes at a simmer until tender, about 30 minutes. Drain and peel potatoes. Put them through a ricer and set aside.

Drain the porcini. In a food processor fitted with the steel blade, process until a smooth paste.

Sprinkle some of the flour on a large board and spread the mashed potatoes on top. Add the porcini paste, eggs, Parmesan cheese, and salt and pepper, and fold the mixture together with your hands until well mixed. Add 2 cups of the remaining flour and mix well. It the mixture seems too wet, add some more flour.

Divide the dough into 8 pieces and roll each into a long strip, about 1 inch in diameter. Line up the strips side by side and cut crosswise into 1-inch pieces. Sprinkle lightly with flour.

Cook the gnocchi according to the instructions on page 115. Remove with a slotted spoon and set aside.

In a small saucepan over medium heat, add the cream and fontina cheese and stir, until the cheese melts and the sauce thickens. Set aside. In a large sauté pan, combine the cooked gnocchi and the sauce and toss lightly. Serve on individual plates, drizzle with just a few drops of truffle oil, and garnish with fresh truffle shavings.

*Wine:* A great silky, velvety wine, a Pinot Noir type. Or a Syrah, where there are so many finishing spices and sensations to attach to the taste of the mushrooms. Wine is essential here to polish the edges.

# POLENTA

*6 servings as a first course, or*

*4 servings as a main course*

Polenta is often served—especially in rural and mountain areas—instead of bread, with tiny deep-fried fish, boiled cotechino, salami, or cheese. Served in this way, it is a perfect complement to meat and fish dishes that are cooked in sauces. Whatever kind of cornmeal is used, be sure that it is dry and without lumps. It should be recently ground; if it has been stored for a long time, the polenta may taste bitter.

The best kind of pot to cook polenta in is the classic *paiolo,* a pot made of copper without a tin lining, with a convex bottom that makes it possible to thoroughly stir at the bottom when using an appropriate wooden paddle. If you don't have one, a deep, heavy-bottomed saucepan will work fine.

The paiolo should only be half full with water; otherwise the water might overflow when you add the cornmeal. The water should be properly salted in the beginning to avoid having to add either salt or water later in the cooking process.

---

*7½ cups water*

*1 tablespoon salt*

*2 cups imported polenta or*
  *farina bramata*

*Preparation:* In a deep, heavy-duty saucepan, bring the water to a boil and add salt. Turn the heat down to low, and slowly add the cornmeal in a very thin stream, to prevent lumps from forming. Using a long wooden spoon, stir constantly while adding the cornmeal, and continue stirring while the polenta cooks. It's ready when the mixture tears away from the side of the pan, about 30 minutes.

*The Dish:* Serve immediately with butter and cheese for a creamy-style polenta, or pour the polenta onto a wet surface and spread it out to a thickness of about ½ inch. Let cool and slice.

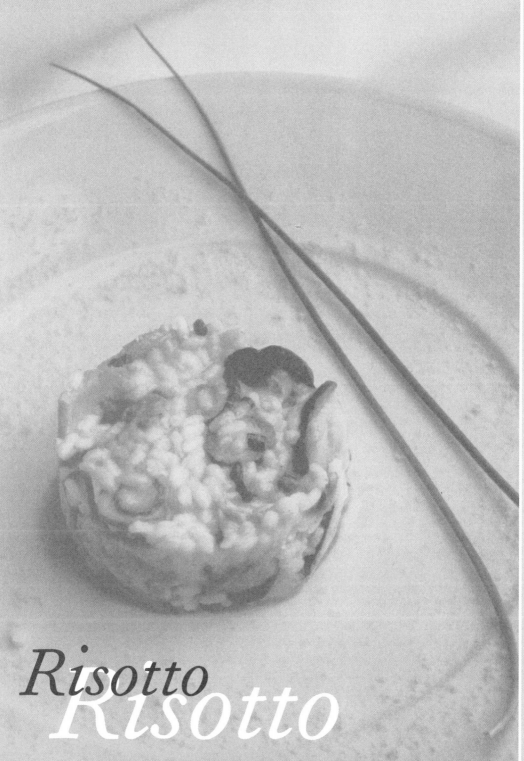

Risotto
*Risotto*

❈

Basic Risotto
*Risotto con Peperoni Rossi e Pannocchie*
**(Risotto with Sweet Peppers and Corn)**
*Risotto con Funghetti e Fiori di Zucca*
**(Risotto with Porcini Mushrooms and Zucchini Flowers)**
*Risotto con Radicchio e Gorgonzola*
**(Risotto with Radicchio and Gorgonzola)**
*Risotto con Gamberi e Pepe Forte*
**(Risotto with Shrimp and Hot Pepper)**
*Risotto con Triglie e Mandorle*
**(Risotto with Red Mullet and Almonds)**
*Risotto con Salsiccia e Spinaci al Vino Rosso*
**(Risotto with Sausage and Spinach in Red Wine Sauce)**
*Riso al Salto con Ragù di Funghi*
**(Rice Cakes with Mushroom Ragù)**

*Risotto*

# ✤ *Risotto*

ARABS BROUGHT RICE TO THE SOUTH OF ITALY, AND IT FOUND ITS CON-secration in risotto in the north. I love to present it, and to have it presented to me—I can always judge a cook by the way he makes risotto. It can't be too al dente *or* too cooked. There has to be creaminess and elegance, and you can't taste the starch. My cooks do it so well that they can tell if it's done just by looking. This is not a dish you make by carefully following a recipe. It requires instinct, and judgment—and good muscles.

But you don't need to be a slave to the dish. You can cook it halfway through, and finish it when you are ready to serve; rice that has been in the refrigerator wakes from its lethargy and has new blood flowing through it—definitely the way to go for quick home use. Or you can follow Luciano's instructions and finish the whole dish in less than 20 minutes, since he does not believe in the standard advice about constant stirring and low heat. Once you have mastered the basic recipe, we offer several variations, but there is no limit to what you can add to the dish, as long as you exercise a little common sense.

If pasta is blue jeans, then risotto is the complete suit. Rice is much more coherent on the plate than pasta. It's not the mess of a pasta presentation. Rice works together with other dishes, as part of a main dish or as a first course with special ingredients like porcini or truffles.

So you need to make the effort to produce a superior, accomplished dish. Risotto does not happen by fluke. It needs excellent broth, perfect handling, and care. I think that rice is a little more intellectual than pasta. There is a sense of art to it.

Risotto may not be as colorful as pasta, but it is more adaptable. I like it the traditional way. You start with nothing, just a wide pan so the rice will swim. Put in a little olive oil and some chopped onion, on low heat, until the onion crackles. Then add the rice, then the wine. Then you add warm broth, and more broth, cuddling the rice with the liquid.

At the restaurant, we usually stop after 10 minutes, when the rice has lost some of its starch and is ready to be married to other ingredients. We spread it on a baking sheet to cool, refrigerate, and finish when we want to serve.

You can cook the other ingredients on the side—vegetables for 10 minutes, meats for 15. When you are ready to eat, heat up your broth, return the rice to the pan, and continue adding broth until the rice is done, 18–20 minutes total. You can keep the flame at medium-high, stir to start and to finish, and watch it in between, but you don't have to stand there forever. Risotto is more forgiving than that, as long as you pay attention at the right moments.

The important thing is the *mantecare*, the vigorous stirring at the end. The last three minutes of preparation are off the heat. You add butter and Parmesan cheese and then you stir vigorously with a wooden spoon so the butter and cheese drip down into the rice. It's *alla mano*, a natural contact you have with the dish. Those last couple of minutes seal everything perfectly, and give you the creamy consistency you want.

There's an art to making pasta, but you raise the level higher when you make risotto. You can even color it with an infusion—saffron, asparagus, beet juice—more for artistry than for texture. At Valentino we make risotto with vegetables, even with fruit, and with seafood and certain meats. Sometimes for fun we make it with black-eyed peas, salami, or little meatballs. One of our most popular dishes is risotto with fresh corn and roasted red bell pepper—a perfect summer dish in a country that loves sweet corn.

Or you can make a beautiful risotto with *carpaccio di porcini,* when they are in season. Add freshly shaved porcini mushrooms to slightly undercooked plain risotto, and then cover them with the still-cooking rice, and finish the dish.

This is a long way from Mamma's rice *arancine,* little fried croquettes, or her boiled rice with lentils. It is a long way from her exuberant pasta. Risotto stands apart from other first courses. It is a different passion, a grown-up passion. There's even a physical difference in the way you eat it. Pasta is like the Chinese slurping noodles, while with risotto you pose, you have a dignity. Pasta is visceral; risotto, I dissect in my head.

## BASIC RISOTTO

*4 servings*

*4–5 cups Chicken Stock (see page 74)*
*2 tablespoons onion, finely chopped*
*2 tablespoons olive oil*
*2 cups (14 ounces) arborio rice, preferably Vialone Nano*
*½ cup dry white wine*
*4 tablespoons (2 ounces) butter*
*¼ cup Parmesan cheese, grated*

*Preparation:* In a small saucepan, bring the chicken stock to a boil and turn the heat to a low simmer. In a medium-size heavy-duty saucepan over medium heat, sauté the onion in the olive oil a few minutes, until translucent. Add the rice and stir to coat it in the oil. Cook 3–4 minutes, stirring frequently, not allowing the rice to color. Pour in the wine, stirring until it evaporates. Add 2 cups of the simmering broth, and cook over medium-high heat until it is absorbed by the rice, 8–10 minutes, stirring with a wooden spoon to prevent the rice from sticking to the pan.

*Chef's Tip:* If you want to work in advance, you can spread the rice on a big platter or baking sheet after the first 10 minutes and aerate it well so that it stops cooking. Rewarm the stock before proceeding. When you are ready to serve the risotto, return the rice to the pan.

*The Dish:* Continue to cook the rice, over medium-high heat, adding ½ cup of the hot broth at a time. Stir so that the rice does not stick, but allow the rice to absorb all of the liquid before adding more broth. Cook for about 10 more minutes for an al dente but creamy risotto. (It should take a total of 18–20 minutes to cook, from the first addition of broth to the last.) Remove the pan from the heat. Vigorously stir in the butter and Parmesan cheese and serve.

*Wine:* There are no rules here: Try a buttery Chardonnay, a fresh young Chianti, or a soft California Merlot. The trick is to pay attention to what you serve with the risotto. These wines work if this is your main course, but if you serve it next to veal, you need to match to the stronger flavors.

## RISOTTO CON PEPERONI ROSSI E PANNOCCHIE /
Risotto with Sweet Peppers and Corn

*4 servings*

I was in a restaurant called Miramonti l'Altro near Brescia, and I was very impressed by this cornucopia—half a yellow pepper stuffed with rice overflowing onto the plate. That was an inspiration fifteen years ago. Then to adapt the dish for America, I thought: What is more appropriate, more a comfort food, than corn? The yellow and red peppers—which are crunchy and peppery but sweeter than the green—combine beautifully with the corn and the sublime risotto. This has become another of our signatures.

*2–3 ears sweet corn, cooked*

*1 red bell pepper*

*1 yellow bell pepper*

*1 tablespoon olive oil*

*2 cups (14 ounces) arborio rice,*
  *preferably Vialone Nano*

*4–5 cups Chicken Stock*
  *(see page 74)*

*1 tablespoon onion, finely chopped*

*½ cup dry white wine*

*6 tablespoons (3 ounces) butter*

*¾ cup Parmesan cheese, grated,*
  *plus extra for garnish*

*Preparation:* Trim the kernels from the cob to equal about 1½ cups.

On a grill or over an open flame on the stove, roast the peppers for 8–10 minutes, turning frequently, until blackened. Place in a paper bag to steam for 10–15 minutes. Remove the blackened peel, cut off the tops without tearing the peppers, and scoop out the seeds and membranes.

Cut each pepper in half and dice half of each. Reserve the remaining 2 halves for garnish.

In a skillet over low heat, sauté the diced peppers and corn in olive oil for 1 minute, just to impart flavor. Set aside.

*The Dish:* Follow the directions for cooking basic risotto (page 128). After the risotto has cooked about 15 minutes and just before it's done cooking, remove the pan from the heat. Add the roasted peppers and corn, and return to the heat. Cook, stirring constantly, for 3–4 more minutes, until the rice is creamy. Vigorously stir in the butter and Parmesan cheese.

Serve the risotto in individual dishes. Cut the roasted pepper halves in half once and place 1 on top of each plate of risotto as garnish. Sprinkle with Parmesan cheese.

*Wine:* Serve a gentle red wine with this dish: a Rosso Conero, a Rubesco from Umbria, a Merlot from Friuli, or a young Barbera. These have great fruit and suppleness, and will not disturb the sweetness of the peppers and corn.

# RISOTTO CON FUNGHETTI E FIORI DI ZUCCA /
## Risotto with Porcini Mushrooms and Zucchini Flowers
*6 servings*

This is a popular dish for us at Valentino. The best time to make it is at the height of fresh porcini season, from the end of August to the end of October, but with new supplies coming from Oregon, North Africa, and France, you probably can find fresh porcini about six months out of the year. Or you can substitute other wild mushrooms.

---

*½ pound zucchini blossoms*
*¼ teaspoon garlic, finely chopped*
*½ pound fresh porcini mushrooms*
  *(or any other fresh wild*
  *mushrooms)*
*2 tablespoons olive oil*
*2 cups (14 ounces) arborio rice,*
  *preferably Vialone Nano*
*2 tablespoons yellow onion,*
  *finely chopped*
*½ cup dry white wine*
*4–5 cups Chicken Stock*
  *(see page 74)*
*Salt and pepper, to taste*
*Pinch of saffron*
*2 tablespoons (1 ounce) butter*
*½ cup Parmesan cheese, grated*

*Preparation:* Remove the pistils from the inside of the zucchini blossoms and set aside 4–6 blossoms for garnishing. Chop the remaining blossoms into thirds.

In a skillet, sauté the garlic and mushrooms in olive oil over medium-high heat, until tender, about 10 minutes.

*The Dish:* Follow the directions for cooking basic risotto (see page 128). After the risotto has cooked about 15 minutes, just before it's done, remove the pan from the heat. Stir in the mushrooms, zucchini flowers, salt and pepper, and saffron and return to the heat. Cook, stirring constantly, 3–4 more minutes, until the rice is creamy and has finished cooking. Remove from the heat and vigorously stir in the butter and Parmesan cheese. Place the risotto on individual dishes and garnish with zucchini blossoms.

*Wine:* There are endless possibilities. Definitely a red, one that mixes fruit and strength because the risotto is so intense in taste. A Nebbiolo would be very adaptable—intense and robust—tasting of blackberry, tea leaves, chocolate, earthiness. Or a Classico Valpolicella, or an aged Chianti—wines that have turned slightly in color and show the fruit, show character. Or try a wine from Tuscany, a Vino Nobile—again, a wine where the berries are reaching perfect maturity.

## RISOTTO CON RADICCHIO E GORGONZOLA /
### Risotto with Radicchio and Gorgonzola

*4 servings*

4–6 cups Chicken Stock
   (see page 74)
2 medium heads radicchio trevisano
2 tablespoons onions, chopped
2 tablespoons olive oil
2 cups (14 ounces) arborio rice,
   preferably Vialone Nano
½ cup dry white wine
4 ounces sweet Gorgonzola cheese
¼ cup (2 ounces) butter
1 tablespoon Parmesan cheese,
   grated
4–6 parsley sprigs

Bring the chicken stock to a boil and turn the heat to a low simmer. Coarsely chop the radicchio, reserving 1–2 leaves for garnish. Chop those 1–2 leaves finely and set aside. In a deep, heavy-duty saucepan, sauté the onions in the olive oil over medium heat until translucent. Add the radicchio and cook for a couple of minutes over low heat. Add the rice and follow the directions for cooking basic risotto on page 128.

When the rice is al dente, remove from the heat and add the Gorgonzola cheese, butter, and Parmesan cheese, and stir vigorously until creamy. Garnish with the finely chopped radicchio and parsley sprigs.

*Wine:* A wine with a lot of fruit and delicate balance. A good Chianti, where you taste cherries and acidity, but not a lot of overpowering tannin. Or try a soft California Merlot—Arrowood or Silverado.

## RISOTTO CON GAMBERI E PEPE FORTE /
### Risotto with Shrimp and Hot Pepper

*4 servings*

---

4–5 cups Lobster Broth
(see page 75)

1 teaspoon garlic, finely chopped

3 tablespoons olive oil

1–2 teaspoons jalapeño pepper,
thinly sliced, to taste

6–8 medium-size uncooked shrimp,
shelled and deveined

2 cups (14 ounces) arborio rice,
preferably Vialone Nano

2 tablespoons onion, finely chopped

¼ cup (2 ounces) butter

¼ cup Parmesan cheese, grated

1–2 teaspoons Garlic-Infused Olive
Oil (see page 7)

Bring the lobster broth to a boil and turn the heat to a low simmer. In a skillet, sauté the garlic for 1–2 minutes in 1 tablespoon of the olive oil. Add the sliced jalapeño and shrimp and cook about 3–4 minutes, over medium heat. Set aside 8 small slices of pepper and 4 shrimp for garnish. Chop the remaining cooked shrimp into small pieces.

Follow the cooking instructions for basic risotto on page 128, using the lobster broth. After the risotto has cooked about 15 minutes, just before it's done, remove the pan from the heat. Stir in the shrimp and jalapeño and return to the heat to finish cooking the rice. Remove from heat. Add the butter, Parmesan cheese, and garlic oil. Mix vigorously until creamy and garnish with shrimp and sliced jalapeño.

*Wine:* This is an aggressive marriage that calls for a wine that is bold and peppery, such as one of the new Syrahs made in the Santa Ynez Valley or the Carneros region of California. Or something from Australia or South Africa; wines from those areas have a rich taste of fruit, spices, and earthiness.

## RISOTTO CON TRIGLIE E MANDORLE /
### Risotto with Red Mullet and Almonds

*4 servings*

Mullet is a popular Mediterranean fish—called *triglie* in Italy, *rouget* in France. You can substitute a small red snapper or sand dabs, but if you ever find mullet, buy it; it has a flavor you can't duplicate. After many years of looking for a reputable supplier, we now get it twice a week at the restaurant, and I'm always thinking about new ways to serve it. Risotto with mullet, pasta with mullet, salads with mullet—there are lots of delicious possibilities.

---

*12 red mullet fillets or small red
  snapper fillets, skin on
2 tablespoons onion, finely chopped
6 tablespoons olive oil
2 cups (14 ounces) arborio rice,
  preferably Vialone Nano
½ cup almonds, finely chopped
½ cup dry white wine
4–5 cups Chicken Stock
  (see page 74)
5 tablespoons (2½ ounces) butter
¼ cup Parmesan cheese, grated
Fresh thyme sprigs*

*Preparation:* Bone the mullet fillets and refrigerate until needed.

*The Dish:* In a deep saucepan, sauté the onion in 2 tablespoons of the olive oil over medium heat until translucent. Add the rice and half of the almonds and, stirring frequently, cook about 3–4 minutes. Pour in the wine and let evaporate. Continue with the cooking directions for basic risotto on page 128. When the risotto is al dente, remove from the heat and vigorously stir in 4 tablespoons of the butter, 2 tablespoons of the olive oil, and the Parmesan cheese, until the rice is creamy.

Meanwhile, bread the mullet fillets, meat-side only, with the remaining almonds. In a sauté pan, heat the remaining olive oil with the remaining tablespoon of butter over high heat. Place the fillets skin-side down and sauté for 2 minutes on each side. Add thyme sprigs and remove from the heat.

Spoon the risotto onto the plates and arrange the mullet on top. Garnish with fresh thyme sprigs and a few drops of olive oil.

*Wine:* Mullet is a fairly robust fish, so I would go with a beautiful red—something soft, a mouthful of fruit to compensate for the starchiness of the risotto and the richness of the almond sauce: a Pinot Noir, a Friulian Merlot, or a Cabernet Franc—grapes that make me taste strawberry or cherry. But if I had to think of a white, it would be a French Burgundy like a big Puligny-Montrachet—a wine with dignity, rich in oak and perfume.

## RISOTTO CON SALSICCIA E SPINACI AL VINO ROSSO /
### Risotto with Sausage and Spinach in Red Wine Sauce
*4 servings*

4 ounces mild Italian sausage,
    *without fennel, casings removed*
2 garlic cloves, thinly sliced
2 tablespoons onion, finely chopped
2 tablespoons olive oil
2 cups (14 ounces) arborio rice,
    *preferably Vialone Nano*
½ cup dry red wine, such as
    *Burgundy or Cabernet*
4–5 cups Chicken Stock
    *(see page 74)*
1 pound fresh spinach, steamed
    *and chopped to equal ½ cup*
2 tablespoons (1 ounce) butter
¼ cup Parmesan cheese, grated

❈ *Chef's Tip:* Make sure that you use sausage that does not contain fennel. It is too pungent an element for this dish and would unbalance the flavors.

*Preparation:* In a skillet, crumble the sausage and cook over medium heat until nicely browned. Add the garlic and cook another 1–2 minutes. Set aside.

*The Dish:* Follow the cooking instructions for basic risotto on page 128. After the risotto has cooked about 15 minutes, just before it's done, remove the pan from the heat. Stir in the sausage and spinach and return to the heat to finish cooking the rice. Add the butter and Parmesan cheese and stir vigorously until creamy.

*Wine:* A Cabernet, or a "Super Tuscan." This dish blends beautifully with the flavor of cassis so typical in a beautiful Cabernet, or with the abundant fruit in the Sangiovese grape. For a good Tuscan, try Castello di Fonterutoli or Castello di Volpaia. Or in California, think about Far Niente Cabernet or any of the other good Napa wines, like the ones made by Mondavi or Silver Oak.

RISO AL SALTO CON RAGÙ DI FUNGHI /
Rice Cakes with Mushroom Ragù

*4 servings*

We use this rice cake as a base. Topped here with mushrooms, it can also be loaded with quail, a meat ragù, or vegetables. It's the best way to use leftover risotto.

---

FOR THE RAGÙ
*4 cups fresh wild mushrooms, sliced*
*2 tablespoons olive oil*
*Salt and pepper, to taste*
*1 cup Chicken Stock (see page 74)*

FOR THE RICE CAKES
*⅓ cup olive oil*
*1½ cups cooked leftover risotto, cold*
*Salad greens, for garnish*

*Preparation:* TO MAKE THE SAUCE: In a medium-size saucepan, sauté the mushrooms in the olive oil until the mushrooms are tender, about 15 minutes. Season with salt and pepper and add the chicken stock. Reduce for about 10 minutes to a creamy consistency.

*The Dish:* In a medium-size nonstick skillet, heat 1 tablespoon of the olive oil over medium-high heat, until it is very hot. Form a thin pancake with about 2 tablespoons of the cold risotto. As soon as it hits the skillet, flatten it further with a spoon or spatula to about ¼ inch thick. Cook the cake for 4 minutes, then flip it over to cook the other side. The pancake should be brown and crispy. Cook the remaining risotto in the same manner, adding more oil for each pancake, as necessary. Keep the rice cakes warm in the oven until ready to serve.

> ❋ *Chef's Tip:* The more ingredients there are in the risotto, the harder it is to fry the pancakes without sticking. Basic risotto works best. The pan has to be very hot to seal the pancake and keep it from cracking when you turn it.
>
> Dip the spatula or spoon in cold water because it keeps the rice from sticking—but not too much water, or it will hit the oil and spatter.

Serve the rice cakes topped with the warm mushroom ragù and the greens on the side.

*Wine:* Some elegant matches would be a Pinot Noir from Oregon, a Barbera aged in oak, or a light burgundy like Volnay, which has body and character and is not overly tannic.

*"Topped here with mushrooms, it can also be loaded with quail, a meat ragù, or vegetables. It's the best way to use leftover risotto."*

# Secondi
*Secondi*

✸

*Tagliata di Tonno in Camicia di Erbe*
**(Tuna with Herb Crust)**
*Filetti di Tonno al Sesamo con Fave e Rafano*
**(Sesame-Seared Tuna with Horseradish and Fava Beans)**
*Bistecca di Tonno con Fave e Pinot Nero*
**(Tuna in Red Wine Sauce with Fava Beans)**
*Salmone ed Asparagi al Vapore con Salsa di Tartaro*
**(Asparagus and Steamed Salmon with Tartar Sauce)**
*Filetti di Salmone al Funghetto* **(White Salmon with Mushrooms)**
*Trota Salmonata con Patate e Crema d'Aneto*
**(Salmon Trout in Potato Crust with Cream of Fennel and Dill)**
*Branzino al Sale* **(Baked Whole Bass in Sea Salt Crust)**
*Pizzaiola di Pesce* **(Whitefish Pizzaiola)**
*Guazzetto di Pesce in Brodo d'Astice*
**(Seared Fish with Roasted Garlic and Lobster Broth)**
*Capesante alle Piccole Verdure*
**(Sautéed Scallops on a Mixed Vegetable Pillow)**
*Astice alla Crema di Peperoni Dolci*
**(Lobster with Sweet Pepper Sauce)**
*Filetti di Triglie con Pomodori e Olive*
**(Red Mullet with Tomatoes and Olives)**
*Filetti di Baccalà al Forno* **(Baked Filet of Codfish with Tomatoes)**
*Bracioline di Pollo con Salsiccia d'Anatra*
**(Rolled Chicken Breast, Stuffed with Duck Sausage)**
*Pollo e Gamberi Allo Spiedo* **(Chicken and Shrimp Skewers)**
*Posto's Barbecue Sauce*
*Spezzatino di Pollo*
**(Chicken Breast in Radicchio Cup with a Mushroom Medley)**
*Petti di Pollo e Carciofi* **(Chicken Breast with Artichokes and Lemon)**
*Portafogli di Pollo alla Valdostana*
**(Chicken "Wallets" with Prosciutto, Cheese, and Asparagus)**

*Secondi*

Quagliette alla Diavola con Rucola e Finocchio
(Spicy Grilled Quail with Arugula Salad and Grilled Fennel)
Ragù di Quaglie (Quail Ragù)
Anatra in Umido alla Toscana (Tuscan Duck with Olives)
Salsiccia d'Anatra a Polpette (Duck Sausage Patties)
L'Oca Arrostita (Roasted Goose)
Petti di Fagiano Avvolti in Pancetta
(Pheasant Breast Wrapped in Pancetta)
Sella di Coniglio Arrosto con Funghi (Roasted Rabbit)
L'Abbacchio di Paola (Roman Lamb)
Tagliata d'Agnello con Polenta e Peperoni
(Lamb Tagliata with Polenta and Peppers)
Costolette d'Agnello al Trittico di Noci
(Lamb with Almonds, Walnuts, and Pine Nuts)
Cosciotto d'Agnello alla Menta
(Roast Leg of Lamb with Red Wine and Mint)
Brasato al Barolo (Beef Braised in Barolo)
Fassu Magru dei Giorni di Festa (Stuffed Beef Rolls for the Holidays)
Stracotto di Costolette di Manzo (Braised Beef Short Ribs)
Scaloppine di Maiale in Agrodolce con Cannellini
(Pork Scaloppine with Sweet and Sour Sauce
and Tuscan Beans)
Rollatini di Vitello (Stuffed Veal Rolls)
Costolette di Vitello con Fonduta (Veal Chops Fonduta)
Filetti di Cervo con Salsa al Melograno
(Venison Medallions with Pomegranate Sauce)
Grigliata di Verdure e Mozzarella
(Grilled Vegetables with Smoked Mozzarella)
Salsa Bruna (Brown Sauce)

# ✿ *Secondi*

I ACCEPT THE MAIN COURSE. I'M NEVER ABSOLUTELY ENCHANTED BY IT, though I have my cravings, like everybody else, for a steak here and there, or a piece of prime rib. I enjoy trying what I call the meats of evolution—buffalo and ostrich and free-range chickens. And I love seafood. But in my heart I am a pasta and antipasto eater. Perhaps it is because of the way I grew up. My family could not afford meat for a *secondi,* and I got used to just small amounts of it as an ingredient in a dish. It was a rare occasion, a special holiday, when we'd have a proper second course, so it holds no memory for me.

Besides, I never sit down to a regular meal at the restaurant, and I don't often have the privilege of a real family meal. At Valentino I eat some pasta at three in the afternoon, or at Posto I'll have a grilled pizza and pasta late in the evening. That makes me more of a taster than an eater.

But I know how to serve secondi, even if they aren't part of my daily life. They are part of the structure of a fine dinner, and we offer an array of them at all the restaurants. On the fantasy menu at Valentino you might get more than one, in smaller portions so you can taste more things. That way I satisfy both the customer's desire for a serious meal, and my love of grazing.

## FISH AND SEAFOOD

Picture this: A guy—his pants still rolled from docking the fishing boat, in his slippers from the boat—is selling the fish he just caught, while it's still so fresh. He has cut the fish into portions and wrapped it in parchment paper, maybe half a kilo of fish in each package, and then he and his friends each go to sell it to different villages near where I grew up. The town of Pozzallo is on the southern coast of Sicily, and the fishermen would come in their motorboats to my hometown, Modica, which was about ten miles away. The fishmongers came a couple of times a week, either early in the morning, after they'd been at sea all night, or at sunset.

It was a beautiful sight, when the boats came at sunset, like Columbus arriving, and we would have the *pronto* market—right then and there. A living market, lots of noise, people buying fish, and the trucks lining up to take some of it far away.

My mamma comes from Pozzallo, so she is a fish nut. Her whole family is oriented toward fish. My grandfather was a fantastic fish cook, and it was a tradition: When the fish arrived, Papá Santo cooked, often *alla ghiotta,* Sicilian fish stew. Or Mamma made smelts; a frying pan ready with oil was all she needed. I remember the joy of eating those little fish, scales and all.

Once my father took me to an area south of Messina called Ganzirri, where they cultivate mussels and shellfish. I still remember the incredible bushels of mussels, something I'd never seen before. I remember we bought quite a few bushels and brought them back to Modica. And because the neighborhood is an extension of family, we went knocking on our neighbors' doors, saying, *"Puttammu i cozzi"*—"We brought the mussels." We passed them out, almost like an allocation. And we steamed ours and served them with garlic, parsley, and good olive oil, and put them on a big plate in the center of the table for the whole family to share.

We ate sardines, a few shellfish indigenous to the island, little shrimp, and sometimes clams. Tuna and swordfish were rich people's food. Sometimes we had tuna at my grandfather's house, and in his hand it was the most succulent steak I'd ever had.

When I started working as a busboy in Los Angeles, I encountered seafood anew, suddenly discovering things I had never seen before—big red Spanish shrimp, lobster, scallops. I learned about texture and delicacy of preparation. Since being in America, I have come to like shellfish more than fish, and I have become very partial to crab: well-prepared soft-shell crab, stone crab with spicy mustard. I particularly like to serve crabmeat with fruit, especially melon and mango, and then with something piquant, like a little cilantro or a pinch of pepper.

With my history, I am very finicky about freshness: I will eat it only if I know it has just come out of the water. I have a great time when we get fish deliveries at Valentino. Of course I look at the eye, which must be bright and shiny. I see that fish staring at me and I say: "Okay, you passed the test." Part of my great satisfaction comes from being demanding. We have suppliers and sources all over the world—a guy who brings us whatever seafood is in season, or, when he can, a delicacy like shad roe. We have another source who flies fish in from Europe.

We treat fish with respect. I flash back to Grandpa and his famous stew, and the family seated at the table eating mussels. We're all digging in, eating *cozzi*. It felt to me like an embrace, which is what I think food and the sharing of the table is all about.

## POULTRY AND GAME

Chicken came from the countryside around my agricultural hometown. If there was a special occasion, we got a chicken from the *massara,* the farm woman, who did the whole operation right there, killed the chicken for us. When I was a good student, or a good boy, I was rewarded with a roasted chicken, so now chicken is endearing for me. It never tasted more delicious than when we had something to celebrate. And we made great broth with the roosters.

Rabbit is one of my favorite meats, and I still recall being served a *stimpirata*, rabbit stew with olives and potatoes. The one pity is that some people have the preconception that "bunny" meat is offensive. Rabbit is a dark, juicy, and interesting meat that doesn't get the attention it deserves.

Other game I like to serve includes small, succulent quail, either grilled in sage or stuffed and served with risotto. Quail is one of our most popular dishes at Valentino no matter how we prepare it. We also have a wonderful recipe for a pheasant breast wrapped in pancetta; it is a beautiful presentation—the breast is sliced, so that you see the herbs at the center—and it's quite simple to prepare. You can always substitute a more available bird, like chicken, or even turkey breast, for these recipes, but you may be in for a pleasant surprise: Many good-quality markets now carry quail and pheasant, and there are retail mail-order outlets, many of which we have listed in the Suppliers section (see pages 263–264).

## MEAT

Sicily is not rich in meats. We don't know much about steak. Growing up, there was a great deal of lamb, but it was more mutton than lamb, served in stews or as a big focaccia turnover. And we had mortadella—but prosciutto? Too expensive. Pork meat or "red veal" from a big steer were much more common staples.

When I was eight or nine, I was already very adventurous, very responsible. I was willing to do all kinds of little services for my family. The slaughterhouse truck came by every Thursday—there was no refrigeration, so everything was consumed by the evening's end. On the day of the slaughter, the *macello,* I would wait in line because if I got there at the right time I could get the beef heart, liver, or some of the innards, and a small piece of veal. Sometimes I could muscle my way in and get some tripe, which was a real treat. I would bring it home like I had a trophy, and Mamma would cook it with sweet onions and lots of broth. But I've lost interest in it—I think it was an emotional thing, when I was a boy, and now that the emotional connection is gone, I do not eat innards very often.

On a very special occasion, Mamma went out of her way to make what Sicilians call *fassu magru,* a big roulade: a flank steak stuffed with eggs and bread crumbs and spinach and provolone, tied and oven-roasted very slowly, and then sliced.

But my first real awakening to fine meats was at my job at The Marquis. Suddenly I saw all these new things—steak Diane, tournedos of beef, veal piccata, and osso buco. And boy, did a veal cutlet Milanese taste better than the one my mother made with that red veal.

Today, meat is a big seller in all my restaurants. We have the advantage of being in a major city, where we have great availability of meats, many raised by small, quality suppliers whose products have wonderful taste and texture. There are enough possibilities to please any chef who wants to be creative and explore new kinds of sauces. We have served veal parmigiana since Valentino opened, and we will continue to serve it, because it is a classic Italian dish, the sort of thing that some people expect when they come to an Italian restaurant. But today you might find it on the menu alongside a rack of lamb in an almond crust or a grilled Napa pigeon in a honey and fig sauce.

# TAGLIATA DI TONNO IN CAMICIA DI ERBE / Tuna with Herb Crust

*4 servings*

The peasant-style tuna Mamma used to make with vinegar and olives is given a delicate treatment here, by searing it with fine herbs that seal the fish. I like the simplicity of this dish, but it has to be absolutely grade-A tuna, sashimi grade, which is as good as it gets. It is an opulent dish, not an everyday one—what you do when you find a great piece of tuna and you want to go all-out. This is one of the easier ways to still do *bella figura*.

FOR THE BLACK OLIVE PESTO
*1 cup olive oil*
*20 fresh basil leaves*
*Pinch of salt*
*3 tablespoons pitted olives, chopped*
*2 tablespoons capers*

*1 cup fresh herbs, finely chopped, at least 5 different kinds, such as rosemary, marjoram, thyme, sage, chive, tarragon, and mint*
*20 ounces sashimi-grade tuna steaks, cut into 3-inch medallions*
*2 tablespoons olive oil*

*Preparation:* TO MAKE THE PESTO: Combine the oil, basil, salt, olives, and capers in a food processor or blender and process until pureed.

Spread the chopped herbs on a cutting board and coat the pieces of tuna on all sides. Wrap each piece in foil to prevent burning.

*The Dish:* In a large skillet, warm the olive oil over high heat. Cook the tuna medallions (in the foil) for 2 minutes on each side. Remove the foil. They should be cooked only about ¼ inch through, and the center of the tuna should be raw.

Serve as an appetizer with the black olive pesto. For a second course, pile the tuna on an assortment of roasted vegetables, including bell peppers, leeks, and mushrooms, and drizzle the pesto over the fish.

*Wine:* An opulent Chardonnay, rich, full of buttery and crispy sensation and enough body to support the meaty tuna—Grgich Hills or Chateau Montelena—or a soft Pinot Noir from Au Bon Climat.

## FILETTI DI TONNO AL SESAMO CON FAVE E RAFANO /
### Sesame-Seared Tuna with Horseradish and Fava Beans
*4 servings*

In Venice, in the summer, you see a lot of fresh horseradish, which has a different consistency than what we are used to seeing in jars. They infuse liquids with it. Here, we use it to spice up a dressing for a cold summer salad.

---

*1 pound ahi tuna*

*¾ cup white sesame seeds*

*1 tablespoon (½ ounce) butter*

*2 tablespoons olive oil*

*8 ounces shelled fava beans*

*2 teaspoons balsamic vinegar*

*1 tablespoon shallot or mild onion, chopped*

*Salt and pepper, to taste*

*½ cup mayonnaise*

*¼ cup horseradish, freshly grated, or prepared horseradish without additives*

*1 teaspoon Dijon mustard*

*Mixed baby greens*

*1 red tomato, finely chopped, for garnish*

*1 yellow tomato, finely chopped, for garnish*

Preheat the oven to 200 degrees.

Coat the tuna on all sides in sesame seeds. In a large skillet, melt the butter with 1 tablespoon of the olive oil. Add the tuna and cook over medium heat on all sides until golden. Do not cook the fish all the way through. Remove the tuna from the pan and keep warm in the oven.

Remove the favas from the pods according to directions on page 96 and steam the beans until tender, about 8 minutes. Season with the remaining olive oil, vinegar, shallot or onion, and salt and pepper, and keep warm.

In a small bowl whisk together the mayonnaise, horseradish, and mustard. Add 1–2 teaspoons hot water to thin down the sauce. Arrange the greens on a serving dish, put the fava beans in the middle of the plate, slice the tuna, and lay it over the beans. Spoon dressing over everything. Garnish with the chopped red and yellow tomatoes.

*Wine:* With tuna I always like white wine that is fat—rich in the mouth, full of different flavors, of the proper amount of acid to sustain the tuna's intense flavor. Try a big Chardonnay with a lot of perfume and body, something like Peter Michael or Grgich Hills. For an Italian wine with the same intensity, try Cervaro della Sala, which is a Chardonnay and Grechetto blend by Antinori. Or a soft red. I love Pinot Noir with tuna: Etude, an Oregon Pinot, Au Bon Climat—all are wines of elegance.

## BISTECCA DI TONNO CON FAVE E PINOT NERO /
### Tuna in Red Wine Sauce with Fava Beans
*4 servings*

California, the land of tuna. We have endless recipes. The ingredients are part of my childhood, so typical of my daily nourishment, but this is not the canned tuna I ate as a kid. Fresh tuna is a very festive fish, and with a wine reduction sauce and the fresh fava, you add a touch of elegance.

---

*2 cups shelled fresh fava beans*

*½ cup balsamic vinegar*

*½ cup plus 1 tablespoon olive oil*

*1 teaspoon fresh rosemary, chopped*

*4 cloves garlic, sliced thinly lengthwise*

*4–8 ounces sashimi-grade tuna steaks, sliced at least 1½ inches thick*

*2 cups Pinot Noir wine*

*½ shallot, finely chopped*

*1 teaspoon whole black peppercorns*

*1 cup Lobster Broth (see page 75) or Chicken Stock (see page 74)*

*Preparation:* Remove the fava beans from the pod. Bring a medium-size pot of water to a boil and blanch the beans for 1–2 minutes. Strain and remove the outer skin, squeezing the bean out with your fingers.

*To make the marinade:* In a large bowl, combine the balsamic vinegar, ½ cup of the olive oil, the rosemary, and the garlic. Place the tuna steaks in the mixture and marinate for 2–3 hours (do not use salt, which would cook the flesh).

*The Dish:* *To make the sauce:* In a large saucepan over high heat, combine the wine, shallot, and peppercorns. Bring to a boil, then reduce to a simmer. Reduce the liquid to a third of its volume.

In a small saucepan, over medium-high heat, reduce the stock by half. Add the stock to the wine mixture and simmer until thickened, about 45 minutes.

In a large nonstick skillet or on a grill over high heat, sear the tuna very quickly, 2–3 minutes on each side. Using a very sharp knife, cut the tuna steaks into thin slices on the diagonal, across the grain of the fish.

In a small skillet, sauté the fava beans in the remaining olive oil for a few minutes, until tender.

To serve, mound about ½ cup of the fava beans at the center of each plate and drizzle the sauce around the edge. Place the fish on top of the beans.

*Wine:* Definitely a Pinot Noir, as a continuation of the sauce.

SALMONE ED ASPARAGI AL VAPORE CON SALSA DI TARTARO /
Asparagus and Steamed Salmon with Tartar Sauce
*4 servings*

We always get requests for lighter dishes, so we look for ways to enrich a mild fish. I like a firm fish, because if the piece is too big, you can have it cold the next day. The sauce provides the kick, whichever way you eat it; you need that extra flavor with a delicately poached fish.

---

*16 large asparagus spears*
*1 cup mayonnaise*
*1 tablespoon pickled onion, chopped*
*1 tablespoon capers, chopped*
*½ teaspoon horseradish (freshly grated if possible)*
*1 small garlic clove, chopped*
*1 tablespoon fresh dill, chopped*
*1 lemon*
*¼ cup dry white wine*
*2 bay leaves*
*½ teaspoon whole cracked peppercorns*
*Salt, to taste*
*1 pound Atlantic salmon fillet, cut into ½-inch pieces*
*1 teaspoon shallot, chopped*
*1 tablespoon olive oil*
*24 leaves Belgian endive*
*1 medium tomato*

*Preparation:* Discard the bottom quarter of the asparagus stems, and cut the spears into 1-inch slices.

In a small bowl, combine the mayonnaise, onion, capers, horseradish, garlic, and dill. Set the sauce aside.

*The Dish:* In a large saucepan, bring enough water to a boil to cover the fish and asparagus. Add the juice of half the lemon, the white wine, bay leaves, peppercorns, and salt. Cook the asparagus for 2 minutes, then add the salmon and simmer for about 3 minutes, or more, if you like your fish well done. Drain the liquid, reserving about ¼ cup. Put the salmon and asparagus in a mixing bowl with the shallot and toss with the remaining lemon juice and the olive oil.

Add some of the reserved fish-poaching liquid to the sauce to thin it down if necessary.

Cut the bottom of the endive leaves to a point, and arrange on each plate to form a flower. Slice the tomato into 6 wedges, then cut each of the wedges into fourths. Put a wedge of tomato on the middle of each leaf. Divide the salmon and asparagus into 4 servings and arrange on top of the endive. Spoon the sauce over the dish.

*Wine:* A many-layered white wine: a big white Burgundy—a Chassagne or Batard Montrachet or a young Corton Charlemagne. Or a big Chardonnay from California, a Chateau Montelena or a Kistler; wines that have strength, crispness, freshness, and a bouquet that can stand up to the dish. You want to smell flowers and dry rose petals.

## FILETTI DI SALMONE AL FUNGHETTO /
### White Salmon with Mushrooms

*4 servings*

This is a fairly modern recipe. This particular white salmon, which comes from the northern seas, is a fish that has delicate texture and finesse—it's almost creamy when you put it in your mouth—and yet it's a firm fish, and it feels like an expensive item, like a steak. We like to serve it with mushrooms and a medley of vegetables.

---

*¾ pound mixed wild mushrooms—*
  *chanterelle, lobster, morel, or*
  *fresh porcini if you can find them*
*1 cup white wine*
*1 cup Fish Stock (see page 74)*
*1 tablespoon shallot, finely chopped*
*¾ cup heavy cream*
*3 tablespoons olive oil*
*1 garlic clove, thinly sliced*
*Salt*
*4–8 ounces salmon fillets, skinned*
  *and deboned*
*Pepper, to taste*
*8–12 sprigs fresh thyme*

*Preparation:* Clean the mushrooms by rubbing with a damp towel or mushroom brush, and chop coarsely.

*The Dish:* In a small saucepan over medium-high heat, reduce the wine by half. Add the fish stock and reduce again by half. Add the shallot and cream, reduce heat to low, and simmer until the sauce thickens slightly.

In a large skillet, warm 2 tablespoons of the olive oil over medium heat. Add the garlic, mushrooms, and a pinch of salt, and sauté until dry, about 3–4 minutes.

In a nonstick skillet, heat the remaining olive oil over medium-high heat. Sear the salmon briefly, about 3 minutes per side, seasoning with salt and pepper. It should not be cooked all the way through.

Spoon the cream sauce into the center of individual plates. Place the salmon on top of the sauce and pile the mushrooms over the fish. Garnish with sprigs of fresh thyme.

*Wine:* A crispy, herbaceous wine, full of hearty sensations and robust flavor—Sauvignon Blanc by Duckhorn, Grechetto from Falesco in Umbria, or Nozze d'Oro of Regaleali in Sicily.

## TROTA SALMONATA CON PATATE E CREMA D'ANETO /
### Salmon Trout in Potato Crust with Cream of Fennel and Dill
*4 servings*

This is as much as we want to cross the border into France. You could very easily think that this is a French recipe, or find it in an American bistro cookbook or a contemporary Italian book. In American cuisine, we have freedom to explore. We wanted an intriguing presentation for this classic dish, but it had to be our own interpretation, so we added tomato and used olive oil instead of butter.

---

*1 fennel bulb*

*2 tablespoons fresh dill, chopped*

*2 tablespoons olive oil*

*1 medium Yukon Gold potato*

*4 baby Coho salmon, skinned and
    butterflied*

*Salt and pepper, to taste*

*2–4 tablespoons (1–2 ounces) butter*

*1 teaspoon garlic, chopped*

*½ cup Lobster Broth (see page 75)*

*1 tablespoon canned tomato puree*

*Preparation:* Cut off the base of the fennel bulb and slice lengthwise into ¼-inch slices. Steam until very tender, about 20 minutes. Process until smooth with 1 tablespoon of the dill, and the olive oil. Set aside.

*The Dish:* Preheat the oven to 450 degrees.

Using a mandoline, slice the potato into paper-thin slices. Season the salmon with salt, pepper, and a pinch of fresh dill. Cover the skinless side with overlapping slices of potato.

In a nonstick skillet, heat the butter over high heat. Sauté the fish, potato-side down, swirling the pan to cool the butter so it doesn't burn. Cook until the potato is crisp, about 2 minutes. Turn the fish over and sear the other side for 20 seconds. Remove to a buttered ovenproof dish. Cook the 3 remaining servings, adding more butter if necessary.

In the same pan, sauté the garlic and 2 pinches of fresh dill in the leftover butter on high heat, for 30 seconds. Add the lobster broth and tomato puree and reduce the sauce until slightly thickened.

To serve, heat the salmon for 1 more minute in the preheated oven. Place a mound of fennel puree on each plate. Place the salmon on top and add any remaining baking juices to the sauce. Thin the sauce slightly with water if necessary, and spoon it over the fish.

*Wine:* A mild Chardonnay like Sonoma-Cutrer, or an Oregon Chardonnay, which is a little more austere. Or a wonderful French Chablis, with lively, crisp sensations. From Italy I would go with a nice medium-bodied white wine, a Trebbiano d'Abruzzo.

*"This is as much as we want to cross the border into France. . . . An intriguing presentation for this classic dish."*

## BRANZINO AL SALE / Baked Whole Bass in Sea Salt Crust

*4 servings*

*Branzino,* a very popular fish from the Atlantic and the Mediterranean, can be prepared in many ways. In this recipe, the fish cooks slowly, wrapped in salt, which comes away easily once cooked.

---

*1 whole sea bass (3½–4 pounds),*
*cleaned and scaled*

*½ lemon, sliced*

*3 whole garlic cloves*

*Salt and pepper, to taste*

*6 sprigs Italian parsley, plus extra*
*for garnish*

*2 sprigs fresh thyme*

*1–2 pounds very coarse sea salt*

*Lemon wedges, for garnish*

*Preparation:* Preheat the oven to 375 degrees.

Wash and dry the fish, then stuff the belly with the lemon, garlic, salt and pepper, and herbs. Place the sea salt in a bowl and stir in 3 tablespoons of water. Pour half of the salt mixture into a baking pan and place the fish on top. Cover the whole fish with the rest of the sea salt.

Bake for 45–55 minutes, until the salt crust hardens and colors slightly. Remove and allow to rest for 10 minutes. Break open the salt covering, and serve the fish with lemon wedges and parsley.

*Wine:* Break the rules about red wine and fish, and serve a beautiful Pinot Noir, a Nero d'Avola, or a Valpolicella. These wines inspire a sense of freshness to go with the marvelous fresh fish—and the complex fruit flavors of the wine work nicely with the crusted fish.

## PIZZAIOLA DI PESCE / Whitefish Pizzaiola

*4 servings*

This dish is as old as I am; it started with the emigrants who used to have chicken pizzaiola, veal pizzaiola, anything pizzaiola. In Italy, the word is used around Naples for a mix of tomato with onion, or tomato with peppers. In this country it has been amplified, and there are different versions. Usually you think of chicken or veal, but I prefer a fish that wants to be richer, with a richer sauce. Our rendition remains robust, but it is a little bit lighter, more digestible than its ancestors.

---

*Eight 3-ounce whitefish fillets*
*Salt and pepper, to taste*
*1–2 teaspoons Garlic-Infused Olive*
  *Oil (see page 7)*
*2 teaspoons fresh thyme,*
  *finely chopped*
*24 thin asparagus spears*
*16 chives*
*4 tablespoons (2 ounces) butter*

FOR THE SAUCE
*1 teaspoon olive oil*
*2 tablespoons yellow onion,*
  *finely chopped*
*2 tablespoons capers*
*1 teaspoon garlic, finely chopped*
*Pinch of fresh thyme, chopped*
*¼ cup tomato sauce*
*½ cup Fish Stock (see page 74)*
  *or clam juice*

*Preparation:* Cut the fillets in half horizontally. Season with salt and pepper, the garlic-infused olive oil, and thyme. Place 3 asparagus spears across each piece of fish, roll the fish around the asparagus, and secure with a chive string.

*The Dish:* Preheat the oven to 375 degrees.

In a large skillet, melt the butter over medium heat. Brown the fish bundles briefly on both sides, about 2 minutes total.

Place the skillet in the preheated oven for 5 minutes, so that the fish cooks through. Remove the fish from the skillet and set aside.

In the same skillet, warm the olive oil over medium heat. Stir in the onion, capers, garlic, and thyme. Add the tomato sauce and fish stock. Reduce until slightly thickened to a sauce consistency. Place the fish in the sauce, and warm the fish a few minutes before serving.

Spoon the sauce into individual shallow bowls. Arrange 2 fish bundles on top and garnish with steamed spring vegetables.

*Wine:* A white wine of great character: Gavi di Gavi from La Scolca in Piedmont, or Lacryma Christi from Feudi di San Gregorio in Campania, or even a Sauvignon Blanc from New Zealand's Cloudy Bay or the Napa Valley's Spottswoode. The earthiness, the rich fruit, and that touch of elegance are predominant. Wines like these are very dry, a little austere at first, but rich on the palate.

*Assembling the fish bundles: "Place 3 asparagus spears across each piece of fish, roll the fish around the asparagus, and secure with a chive string."*

## GUAZZETTO DI PESCE IN BRODO D'ASTICE / Seared Fish with Roasted Garlic and Lobster Broth

*4 servings*

My grandpa Santo, my mother's father, used to make *ghiotta,* fish stew, on fish market days, which were Mondays, Wednesdays, and Fridays. He was an excellent cook, and he was especially good with fish. He lived in Pozzallo, a little fish town, and we saw him three or four times a week. His ghiotta was just floured pieces of fish, fried with garlic, olives, and tomatoes, and then simmered—a ragù of fish, a true marinara. Of course at the time I didn't appreciate any of these dishes—thank God there was no McDonald's. But when I got older, I ate San Francisco *cioppino* and *caciucco alla livornese*—more technical dishes, delicate and refined. And here, we try another interpretation. We steam the fish—*a vapeur*—with the vegetables and just a little oil, in an emulsion. And what better elegant finish than lobster broth?

---

*¼ cup plus 2 tablespoons olive oil*
*1 tablespoon (½ ounce) butter*
*1 pound mixed fish such as salmon, whitefish, or John Dory*
*¼ cup onion, finely chopped*
*4 tablespoons Toasted Garlic (see page 7)*
*8 basil leaves*
*1 pound mixed shellfish, such as 4 mussels, 4 clams, and 4 scallops*
*2 cups white wine*
*1⅓ cup diced fresh tomato*
*1 cup Lobster Broth (see page 75)*
*1 tablespoon canned tomato puree*

FOR GARNISH

*Salt and pepper, to taste*
*1–2 teaspoons olive oil*
*2 tablespoons parsley, chopped*

*Chef's Tip:* Luciano Pellegrini checks clams by twisting their shells between his fingers. If there is a clam inside, the shell will not give. If there is only sand, it will split apart under pressure.

*Preparation:* Cut the fish into 1½-inch chunks and clean the shellfish.

In a large skillet over high heat, heat 2 tablespoons of the olive oil, and the butter. Sear the fish for 1–2 minutes, until the outside is very lightly colored. Remove the fish to a cold plate or pan to stop the cooking process.

Turn the heat down to medium and add the remaining olive oil, the onion, toasted garlic, basil, and shellfish. After 1 minute add the white wine and diced tomato. Cook until most of the liquid has evaporated, removing the shellfish to a plate or bowl as they open. If you cover the pan they will open more quickly.

When the shellfish are done, add the lobster broth and tomato puree to the pan and boil on high until reduced by a third, about 5 minutes.

Let everything cool, and then cover the fish and broth. Refrigerate.

*The Dish:* Ten minutes before serving, reheat the broth. Add the seafood and shellfish for 2 minutes to warm them up.

Divide the seafood and shellfish into 4 individual shallow bowls. Taste the sauce and adjust seasonings, and spoon over the fish. Garnish with the olive oil and a handful of chopped fresh parsley.

*Wine:* A wine that is intense and hearty, and has character. A Trebbiano d'Abruzzo or a Pinot Bianco from Friuli, both white wines with no oak, little bottle aging, and great flavors. From California or Oregon, a Vin Gris or some of the new interpretations of Italian varietals, like a Tocai or a Fiano, all with intense flavors.

## CAPESANTE ALLE PICCOLE VERDURE /
### Sautéed Scallops on a Mixed Vegetable Pillow
*6 servings*

This doesn't have anything to do with tradition. In fact, in Italy we would have a hard time translating scallops, *capesante*. There they are very, very hard to obtain, mostly farm-raised, and usually expensive. But here we can get very high quality scallops that have a meaty flavor, a little bit like lobster and shrimp. They are adaptable to many different recipes.

If you are able to get *bottarga,* cured tuna roe, that touch of saltiness will add a great deal to the taste of the scallops.

---

*2 tablespoons (1 ounce) butter*

*6 sea or 12 bay scallops*

*1 fennel bulb*

*1 handful fagiolini (haricots verts)*

*1 bunch baby carrots*

*Salt and pepper, to taste*

*2 tablespoons all-purpose flour*

*4 radishes, finely chopped*

*2 fresh Roma tomatoes,*
*    finely chopped*

*1 head baby frisee, finely chopped*

*¼ recipe Basic Vinaigrette*
*    (see page 53)*

*Baby lettuce leaves, for garnish*

*Optional: grated bottarga—*
*    ¼ teaspoon per serving*

*Preparation:*  To clarify the butter, melt it over low heat in a small heavy-duty saucepan. Let cool, then skim the foam from the surface and pour the clarified butter into a cup, discarding the solids at the bottom of the pan.

Clean the membrane from the scallops, wash, dry, and set aside.

In a small pot of boiling salted water, separately blanch the fennel, fagiolini, and carrots. Immerse in cold water to stop the cooking process, and chop finely.

Cut off the end of the fennel bulb and the green tips. Remove the tough outer leaves.

*The Dish:*  Add a pinch of salt and pepper to the flour and lightly dust the scallops with the flour. In a skillet, melt the clarified butter over medium heat. Add the scallops and cook 2–3 minutes per side. Set aside.

Combine cooked and raw vegetables in a bowl and mix with the vinaigrette dressing, to taste.

Mound 1 cup of vegetables in the middle of each plate. Arrange 1–2 scallops on top and garnish with the baby lettuce leaves. Sprinkle a small amount of grated bottarga over the salad.

*Wine:*  This is a rich, festive dish, so you have to have a beautiful, almost decadent Chardonnay or the equivalent, a wine that is wrapped in the sensation of new oak, that speaks of vanilla, pineapple, and exotic fruit; a wine with a creaminess that will enhance the morsel of fatty scallop, the last taste of crunchiness given by the vegetables. A good Mersault or Puligny-Montrachet if you want to splurge, or a consistent Chardonnay like Chateau Montelena or Mondavi Reserve.

## ASTICE ALLA CREMA DI PEPERONI DOLCI /
### Lobster with Sweet Pepper Sauce

*4 servings*

We are so lucky to have Maine lobsters; this incredible tender, juicy meat is definitely one of the greatest foods anybody can think of. There's the American tradition of lobster with drawn butter, a comfort food that will be around for generations. But you can do a lot of other things. Here, we adapt it for a salad in an easy yet elegant dish. Make it with an interesting sauce—something sublime like this sweet red pepper cream.

*1 large yellow onion, sliced*

*1 garlic clove, smashed*

*½ cup olive oil*

*3 Roma tomatoes, peeled, seeded, and diced*

*1 pound red bell peppers, cut in eighths*

*Salt and pepper, to taste*

*¾ cup heavy cream*

*Two 1-pound Maine lobsters*

*Preparation:* In a skillet, sauté the onion and garlic in the olive oil over medium heat, until the onions are translucent. Add the tomatoes, peppers, salt and pepper, and half of the cream. Cover and simmer until tender, about 15 minutes.

Puree the vegetable mixture in the food processor. Stir in the remaining cream and chill.

*The Dish:* In a large stockpot of salted water, boil the lobsters for about 5 minutes.

Let cool. Halve the lobsters, remove the tail meat, rinse, and remove the claw meat.

To serve, arrange the lobster meat on individual dishes and serve with the chilled sauce.

*Wine:* Lobster and Chardonnay are a great pairing, because they are two elegant complements—rich, opulent, full of sensation. I would serve a Chardonnay from Grgich, Kistler, or Sonoma-Cutrer. As an alternative, if you want to splurge, choose a sensuous white Burgundy from the Montrachet family.

## FILETTI DI TRIGLIE CON POMODORI E OLIVE /
### Red Mullet with Tomatoes and Olives

*4 servings*

---

*2 ripe tomatoes, peeled, seeded,
    and diced*
*10 small pitted black olives, chopped*
*5 chives, chopped*
*2 basil leaves, finely chopped*
*Pinch of marjoram*
*½ cup olive oil*
*Salt and pepper, to taste*
*3–4 tablespoons flour*
*Twelve 3-ounce mullet fillets*

In a sauté pan over medium-high heat, combine the tomatoes, olives, chives, basil, and marjoram. Add half of the olive oil and a touch of salt and pepper. Turn down the heat to low and cook slowly for about 15 minutes, stirring frequently.

In a skillet, heat the remaining olive oil over medium-high heat. Lightly flour and season the fish, and brown on both sides for about 3 minutes total. Place the fish on a large platter, and cover with the sauce. Serve with your favorite vegetables.

*Wine:* A Sauvignon Blanc from Friuli (producer Mario Schiopetto or Yosko Gravner) or a Sancerre from the Loire region of France, or an American Sauvignon Blanc (Duckhorn or Araujo, both Napa vineyards). These are wines with a nice fruit-acid balance, elegant and flowery.

## FILETTI DI BACCALÀ AL FORNO /
### Baked Filet of Codfish with Tomatoes
*6 servings*

Cod and I have a love-hate relationship—mostly hate in my childhood, through eight years of boarding school. Prepared by unskilled nuns, it was barely soaked in water, so the saltiness was not washed out, then fried or baked with olives until it was a tasteless piece of cardboard. Every Friday I had to find an excuse to leave it untouched until the plates were removed.

Much later, one of my chefs prepared a cod soufflé for several hundred people and I was forced to taste it, to give my opinion. I began to acquire a taste for it. Now it has become a gratifying fish, very rich in tradition and memories. It is a must on the night before Christmas, one of the seven fish that are served. There is no Christmas Eve without *baccalà*.

---

2¼ pounds salt cod

⅓ cup olive oil

1 pound fresh tomatoes,
　sliced

1 garlic clove, finely
　chopped

1 small bunch parsley,
　finely chopped

1 small bunch basil,
　finely chopped

Pepper to taste

*Preparation:* To tenderize the cod and get the salt off, soak it for at least 24 hours in milk or water, changing the liquid 3 times.

Wash the cod, bone it completely, and cut into pieces that weigh about 2 ounces each.

*The Dish:* Preheat the oven to 375 degrees.

Spread the fillets in a single layer in a pan, cover them with water, and cook for 2–3 minutes over medium heat, to firm up the fish. Drain well and arrange on an oiled baking pan. Cover with the remaining ingredients. Bake for 30 minutes.

*Wine:* I would serve it with a very intense white wine— a Spanish Rioja, a Neapolitan Lacryma Christi, a French Chablis, or a Trebbiano d'Abruzzo.

## BRACIOLINE DI POLLO CON SALSICCIA D'ANATRA / Rolled Chicken Breast, Stuffed with Duck Sausage

*4 servings*

A restaurant cannot stand still. In a steak house, you know that you can come up with an innovative side dish here and there and that is enough. But at a restaurant like Posto, where the chef is famous for innovation and seasonal menus, we must always ask: What else can we do that is light, creative, and a nice mix of ingredients? Combine my love for *rollatini,* little rolls, with Luciano's talent for sausage making, and out of that comes a new dish. This dish is interesting because the flavors of chicken breast and duck sausage are so completely different, and there is a balance between the leanness of the fowl and the fattiness of the duck. It's very adaptable on the grill, and you can serve it for lunch or dinner with some wonderful creamed spinach, or spinach sautéed in garlic.

---

FOR THE BRACIOLINE

*6 ounces mild chicken and duck sausage*
*16 chicken tenderloins or 4 chicken breasts, skinned and deboned*
*1 tablespoon (½ ounce) butter*
*2 tablespoons olive oil*
*1 tablespoon yellow onion, chopped*
*2 teaspoons garlic, chopped*
*1 teaspoon fresh sage, finely chopped*
*1 teaspoon fresh rosemary, finely chopped*
*1 teaspoon fresh thyme, finely chopped*
*⅓ cup dry white wine*
*3 ounces soft white bread, cut into 1-inch chunks*
*2 tablespoons Chicken Stock (see page 74), optional*
*Salt and pepper, to taste*
*1 teaspoon Garlic-Infused Olive Oil (see page 7)*

*Preparation:* Remove the sausage from their casings, crumble, and set aside.

Pound the chicken tenderloins or breasts to ⅛-inch thickness. If using whole breasts, cut into 3–4 vertical sections.

> *Chef's Tip:* Slit open a large food storage bag and place the chicken tenderloin or breast inside to flatten; the bags hold up better than plastic wrap does.

*The Dish:* TO MAKE THE STUFFING: In a large skillet, melt the butter with the olive oil over medium-high heat. Add the onion, garlic, crumbled sausage, and herbs. Stir in the wine and reduce over medium-high heat for 5 minutes. Add the cubed bread and stir to coat. Cook for 5 minutes, transfer to a food processor, and process mixture until smooth. Add 2 tablespoons of chicken stock if necessary, to make a thick paste. Do not salt and pepper the stuffing. The sausage is highly seasoned, and does not require additional help.

*3 tablespoons Herb-Infused Olive Oil (see page 7)*

FOR THE BRAISED ENDIVE

*4 Belgian endive*

*1–2 tablespoons olive oil*

*1 teaspoon Toasted Garlic (see page 7)*

*1 teaspoon whole-grain mustard*

*1 teaspoon butter (1/6 ounce)*

*Salt and pepper, to taste*

*Tomato slices, for garnish*

TO MAKE THE BRACIOLINE: Season the pounded chicken breast sections with salt and pepper, and drizzle lightly with the garlic olive oil. Spread 1 tablespoon of the stuffing across each piece, starting 1 inch from either end. Roll up the chicken pieces into "bracioline."

Brush rolls with the herb olive oil. On a medium-hot to hot grill, sear quickly on all sides. Move to a cooler section of the grill and continue to cook until done, about 7 minutes. Turn once or twice.

Touch to test for doneness: If the roll gives and feels gummy, it's still raw inside. When it springs back, it is done. Total cooking time depends on the thickness of the pounded chicken breast.

> *Chef's Tip:* Start to test the bracioline after about 5 minutes. "When it's raw it still feels like flesh, but as it cooks it firms up," says Luciano Pellegrini. But be careful not to wait too long. "When it's well done, it feels like a shoe sole."

TO MAKE THE BRAISED ENDIVE: Slice the endive in half lengthwise, remove the core, and slice into 1-inch segments.

In a 9-inch skillet, warm the olive oil over high heat. Add the garlic, mustard, butter, endive, and salt and pepper and cook for 2 minutes, until the endive is coated but still crunchy.

Pile the endive on individual plates and place 4 bracioline on top. Garnish with the tomato slices for color.

*Wine:* A slightly spicy wine, like a Pinot Noir, that has character and rich texture. I like an Oregon Pinot Noir. I could also stretch and go with a Merlot from Umbria, because I like the spiciness and the fruit. It is light, supple, and yet has an after-character that is very interesting, to cut whatever fattiness a dish like this will leave.

## POLLO E GAMBERI ALLO SPIEDO / Chicken and Shrimp Skewers

*12 skewers*

This is what having fun with food is all about. Luciano Pellegrini, who is now at Valentino in Las Vegas, devised this dish when he was the chef at Posto. It's a quintessential American dish with an Italian twist, from an Italian chef interpreting his new home. There's nothing wrong with going this far, as long as you do it well.

*12 chicken tenderloins*
*12 medium-large shrimp,*
   *shelled and deveined*
*3 tablespoons olive oil*
*Salt and pepper, to taste*
*1 tablespoon fresh dill,*
   *finely chopped*
*½ cup Posto's Barbecue Sauce*
   *(see page 167)*

*Preparation:* Put 1 piece of chicken and 1 shrimp on a skewer with the chicken flat and the shrimp straight up and down, so both will cook in the same amount of time. Place on a large platter or cutting board, brush with olive oil, and season with salt and pepper and chopped dill. Marinate for approximately 1 hour in the refrigerator.

*The Dish:* Place skewers on a hot barbecue grill, and quickly sear each side. Turn down the heat of the grill or move them to a cooler area farther away from the coals. Brush with the barbecue sauce and cook for about 5 more minutes, turning frequently so they don't burn. Use the remaining sauce as a dip.

*Wine:* If you want a spicy red wine, I like a Syrah by Qupé or Turley, with the cassis and currant flavors against the barbecue spiciness. Or you might want an ale, a nice yeasty young beer.

# POSTO'S BARBECUE SAUCE

*½ cup*

---

*1 tablespoon shallot, finely chopped*

*2 tablespoons balsamic vinegar*

*3 tablespoons olive oil*

*Salt and pepper, to taste*

*1 tablespoon fresh rosemary,
   finely chopped*

*1 tablespoon fresh thyme,
   finely chopped*

*1 tablespoon fresh sage,
   finely chopped*

*1 tablespoon garlic, finely chopped*

*Preparation:* In a stainless-steel bowl set over a pot of gently simmering water, whisk together all of the ingredients. Cook over medium heat for 1 hour. Let stand at room temperature for 1 hour and serve with grilled meats and vegetables.

## SPEZZATINO DI POLLO /
### Chicken Breast in a Radicchio Cup with a Mushroom Medley

*4 servings*

I don't think we cook enough stews at the restaurants, so I am always happy when we can create a family-style, basic dish. The inspiration for the *spezzatino* starts at home, where my mother used little pieces of "poor" ingredients, like potato and chicken cooked together with olive oil, onion, and a little tomato. At Valentino, we have the luxury of fine ingredients, but the idea here is the same. Sometimes this is our "family" dish at the restaurant, the one we make for the employees. When you do it the elegant way—with free-range chicken breasts, radicchio, and mushrooms—it's a chicken dish dressed for the holidays.

---

*1 large head radicchio*

*Four 8-ounce chicken breasts, skinned, deboned, and fat removed*

*2 teaspoons (⅓ ounce) butter*

*2 tablespoons olive oil*

*½ teaspoon garlic, finely chopped*

*1 cup mixed mushrooms, sliced*

*4 fresh sage leaves*

*1 teaspoon fresh horseradish, grated*

*½ cup dry white wine*

*½ cup Chicken Stock (see page 74)*

*½ cup cream*

Peel 8–12 whole leaves from the radicchio and set aside. Chop the remaining inner leaves.

Cut the chicken breasts into 1-inch chunks. In a large skillet over high heat, melt the butter and olive oil and sear the chicken pieces for 2 minutes. Set aside.

In the same skillet, combine the garlic, mushrooms, chopped radicchio, and sage leaves and cook for 2 minutes. Add the horseradish and wine and cook for 2 minutes. Add the chicken stock and cream and remove from the heat.

Five to 10 minutes before serving, bring the sauce to a boil and add the chicken pieces. Cook at high heat until the sauce reduces, about 5 minutes.

When the sauce is very thick, taste and adjust seasonings. Overlap 2–3 radicchio leaves on each plate, to form a cup. Mound the chicken inside and cover with the sauce.

*Wine:* Try a red of good structure, complex and full-bodied, like a Robert Mondavi Cabernet or a rich and elegant Barbaresco by Bruno Giacosa or Albino Rocca.

## PETTI DI POLLO E CARCIOFI /
### Chicken Breast with Artichokes and Lemon
*8 servings*

Sometimes you're looking for an uncomplicated food. This is a dish of great simplicity; it has a very basic, almost dietetic flavor. The artichoke mixes with the lemon, which cuts it and balances it out.

---

*8–12 baby artichokes*
*¼ cup olive oil*
*1 bunch Italian parsley, chopped*
*2 tablespoons fresh tarragon,*
  *chopped*
*2 tablespoons fresh rosemary,*
  *chopped*
*2 tablespoons fresh thyme, chopped*
*8 chicken breasts, 6–7 ounces each*
*3–4 tablespoons all-purpose flour*
*¼ cup (2 ounces) butter*
*2 garlic cloves, minced*
*1 cup dry white wine*
*2 lemons, juiced*
*Salt and pepper, to taste*
*2 cups Brown Sauce (see page 201)*

*Preparation:* Remove the outside leaves of the artichokes until you reach the yellow inner leaves. Remove the choke and cut the artichokes into wedges. In a skillet, sauté the wedges in 2 tablespoons of the olive oil over medium-high heat. Add 2 tablespoons of the parsley and the rest of the herbs and cook for 4–5 minutes, until the artichokes are slightly crispy. Set aside.

*The Dish:* Preheat the oven to 375 degrees.

Lightly coat the chicken breasts in flour. In a large oven-proof skillet over medium heat, sauté the chicken in the remaining olive oil, on both sides, until golden. Remove the chicken and set aside. Drain the olive oil from the skillet. Add the butter, garlic, and artichokes. Pour in the wine and reduce until the wine evaporates.

Add the juice of the lemons, the remaining parsley, salt and pepper, and brown sauce. Put the chicken into the sauce and bake in the oven for 10 minutes. Serve immediately.

*Wine:* A very serious white wine to cut through the acidity of the lemon and artichoke. A steely white Rhone, a Viognier, a Gavi, or a Tocai Friulano. Artichokes by themselves are definitely too harsh, and can change the flavor of the wine, but here the flavor will mix with the other ingredients.

## PORTAFOGLI DI POLLO ALLA VALDOSTANA /
### Chicken "Wallets" with Prosciutto, Cheese, and Asparagus

*4 servings*

"Valdostana" is used to describe the topping of prosciutto, asparagus, and fontina cheese. You can use it on any cold cutlet—turkey, veal, chicken, pork. What gives it a sense of elegance is top-notch products. We use white asparagus when it's in season, San Daniele prosciutto, and free-range chicken. This is a quick and delicious dish.

---

*4 skinless, deboned chicken breasts,*
  *flattened*
*¼ cup olive oil*
*12 spears fresh asparagus*
*4 slices imported prosciutto*
*4 slices imported fontina cheese*
*1 cup dry white wine*
*½ cup Chicken Stock (see page 74)*
*¼ cup (2 ounces) butter*

Preheat the oven to 350 degrees.

In a skillet over medium-high heat, sauté the chicken breasts in the olive oil for 2–3 minutes per side. Transfer to a baking sheet.

Boil or steam the asparagus until just tender. Roll 3 asparagus spears in each slice of prosciutto and place on top of each chicken breast. Top with a slice of fontina cheese and bake for 5 minutes.

Pour the white wine into the same skillet you used for the chicken and reduce until almost completely evaporated. Add the chicken stock and butter. Place the chicken breasts on a platter or on individual plates and drizzle with the wine sauce.

*Wine:* A Barbera. It's a wine that has structure and character, that is very traditional, and it's intense enough to cleanse the cheese, the salt, and the richness. As an alternative, another very intense wine called Teroldego, which matches very well with fontina dishes.

# QUAGLIETTE ALLA DIAVOLA CON RUCOLA E FINOCCHIO /
## Spicy Grilled Quail with Arugula Salad and Grilled Fennel

*4 servings*

FOR THE QUAIL MARINADE

*1 cup olive oil*

*1 teaspoon fresh sage, finely chopped*

*1 tablespoon fresh rosemary,*
*  finely chopped*

*1 garlic clove, finely chopped*

*White pepper, to taste*

---

*2 large fennel bulbs, roots sliced off,*
*  cut into ¼-inch wedges*

*8 boneless quails*

*16 thin slices smoked bacon*

*2 tablespoons olive oil*

*Sea salt*

*8 ounces arugula*

FOR THE DIAVOLA SAUCE

*6 tablespoons olive oil*

*2 tablespoons red wine vinegar*

*1 tablespoon whole-grain Dijon*
*  mustard*

*2 small garlic cloves*

*1 medium jalapeño pepper*

*1 pinch sage*

*1 pinch rosemary*

*Salt and pepper, to taste*

FOR THE SALAD DRESSING

*1–2 tablespoons balsamic vinegar*

*1 tablespoon shallot, chopped*

*¼ cup olive oil*

*Preparation:* TO MAKE THE MARINADE: In a small bowl, whisk together the olive oil, sage, rosemary, garlic, and white pepper.

Cut the quails in half lengthwise. Wrap each half with a slice of bacon and skewer them, 2 halves to a stick. In a large bowl or baking dish, marinate them for 1 hour.

Steam the fennel until just tender, about 5 minutes. Brush with olive oil and set aside.

TO MAKE THE DIAVOLA SAUCE: In a food processor or blender, combine the olive oil, vinegar, mustard, garlic, jalapeño, herbs, and salt and pepper, and let sit for a while.

TO MAKE THE DRESSING: In a small bowl, whisk together the vinegar and shallot and allow to sit for 10 minutes. Add the olive oil and set aside.

*The Dish:* Over medium-to-hot charcoal or a grill, grill the quails for 5–7 minutes, turning them consistently so they don't char on either side. Brush them a few times with the diavola sauce. Grill the fennel slices for a few minutes on each side. Brush the fennel with the diavola sauce. Remove the quails and fennel from the grill and sprinkle with sea salt.

Toss the arugula with the dressing and arrange in the center of each plate. Place the quails on top and arrange fennel around the arugula.

*Wine:* Think of this dish as the beautiful main course in an elegant 5- or 6-course meal, and try one of the Premier Grand Cru Bordeaux wines, a big Cabernet from California, or an intense grape from Sicily, like Nero d'Avola's

Regaleali Rosso del Conte or Duca Enrico from Duca di Salaparuta—beautiful wines that can stand against a rich and complex main course like this one.

## RAGÙ DI QUAGLIE / Quail Ragù

*4 servings*

*2 large boneless quails*
*Salt and pepper, to taste*
*1 pound fusilli*
*4 tablespoons (2 ounces) butter*
*2 garlic cloves, thinly sliced*
*2–3 fresh sage leaves, chopped*
*2 slices smoked bacon or pancetta, chopped*
*½ cup dry white wine*
*½ cup Chicken Stock (see page 74)*
*2 tablespoons heavy cream*
*2 tablespoons Parmesan cheese, grated*

With a sharp knife, cut the legs and the wings off the quails and slice the breasts into small pieces. Season everything with salt and pepper.

Bring a large pot of salted water to a boil and cook the pasta while you make the ragù. In a skillet, melt the butter over high heat until it sizzles. Add the garlic, sage, bacon, and quails. Stir the meat with a fork to help it color evenly and quickly. Remove the meat from the pan and keep warm in a 200-degree oven. Add the wine to the skillet and reduce over medium-high heat. Add the chicken stock and cream and reduce again to desired thickness. Season with salt and pepper, and place the meat back into the sauce at the last minute. Toss the pasta in the skillet with the sauce and sprinkle with Parmesan cheese.

*Wine:* The quail ragù is great over pasta, with a robust aged Chianti or one of the new "Super Tuscan" wines, where texture and fruit provide a backbone.

# ANATRA IN UMIDO ALLA TOSCANA / Tuscan Duck with Olives

*4 servings*

The Tuscans call this dish *anatra muta*. We learned it from a chef who visited Primi in 1985 as part of a UCLA class on gastronomy and history. Pierluigi Stiaccini, a fourth-generation chef, came to us from the restaurant La Torre in Castellina in Chianti, where he cooked dishes taught to him by his mother and grandmother, who in turn had learned from their ancestors. He cooked big bowls of food, family-style, and for the *secondi*, he usually had a choice of rabbit, duck, or mixed roast meats. We are not talking about novelty here, but about an abiding reverence for the past.

*1 whole 5-pound Muscovy duckling*
*3 tablespoons olive oil*
*1 small yellow onion, chopped*
*1 medium carrot, peeled and*
  *chopped*
*1 stalk celery, chopped*
*12 ounces prosciutto, chopped*
*Salt and black pepper, freshly*
  *ground, to taste*
*1 cup dry white wine*
*1 cup brine-cured black olives,*
  *pitted and halved*
*2 tablespoons Italian parsley,*
  *chopped*
*1 bay leaf*

*Preparation:* Remove the excess fat from the duck cavity. Cut off the neck, chop off the wing tips and reserve with gizzards for broth. Place the duck breast-side up and cut through the breastbone. Turn it over, push down on the breast halves, and cut down the backbone. Turn each half skin-side up and feel for the end of the rib cage. Cut each piece in half just below the ribs. Trim off the excess fat and skin.

In a large skillet, warm the olive oil over medium heat. Add the onion, carrot, and celery, and cook about 5 minutes. Add the prosciutto and cook another few minutes, until the onion is golden in color.

*The Dish:* Preheat the broiler.

Place the duck skin-side up on a rack in a broiler pan and broil for 5 minutes, 6 inches away from the heat. Remove from the oven and prick the skin all over to release the fat, being careful not to pierce the meat. Broil another 5 minutes and prick the skin again. Turn the duck over and broil for 5 more minutes.

Transfer the broiled duck to the pan with the onion mixture. Season with salt and pepper and add the wine. Bring to a boil over medium-high heat and turn the heat down to low. Simmer the duck for 15 minutes, covered.

Add the olives, parsley, and bay leaf and cook, covered, for another 20 minutes, or until the duck is tender. Remove the duck to a serving platter. If there is excess liquid in the pan, reduce over high heat. Pour the vegetables over the duck and serve.

*Wine:* Serve Tuscan with Tuscan: Morellino di Scansano (Fattoria le Pupille), Sangioveto by Badia a Coltibuono, or Vino Nobile di Montepulciano (Poliziano). These are wines that emphasize the Sangiovese grape, rich with fruit extracts, with delicate but intense nose and body that should support the gamey flavor of the bird and the rich sauce.

## SALSICCIA D'ANATRA A POLPETTE / Duck Sausage Patties

*4 servings*

Before Posto opened, we sent our chef, Luciano Pellegrini, to Italy for six months to learn the art of sausage making. First we sent him to Gioacchino Palestro, the maven of all things related to goose and duck, who makes his own sausages, prosciutto, and foie gras. Next, we sent him to one of the oldest grill restaurants in Italy—Da Toso, in the Friuli region. Toso has a big grill, a *focolare,* where the chef basically entertains his friends and customers. He'll tell them, "What do I have today? A beautiful *fiorentina,*" a Florentine steak, and the customer will say, "Okay, I'll take ten ounces." He cooks it on the open flame and serves it up. Luciano was his assistant for a while, and when he came back to Posto his repertoire included sausages, birds, and all kinds of meat and game. Now he thinks he can make sausage out of anything.

---

*20 ounces lean duck meat*

*5 ounces duck fat*

*1 tablespoon sea salt*

*1 teaspoon mixed peppercorns,*
*    crushed*

*½ cup red wine*

*1 small garlic clove, chopped*

*1 teaspoon fresh thyme,*
*    finely chopped*

*8 medium-size savoy cabbage leaves*

*Posto's Barbecue Sauce*
*    (see page 167)*

*Preparation:* In a meat grinder, grind the duck meat and fat together. Transfer to a bowl and add the salt, peppercorns, red wine, garlic, and thyme. Cover and refrigerate overnight.

*The Dish:* In a medium-size pot of salted boiling water, blanch the cabbage leaves for a few minutes, then plunge the leaves into cold water to stop the cooking. Form flat, round patties with the sausage mix and put them on a medium-hot barbecue grill. Cook until medium-rare, about 2–3 minutes on each side. Wrap the patties in cabbage leaves, and continue grilling until cabbage is golden brown. Remove from the grill, slice as thick as you want, and serve with Posto's Barbecue Sauce (see page 167).

*Wine:* A Chauteauneuf du Pap, a Syrah, or a Gigondas. These are dark, intense red wines that support the spiciness and saltiness of the duck sausage.

*1 whole 2-pound goose breast,*
    *deboned*

*Salt and pepper*

*1 teaspoon fresh rosemary,*
    *finely chopped*

*2½ teaspoons sage, finely chopped*

*1 cup Marsala wine*

*½ cup (4 ounces) butter*

*4 ounces dry porcini mushrooms,*
    *soaked in water*

*2 dozen pearl onions, peeled and*
    *steamed*

*2 teaspoons garlic, chopped*

*1 tablespoon shallot, chopped*

*¾ cup Chicken Stock (see page 74)*

*2 cups savoy cabbage, coarsely*
    *chopped*

*1 tablespoon olive oil*

*1 recipe Polenta (see page 122)*

Preheat the oven to 375 degrees.

Season the goose breast with salt and pepper, half the rosemary, and half the sage, and add 2 teaspoons of the Marsala wine. Tie the breast together tightly with twine, and in a hot skillet, sear on all sides over high heat for about 5 minutes. Place in the oven and roast for 45–50 minutes.

Remove the meat from the pan and set aside. Discard the fat and add 4 tablespoons of the butter to the pan. Over medium heat, sauté the porcini, onions, garlic, shallot, the remaining rosemary, and 1 teaspoon of the sage. When the garlic becomes golden in color, add the remaining wine and reduce. Add ½ cup of the chicken stock and simmer until reduced to desired thickness.

Meanwhile, in a large skillet, sauté the cabbage in the olive oil over medium heat. Add the remaining chicken stock and cook on low heat for about 20 minutes.

Untie the breast and slice very thin, just under ¼ inch thick. Place the slices in a baking dish. In a separate small skillet, brown the remaining butter with the remaining sage over medium-high heat, then pour it over the goose. Return the goose to the oven for a few minutes.

While the cabbage cooks, prepare creamy polenta according to the recipe on page 122. Keep the cabbage warm until the polenta is done. Arrange the slices of duck over the braised cabbage. Spoon some sauce over the duck and garnish with polenta.

*Wine:* This is an American holiday dish with an Italian twist—the addition of porcini and polenta. It requires a glorious red wine to celebrate a festive occasion. I suggest a great Bordeaux or Brunello, or an aged Chianti or Cabernet Sauvignon, something that will stand up to a rich, fatty bird.

"*An American holiday dish with an Italian twist—
the addition of porcini and polenta.*"

PETTI DI FAGIANO AVVOLTI IN PANCETTA /
Pheasant Breast Wrapped in Pancetta

*4 servings*

We always think of pheasant as a festive dish of almost royal connotation, and combining it with pancetta is the traditional technique—we cook the bird with fat to enrich the flavor and keep the moisture in. If you're not a bacon or pancetta lover, you can remove it at the end, as you would fish skin. Serve this with a bed of soft polenta or creamed spinach.

*3 tablespoons (1½ ounces) butter*
*1 teaspoon fresh rosemary,*
    *finely chopped*
*1 teaspoon fresh thyme,*
    *finely chopped*
*4 fresh sage leaves, finely chopped*
*4 full pheasant breasts*
*Salt and pepper, to taste*
*½ pound pancetta, sliced thin*
    *(about 32 slices)*
*1 recipe Polenta (see page 122)*

FOR THE SAUCE
*½ cup Marsala wine*
*1 cup Brown Sauce (see page 201)*
*½ cup heavy cream*

�֍ *Chef's Tip:* You can probably find frozen pheasant breasts at your market, but if not, you can substitute either boneless, skinless chicken breasts or even turkey breasts—skinned, cut away from the bone, and divided into four sections.

*Preparation:* To clarify the butter, melt it in a small heavy-duty saucepan over low heat. Let cool, then skim foam from the surface and pour the clarified butter into a cup, discarding the solids at the bottom of the pan.

In a small bowl, combine the herbs. Season the pheasant breasts with salt and pepper and the chopped herb mixture. Place the breasts together like a sandwich.

Make a "skin" of overlapping strips of pancetta, and roll up the pheasant breast in it. Make sure the pheasant is completely covered. Refrigerate for 2 hours (this helps the pancetta stick to the fowl).

*The Dish:* Preheat the oven to 375 degrees.

In a skillet over medium-high heat, sear the pheasant meat on all sides in the clarified butter, about 3 minutes per side. Bake in the oven for 10–12 minutes and then remove fowl to a warm plate.

While the pheasant is in the oven, make the creamy polenta according to the recipe on page 122.

TO MAKE THE SAUCE: Pour off the fat from the skillet. Add the wine and reduce by half. Add 1 cup brown sauce. Reduce for a few more minutes, add the cream, and bring to a boil.

Cut the pheasant breast into 1-inch slices. Serve over the creamy polenta and top with the sauce.

*Wine:* A Zinfandel, because it offers fruits—cherries and black currant—that are very distinct in your mouth, and because the high alcohol level is a good foil for the fattiness of the bird and the bacon. Or serve an Amarone, whose raisiny flavor and intense body are a substantial accompaniment to the dish.

Rabbit, with its delicate dark meat, is a parent to chicken. Mamma used to roast it and add big, beautiful green olives, celery, sometimes sweet peppers, and lots of vinegar. Other times it was sweet and sour, with a little sugar—the perfect match for a meat that can be gamey. For me, rabbit is always a dish of special occasion—growing up, that was the only time I saw it. The advantage of this dish is that you can prolong the pleasant sensation—this tastes just as good reheated the next day.

---

*1 recipe Polenta (see page 122)*

*5 garlic cloves*

*2 tablespoons olive oil*

*6 ounces fresh chanterelle or porcini mushrooms, sliced ¼ inch thick*

*Salt and pepper, to taste*

*½ cup dry white wine*

*2 rabbit saddles, deboned by the butcher*

*4–6 fresh sage leaves*

*6–7 slices pancetta*

*2 tablespoons (1 ounce) butter*

*1 teaspoon garlic, finely chopped*

*1 cup Brown Sauce (see page 201)*

*Preparation:* Prepare the polenta according to the directions on page 122.

In a large skillet over medium heat, lightly brown 1 clove of the garlic in the olive oil. Add the sliced mushrooms, salt and pepper, and a few tablespoons of the white wine, and sauté for a few minutes, until the mushrooms are tender.

*The Dish:* Preheat the oven to 375 degrees.

Season the rabbit meat with salt and pepper. Place the sage leaves and remaining garlic on the meat, roll it up, and wrap with pancetta. Secure with twine.

In a sauté pan, brown the butter for 2 minutes over medium-high heat. Add the rabbit, and sear it all over. Place it in a baking dish and bake for about 10 minutes. Turn the oven off, but leave the rabbit in to keep it warm. Add the chopped garlic, then the remaining sage to the pan. When the garlic is light brown, deglaze the pan with the remaining white wine. Let the wine evaporate, and add the brown sauce. Bring to a boil and turn the heat down to a simmer. In the meantime, warm the mushroom mixture over low heat and untie the rabbit pieces. Arrange the rabbit around a scoop of polenta on each plate, placing the rabbit on the side and the sautéed mushrooms on top. Spoon the sauce over it all.

*Wine:* A great Cabernet—the chocolate, the earthiness, the berries, the tannic fruit—is a classic match. And there are so many wonderful Cabernets, from Jordan to Caymus to Altamura. Or if I think about Tuscany, because rabbit is so popular there, a big Sangiovese, like a Montevertine, or something from Fonterutoli or Castello di Ama.

*Angelo Auriana wraps delicate, dark rabbit meat with pancetta and secures with twine.*

## L'ABBACCHIO DI PAOLA / Roman Lamb
(printed with permission from Paola Di Mauro)

*4 servings*

The first time I went to Rome as a restaurateur, one of the highest-rated restaurants in my guidebook was called Papa Giovanni, and I went out of my way to eat there. I went for lunch. It was kind of funky—it still is—but for me it was a wonderful experience. The wine they served me was a Colle Picchionne Bianco, by Paola Di Mauro, and when I asked about her they said, "She's a legend around here." My reaction was "Can I meet her?" So Renato, the restaurant owner, told me to be there tomorrow at ten and he would take me to meet her. She lived about forty-five minutes outside the city, and to get there we had to get a permit to drive along the old Appian Way. When we got there, she embraced me as though we had known each other forever.

Whenever I send a chef to Italy to apprentice at various fine restaurants, I always finish his education by sending him to Paola, my other mother. I tell them: Steal and grab every little secret this lady gives you. She has a touch with flavors like no one else. This *abbacchio* is a straightforward Roman dish, but what makes it Paola's is the second part, where she makes an emulsion with chopped rosemary and anchovies. Emulsions are not a traditional part of Roman cuisine. She takes an ancient dish and makes it modern.

---

*2¼ pounds young lamb leg or shoulder, bone in, cut into 8 chunks*
*2 tablespoons olive oil*
*6 garlic cloves, coarsely chopped*
*Salt and black pepper, freshly ground, to taste*
*1 tablespoon instant flour, like Wondra*
*¾ cup dry white wine*
*1 tablespoon fresh rosemary, coarsely chopped*
*4 oil-packed anchovy fillets, coarsely chopped*
*3 tablespoons red wine vinegar*

Preheat the oven to 350 degrees.

Rinse the lamb chunks under cold running water and pat dry with paper towels. In a casserole or roasting pan large enough to hold all the lamb, heat the olive oil over medium-high to high heat. When the olive oil is almost smoking, add the lamb chunks and brown quickly, turning frequently for 10–15 minutes. Add half the garlic to the lamb as it browns. When all the lamb is browned, add salt and abundant pepper. Sprinkle flour over the lamb pieces, and turn them to mix well.

Add the wine, and when it comes to a boil, immediately cover the pan and place in the oven to roast for 30 minutes.

While the lamb is roasting, use a mortar and pestle to pound the remaining garlic and rosemary into a coarse paste. Add the anchovies and continue pounding. Once the paste is fairly smooth, mix in the wine vinegar, 1 tablespoon at a time, pounding to make a smooth emulsion. When the lamb has roasted for 30 minutes, remove it from the oven and pour the vinegar emulsion over it. Turn the pieces to coat them well with sauce. Return to the oven uncovered, to roast an additional 30 minutes. When the lamb is done, with no trace of red in the meat, remove it from the oven, and let stand for 5 minutes. Transfer the lamb to a heated serving platter. Bring the pan juices to a boil over high heat and cook rapidly for about 45 seconds, or just long enough to reduce and thicken the juices slightly. Add salt and pepper to taste. Pour the juice over the lamb chunks and serve immediately.

*Wine:* Colle Picchione makes a red called Vigna del Vassallo: a blend of Merlot and Cabernet, dry, full-bodied, with elegant balance of fruit and flavors. It is a wine of great structure that perfectly complements rich red meat.

1½ pounds whole lamb loin

3 garlic cloves, 2 minced and
    1 whole

½ cup olive oil

1 bunch of fresh rosemary

1 teaspoon fresh sage, finely chopped

1 teaspoon fresh thyme,
    finely chopped

Salt and pepper, to taste

1 pound sweet red and yellow
    peppers

1 recipe Polenta (see page 122)

½ onion, finely chopped

10 basil leaves, roughly chopped

4 ounces Lamb Stock (see page 73)
    or Brown Sauce (see page 201)

3 tablespoons (1½ ounces) butter

*Preparation:* Rub the lamb loin with the whole garlic clove. In a deep dish, marinate the lamb loin with ¼ cup of the olive oil, several sprigs of rosemary, half of the sage and thyme, and freshly ground pepper. Let it marinate for over 1 hour.

On a grill or over an open flame on the stove, roast the peppers, about 10 minutes, turning frequently, until blackened. Place in a paper bag to steam for 10 minutes. Remove the blackened peel, cut off the tops, and scoop out the seeds and membranes. Cut the peppers into large squares. Set aside 2–3 red and yellow squares for garnish, and chop the rest.

Prepare the polenta according to the directions on page 122, adding a little sprinkle of rosemary. Set aside.

*The Dish:* Preheat the oven to 450 degrees.

In a large saucepan over high heat, sauté the minced garlic and onion in 2 tablespoons of the olive oil. Add a sprinkle of rosemary, the chopped roasted peppers, and the basil leaves, reduce heat to medium-low, and let simmer for about 5 minutes. Add the lamb stock or brown sauce and reduce for 2 minutes. Add a pinch of salt and pepper and set aside.

Remove the loin from the marinade. In a large ovenproof skillet over high heat, brown the loin on all sides in 2 tablespoons of the butter and the remaining olive oil. Cook about 1 minute on each side. Place in the oven and bake for 6–8 minutes, if you like it rare.

Serve the lamb by molding the polenta on individual plates into a standing triangle or cone shape. Slice the lamb and wrap it around the polenta. Heat up the sauce and add the remaining butter. Spoon over the lamb and sprinkle the colorful pieces of peppers on the edges. Garnish with a small sprig of fresh rosemary.

*Wine:* Go with a big wine. This is the perfect opportunity to open and let breathe a big Brunello like the 1990 or 1995 vintage of Lisine or Biondi-Santi, or that special Bordeaux you keep in the cellar for a special occasion.

## COSTOLETTE D'AGNELLO AL TRITTICO DI NOCI /
### Lamb with Almonds, Walnuts, and Pine Nuts
*4 servings*

Lamb is always the meat of choice for political or religious reasons. It's not politically correct to eat veal, but lamb is safe—and wonderful. We like to use great Colorado or Eastern lamb, even New Zealand lamb—meats that don't have that muttony smell but instead have a wonderful, rich texture.

The chop is the best part. Basically, we have interpreted a breaded lamb cutlet with a twist, using nuts instead of bread crumbs. The texture of the nuts is so completely different, and the lovely crunchiness of the outside contrasts with the juiciness of the medium-rare inside.

---

*½ cup (4 ounces) butter*

*½ cup unblanched almonds, sliced*

*½ cup walnuts, coarsely chopped*

*½ cup pine nuts*

*1 cup bread crumbs, finely ground*

*12 single-rib lamb chops, trimmed and bones scraped (French style)*

*2–3 tablespoons all-purpose flour*

*4 large eggs, beaten*

*Salt and pepper, to taste*

FOR THE SALAD

*12 ounces mixed baby greens*

*¼ cup fresh mint, finely chopped*

*¼ cup fresh basil, finely chopped*

*½ cup Citrus Vinaigrette (see page 53)*

*Preparation:* To clarify the butter, melt it over low heat in a small heavy-duty saucepan. Let cool, then skim the foam from the surface and pour the clarified butter into a cup, discarding the solids at the bottom of the pan.

In a food processor fitted with the metal blade, pulse to combine the almonds, walnuts, pine nuts, and bread crumbs. Transfer to a shallow bowl.

Pat the lamb chops dry and dredge the meat lightly in flour. Dip them in the beaten eggs, allowing the excess to drip back into the bowl. Coat them completely with the nut mixture and set aside.

*The Dish:* In a large, nonstick skillet, heat a few tablespoons of the clarified butter over medium heat. Cook the lamb chops (4–6 at a time) to the desired degree of doneness—2–3 minutes per side for medium-rare. Remove from the skillet and drain on paper towels. Season with salt and pepper and arrange 3 chops on each plate.

In a large bowl, toss together the greens, mint, basil, and citrus vinaigrette. Serve the salad on the side with the chops.

*Wine:* I would choose a wine that is very, very intense: a light, late harvest type from the Veronese called Ripasso, by a producer like Masi or Quintarelli, or a new Sangiovese made in California. I don't want just a normal big, bold wine, but one that has a certain resiny taste, a spiciness. Maybe an Australian Shiraz—that may be the best of the bunch.

## COSCIOTTO D'AGNELLO ALLA MENTA /
### Roast Leg of Lamb with Red Wine and Mint
*4 servings*

I like the fact that you can do a lot of things with this dish afterward. Definitely sandwiches, or shredded on top of a salad. It's a dish that will hold for a day or two. And there is nothing more comforting than the real texture of lamb that comes out in a well-cooked, marinated dish with red wine, spices, and aromatics. Angelo Auriana, the chef at Valentino, likes to cut pieces of meat from the leg and cook them individually, but I also think, as with a whole prime rib or whole sirloin, there is also the pleasure of carving, of getting all the juices and flavors. You can do the whole leg the same way—brown it, add liquid, and cover—but it is a longer cooking process.

---

*Four 7-ounce pieces of lamb, about 1½ inches thick, cut from the leg*
*½ cup (4 ounces) butter*
*4 teaspoons shallot, chopped*
*24 fresh mint leaves*
*½ cup red wine or Chicken Stock (see page 74)*
*1 cup Brown Sauce (see page 201)*
*Salt and pepper, to taste*

*Preparation:* Sear the lamb over high heat in 2 tablespoons of the butter. After 5 minutes, remove the meat and discard the excess butter. Drain any meat juices back into the pan. Add 2 more tablespoons of the butter to the pan, along with the shallot and half the mint. Add the wine or stock and reduce until the juices stick to the pan again, 2–3 minutes. Add the brown sauce and reduce for 4 minutes.

Cut the lamb into ¼-inch slices with a serrated knife, cutting against the grain. Arrange in 4 individual spirals on a baking dish and drain any additional juices from the cutting board into the sauce. Salt and pepper the meat to taste.

In a small pan, brown the remaining butter and mint leaves. Remove the mint leaves after 1 minute and place on top of the meat.

The dish can be prepared in advance to this point. Wrap the meat and store it in the refrigerator.

*The Dish:* When ready to serve, preheat the oven to 400–450 degrees.

Heat the sauce over medium heat. Warm the meat in the oven for a couple of minutes, and then remove with a spatula to individual dinner plates. If there are any juices left in the baking dish, add them to the sauce. Thicken the sauce with a little butter if necessary, and spoon it over the meat.

*Wine:* No surprises here. A good Merlot that is very robust, very intense in fruit, with nice tannin that will evolve and develop in the mouth, cutting some of the fattiness of the lamb. A good Bordeaux always goes with lamb, especially a fairly old one, if you can afford a second or third growth. And I believe that a four- or five-year-old Chianti, especially a Riserva, would be perfect. From California, try a big Napa Cabernet or a Merlot from one of the best producers, Matanzas Creek of Sonoma.

# BRASATO AL BAROLO / Beef Braised in Barolo

*6 servings*

*Brasato* is part of what home-and-hearth Italian food is all about. Other cuisines do this dish their own way. We love it because it can be done for large parties, it doesn't have to be the finest cut of meat, and, once you get into the habit, it is actually an easy process. It is a very practical and convenient restaurant dish—a traditional food that is very appealing for either a Piedmontese regional dinner or a very hearty winter meal. I think of it as Italian pot roast, slow-cooked with vegetables and herbs and then cut into individual slices to serve.

*3–4 pound top sirloin, well tied*

*1 bottle Barolo wine, or other robust red wine*

*2 carrots, peeled and coarsely chopped*

*2 stalks celery, coarsely chopped*

*2 medium yellow onions, halved*

*3 bay leaves*

*4–6 fresh sage leaves*

*2 sprigs rosemary, roughly chopped*

*¼ cup Italian parsley, chopped*

*Salt and pepper, to taste*

*½ cup (4 ounces) butter*

*1 cup brandy*

*Preparation:* In a large covered roasting pan, marinate the meat for 12 hours with the wine, carrots, celery, onions, herbs, and salt and pepper. Keep the pan in a cool place.

*The Dish:* In a large skillet, heat the butter over high heat and sear the meat until it is evenly colored on all sides. Pour in the brandy and add the marinating ingredients to the pan.

The brasato can continue to cook over low heat on the stove, or you can roast it in the oven at 375 degrees. Total cooking time is 3–3½ hours, but after 2 hours remove the vegetables and herbs. Pass them through a sieve to form a puree with the marinating liquid.

When the meat is done, slice into 1-inch-thick pieces and serve at once, with the puree.

*Wine:* It has to be a Nebbiolo, because this dish needs the heartiness and powerful texture, the emphasis on chocolate, dried flowers, rich blackberries, and the hint of smokiness that is typical of big red wines. Try a Giacosa, a Conterno, or a Barolo by Pio Cesare or Altare, some of the Piedmontese producers.

## FASSU MAGRU DEI GIORNI DI FESTA /
## Stuffed Beef Rolls for the Holidays

*8 servings*

*Fassu magru* means "false lean," maybe because you use a lean meat but a big rich stuffing. My mother made this dish two or three times a year, for special occasions—an important guest's arrival or Christmas lunch. It was what she brought when she was asked to help provide food after someone died, which is called the *consolo,* as in consolation, where everyone brought food to the grieving family so that they would not have to worry about cooking. It is a dish of the past; she does not make it anymore.

*4 large eggs, hard-boiled*

*¼ pound salami, diced into small cubes*

*¼ pound prosciutto, diced into small cubes*

*¼ pound pancetta, diced into small cubes*

*½ pound caciocavallo cheese, diced into small cubes*

*1 garlic clove, finely chopped*

*2 tablespoons olive oil*

*2 tablespoons fresh Italian parsley, finely chopped*

*1½ cups bread crumbs*

*Salt and pepper, to taste*

*1½ pounds beef rib or beef chuck shoulder, in 1 piece*

*1 yellow onion, chopped*

*¼ cup canola or vegetable oil*

*1 cup white wine*

*2 cups canned peeled tomatoes, drained, seeded, and chopped*

*½ cup water*

*Preparation:* Chop 2 of the hard-boiled eggs.

To prepare the stuffing, in a bowl combine the chopped eggs, salami, prosciutto, pancetta, caciocavallo cheese, garlic, olive oil, parsley, bread crumbs, and salt and pepper and mix thoroughly.

Slice the remaining 2 eggs into ¼-inch-thick slices.

Pound the beef to about ¼ inch thick. Sprinkle with salt and pepper and distribute the stuffing evenly. Cover with a layer of sliced hard-boiled eggs.

Roll the meat up carefully and secure with string. The beef roll can be refrigerated at this point.

*The Dish:* Preheat the oven to 475 degrees.

In a large sauté pan, brown the onion in the canola oil over medium heat. Add the beef roll and cook until nicely browned on all sides. Sprinkle the wine over the roll and cook another 5 minutes, until the wine evaporates. Add the tomatoes and water and bring to a boil.

Place the roll in the oven for about 1 hour, turning and basting every 15 minutes. Remove from the oven and let rest for 15 minutes. Remove the string and cut the roll into 8–10 ½-inch-thick slices. Return the cooking liquids to the stove, add the olive oil, and simmer for a few minutes over medium heat. Strain and pour the sauce over the slices.

*Wine:* This needs a Sicilian wine, a big Nero d'Avola or Perricone, like Rosso Riserva del Conte by Regaleali. Or a Sicilian-Bordeaux blend: Ceuso Custera by Antonino Melia. These are wines of tradition, wines that reflect a noble Sicilian history. They are the sentimental match for a dish with the same heritage. Dignity has to be matched with dignity, strength with strength.

## STRACOTTO DI COSTOLETTE DI MANZO / Braised Beef Short Ribs

*6 servings*

*3 tablespoons olive oil*

*6 short ribs, 3 ribs apiece, each
section weighing 1 pound*

*Salt and pepper, to taste*

*3 tablespoons (1½ ounces) butter*

*3 yellow onions, chopped*

*4 garlic cloves, peeled*

*1 ounce chili flakes*

*8 Roma tomatoes, peeled and seeded*

*4 cups robust red wine, a Barolo,
Chianti, or Cabernet*

*4 cups Beef Stock (see page 73) or
Chicken Stock (see page 74)*

*4 sprigs fresh thyme*

Preheat an ovenproof skillet in a 450-degree oven. When hot, add the olive oil and place the ribs in the pan. Season with salt and pepper and place in the oven, turning to sear on all sides, about 5 minutes total. Set aside. Reduce the oven heat to 375 degrees.

In a large ovenproof casserole dish over medium heat, melt the butter and add the onions, garlic, and chili flakes. Sauté for a few minutes, until the onions are translucent, and then add the tomatoes. Arrange the beef ribs on top and pour the wine and stock over them. Add the thyme.

Cover with foil and place the casserole dish in the oven for 3½ hours.

Remove the casserole dish from the oven and set the meat aside. Strain the sauce and pour it over the ribs. Serve immediately, or reheat for 5–10 minutes over medium heat when ready to serve.

*Wine:* For this intense dish, try a Cabernet Sauvignon or Merlot that is three to four years old, from Italy, California, or France. Both these wines have a note of fruit richness, vegetables, and herbs that will blend with the sauce. For an alternative, try an Australian Shiraz, a deeply flavored, peppery wine that will complement the many concentrated flavors of the dish.

## SCALOPPINE DI MAIALE IN AGRODOLCE CON CANNELLINI /
### Pork Scaloppine with Sweet and Sour Sauce and Tuscan Beans

*6 servings*

1 pound cannellini beans

¾ cup olive oil

10 tablespoons (5 ounces) butter

1 cup Beef Stock (see page 73)

1 onion, chopped

1 stalk celery, chopped

1 carrot, chopped

3 ounces prosciutto, chopped

3-pound pork loin

All-purpose flour

Salt and pepper, to taste

2 ounces capers

1 tablespoon sugar

1 cup red wine vinegar

*Preparation:* Soak the cannellini beans overnight. Drain, then bring them to a boil in abundant water. Reduce the heat to medium-low, and simmer until tender, about 1–2 hours. You can do this a day in advance, but warm the beans when you are ready to make the dish.

In a casserole, combine ¼ cup of the olive oil, ¼ cup of the butter, and ½ cup of the broth. Add the chopped vegetables and prosciutto and cook slowly until the vegetables are tender but not browned. Remove from heat. When cool, pass the mixture through a strainer or puree in a blender until smooth.

*The Dish:* Slice the loin into 6 medallions, about 3½ inches thick. Pound the meat gently until it is about 1½–2 inches thick. Dust with the flour mixed with a pinch of salt.

Wash and dry the capers and chop very fine.

In a saucepan over low heat, combine the sugar and 2 tablespoons of the butter. When the sugar is dissolved in the melted butter, add the vinegar and let it reduce slightly. Add the capers and ¼ cup of the olive oil, and whisk the mixture for about 3 minutes. Add the blended vegetables, season with salt and pepper to taste, and keep warm.

In a frying pan over medium heat, combine the remaining butter and olive oil. Place the floured scallopine in the pan and cook for about 3 minutes on each side. Remove the meat to parchment paper to drain while you finish cooking the remaining pieces. Place the drained scallopine on a serving plate and pour the warm sauce on top of them. Arrange the beans on the side.

*Wine:* With pork I love red wines with great layers of fruit extract that feel almost like a marmalade of black fruits: a Brunello di Montalcino, with sensations of licorice and cherries, like Il Poggione or Col d'Orcia, or a dark, sweet Zinfandel enlivened by blackberry and maple syrup— Ravenswood, Turley, or Ridge.

*2 cups bread crumbs*

*2 cups Parmesan cheese, grated*

*4 tablespoons Italian parsley,
    finely chopped*

*1 yellow onion, cut into ¼-inch
    slices*

*¼ cup olive oil*

*2 pounds veal cutlets, pounded very
    thin and cut in half*

*Salt and pepper, to taste*

*½ pound prosciutto cotto, cut into
    paper-thin slices*

*⅓ pound salami, thinly sliced*

*½ pound provolone or mozzarella
    cheese, thinly sliced*

*½ cup all-purpose flour*

*½ cup (4 ounces) butter*

*½ cup Marsala wine*

*1 cup Beef Stock (see page 73)*

*Preparation:* In a bowl, combine the bread crumbs, Parmesan cheese, and 3 tablespoons of the parsley and set aside. In a large sauté pan, cook the onion in 1 tablespoon of the olive oil over medium heat for about 10 minutes, until the onion starts to brown. Remove the onion from the pan.

Lay out the veal cutlets and sprinkle with salt and pepper. Cover each with a layer of prosciutto and salami, then some onion and a slice of provolone or mozzarella cheese. Roll the veal cutlet up tightly, tuck in the ends, and secure the center with a toothpick or two. Repeat until all the veal and stuffing are used. Refrigerate until ready to use.

*The Dish:* Dust the veal rolls with flour, brushing off the excess. In a large sauté pan, fry the rolls in the remaining olive oil until golden brown on all sides, about 3 minutes per side.

Remove the veal from the pan, set aside, and keep warm in a 200-degree oven. Add the butter, the Marsala, and the beef broth to the pan and reduce, on high heat, until the liquid thickens into a sauce, about 4–5 minutes.

Remove the toothpicks from the veal rolls and spoon the sauce over them. Sprinkle with the remaining parsley.

*Wine:* I love this with a wine from the south of Italy. Calabria makes a very rich Gravello by Librandi, or try a Merlot by Planeta from Sicily, or a Cannonau by Cantina Sociale di Santadi from Sardinia. They are all powerful wines, full of character, earthy, and thick enough to stand up to this dish.

## COSTOLETTE DI VITELLO CON FONDUTA / Veal Chops Fonduta

*4 servings*

When I was a busboy at The Marquis in Los Angeles, I started seeing veal chops and scallopine that were absolutely tender and pure white. It was so different from the *vitelloni* I was used to from my childhood, slaughtered the same day and sold so the meat was fresh, but tough.

One of the specialties of any Italian restaurant is veal, and we are no different. The height of a main course is a chop. In a chop house it would be grilled, in a French restaurant, served with morels and cream sauce, and in the Italian version, the usual routine is mushrooms or deglazed red wine. We felt that a cheese that was elegant, soft, and full of flavors, like fontina, was perfect as a topping.

---

*Four 12-ounce veal chops*
*¼ cup olive oil*
*1 tablespoon shallot, finely chopped*
*½ cup brandy*
*Salt, to taste*
*1 teaspoon white pepper*
*2 tablespoons (1 ounce) butter*
*½ cup Chicken Stock (see page 74)*
*4 paper-thin slices fontina cheese*
*Fresh truffle (as much as you*
*    like to splurge)*

In a large nonstick skillet over medium to high heat, sear the veal chops in the olive oil for about 3 minutes on each side. Discard the oil. Add the shallot, brandy, salt and pepper, and butter. Cook the chops in the sauce, about 10 more minutes for medium-rare. Remove the chops and set aside on a warm platter. Add the chicken stock to the pan and reduce for 2–3 minutes on medium-high heat. Meanwhile, place the slices of fontina cheese on top of the veal chops and melt under a broiler for 1–2 minutes. Top with sauce and garnish with thinly sliced truffle.

*Wine:* You have plenty of choices. This dish goes with any red wine of structure—such as a Sangiovese with rich body, good fruit, and a solid feeling in the mouth; when you drink it, it stays there. Or a Merlot, which gives you a mouthful of rich fruit and polishes your palate after the cheese. You want a wine that can stand up, but that also has finesse.

We like to create new dishes with game. With venison, we like to combine it with fruit sauces—either dried fruits like figs, cherries, and raisins, or fresh apples and pomegranates. These provide clean, bracing flavors to contrast with the complex flavor of the meat.

---

*6 tablespoons (3 ounces) butter*

*Four 6-ounce venison medallions*

*Salt and pepper, to taste*

*2 teaspoons fresh sage,*
  *finely chopped*

*1 teaspoon fresh rosemary,*
  *finely chopped*

*1 garlic clove, crushed*

*1 tablespoon shallot, finely chopped*

*12 juniper berries*

*1 cup red wine*

*2 tablespoons heavy cream*

*4 tablespoons pomegranate seeds,*
  *plus additional for garnish*

*¼ cup water*

In a large skillet over high heat, brown 2 tablespoons of the butter. Add the medallions and season with salt and pepper. Cook until the venison is a reddish brown, about 4 minutes on each side. Remove the venison medallions and discard the fat.

Add 2 more tablespoons of butter to the skillet and stir in the herbs, garlic, shallot, and juniper berries. Cook over medium heat until the shallot is translucent. Add the wine and reduce for a few minutes on high heat. Add the cream, pomegranate seeds, water, and remaining 2 tablespoons of butter. Simmer until the sauce is slightly thickened.

Slice the medallions about ¼ inch thick; if the venison is too rare, put it in a hot oven, about 400 degrees, for a few more minutes. Fan the slices on a serving dish. Spoon on the sauce and garnish with pomegranate seeds.

*Wine:* Game dishes provide the ultimate challenge for red wine. Game has a bitter, intense taste and can tire out your palate, so it needs to be modulated with other flavors, particularly sweet and sour fruit. They balance the game by cutting into the flavor, so you need a rich wine with strength and power. Try any of the major Château wines from Bordeaux—the Château classification was made in 1860. These are the famous wines, like a first-growth Château Margaux or Haut-Brion. For something a bit less expensive, try a Rhone varietal like an Hermitage or a Cote-Rotie. Or try the new proprietal reserves of California, like a Dominus, or an Insignia by Phelps. In Italy, there is the Montepulciano d'Abruzzi, the Taurasi from the Campania area, or the Turriga from Sardinia. With venison you have plenty of choices.

## GRIGLIATA DI VERDURE E MOZZARELLA /
### Grilled Vegetables with Smoked Mozzarella
*6 servings*

Grilling is part of our religion now. The Mediterranean diet, the healthy approach—these are the inspirational reasons for this dish. And vegetables abound. We have never had better ones. So we created a very colorful and flexible vegetable dish, based on what the market offers.

---

*4 yellow bell peppers, sliced into 1-inch pieces*

*4 red bell peppers, sliced into 1-inch pieces*

*2 Maui, Tropea, or purple onions*

*4 zucchini, sliced lengthwise into ½-inch-thick strips*

*6 small radicchio hearts*

*3 leeks, green tops removed*

*6 portobello mushrooms*

*4 garlic cloves, finely chopped*

*4 sprigs fresh rosemary, chopped*

*1 cup olive oil*

*Salt and pepper, to taste*

*¼ cup plus 2 tablespoons balsamic vinegar*

*6 ounces smoked mozzarella or scamorza cheese, thinly sliced*

Place the vegetables on a large platter or baking sheet. In a large bowl combine the garlic, rosemary, olive oil, and salt and pepper. Whisk lightly and brush onto the vegetables.

Grill the vegetables outdoors on a grill or inside in the broiler. Transfer to a baking sheet and arrange in a single layer. Sprinkle with balsamic vinegar and top with slices of mozzarella or scamorza cheese. Heat under the broiler until the cheese is melted. Serve immediately.

*Wine:* A Pinot Noir (Martinelli, Hanzell, Ponzi) or a Piedmontese Dolcetto (Altare, Sandrone)—wine of supple fruit, clean finish, and enough structure to stand up to the crunchiness of each vegetable.

## SALSA BRUNA / Brown Sauce

*8 cups*

---

5 pounds veal, lamb, or venison
    bones
1 head garlic, cut in half
    horizontally
3 tablespoons olive oil
1 large onion, coarsely chopped
4 carrots, coarsely chopped
1 bunch celery, coarsely chopped
2–3 bay leaves
A few sprigs fresh rosemary, thyme,
    and sage
1 tablespoon whole black
    peppercorns
One 6-ounce can tomato paste
2½ gallons (40 cups) water

Preheat the oven to 375 degrees.

Place the bones and garlic in a large roasting pan and brown in the oven for 1–2 hours, turning the bones a few times. Remove from the oven, allow to cool about 20 minutes, and trim off and discard the fat.

In a large stockpot, combine the olive oil, onion, carrots, and celery. Sauté for a few minutes over medium heat. Add the bones and garlic, herbs, peppercorns, tomato paste, and water and bring to a boil. Turn the heat down and skim the foam off the top of the liquid. Simmer uncovered for about 6 hours. Check to make sure there is enough liquid, adding water if necessary. Strain the sauce and reduce further until you have 8 cups of sauce.

*Dolci*
*Dolci*

✳

*Budino di Mascarpone* **(Mascarpone Pudding)**
*Biancomangiare*
*Terrina di Ricotta Sarda* **(Ricotta Terrine)**
*Cannoli*
*Cassata di Ricotta*
*Pan di Spagna* **(Sponge Cake)**
*Crema Fritta al Grand Marnier* **(Fried Cream with Grand Marnier)**
*Crostata di Ricotta e Castagne* **(Ricotta Chestnut Crostata)**
*Torta di Castagne* **(Chestnut Cake)**
*Croccante Semifreddo*
*Raviolini Dolci alla Crema di Ciliegie*
**(Sweet Ravioli with Cherry Custard Sauce)**
*Pere Cotte al Mascarpone*
**(Poached Pears in Burgundy Wine with Mascarpone Mousse)**
*Torta di Formaggio con Fragole e Vecchio Balsamico*
**(Mascarpone Cheesecake with Strawberries in Balsamic Vinegar)**
*Crostata di Pignoli con More e Conserva di Fichi*
**(Pignoli Crostata with Blackberry and Fig Compote)**
*La Pasta Frolla* **(Pastry Dough)**
*Semifreddo al Limone con Salsa di Lamponi*
**(Lemon Semifreddo with Raspberry Sauce)**
*Bavarese con Frutta della Passione, Salsa di Lamponi*
**(Bavarian Cream with Passion Fruit and Raspberry Sauce)**
*Millefoglie di Pesca con Frutti di Bosco*
**(Peach Millefoglie with Berries)**
*Spumone d'Arancia* **(Orange Semifreddo)**
*Crostata di Grappa e Limone* **(Lemon and Grappa Crostata)**
*Frutta Candita* **(Candied Fruit Peel)**

*Dolci*

*Polenta Dolce alla Nocciola* **(Sweet Polenta with Hazelnut Sauce)**
*Torta di Ricotta con Sentori d'Arancio e Cioccolato*
**(Ricotta, Orange, and Chocolate Torte)**
*Torta di Cioccolato all'Essenza di Amaretto*
**(Chocolate and Amaretti Torte)**
*Dolce Valentino* **(Valentino's Chocolate Truffle Cake)**
*Terrina di Cioccolato Agrodolce ed*
*Amaretti con Granita di Caffè*
**(Terrine of Bittersweet Chocolate and Amaretti with Espresso Granita)**
*Salame di Cioccolato allo Zabaglione*
**(Salami-Shaped Chocolate with Zabaglione)**
*Il Bonet* **(Traditional Piedmontese Chocolate Pudding)**
*Budino di Espresso* **(Espresso Chocolate Custard)**
*I Tre Tartufi* **(The Three Truffles)**
*Biscotti di Semolina* **(Semolina Cookies)**
*Biscotti Caramellati al Cioccolato* **(Dark Chocolate Fudge Cookies)**
*Traditional Amaretti*
*Amaretti Soffici* **(Seventeenth-Century Amaretti Cookies)**
*Panettone di Luciano*
*Tronco Natalizio* **(Christmas Log)**

# ✜ *Dolci*

THE IDEA OF HAVING DESSERT IN AN ITALIAN RESTAURANT IS A FAIRLY recent one, when you consider our history. When I grew up, we took a break after a big meal. We walked to the bar, to the *caffè*, and then, after a while, we would have a sweet. Remember that we took our main meal at midday. We strolled to the local bar to get a *granita*, a little *gelato*, or a *cannoli*. There were no fancy desserts, not even on special occasions like a birthday. We might buy cannoli or rum *baba*, or my mother would make *biancomangiare*, but that was all. There was no big cake with lots of frosting. Fruit was the way to finish a meal.

Now, slowly, the Italian dessert has evolved, thanks to the explosion of fine restaurants in Italy, and to the demand from people who want a good dessert. Suddenly, we have started to take this course more seriously. At Valentino, we started with cannoli or spumoni. Then we moved to the new wave: *tiramisu* and *panna cotta.* But there are so many more types of desserts to try, because there are products that are unique and very much ours, like ricotta and almond paste. There are things we can do with custards, fruit, and even chocolate that are specifically Italian, like *zabaglione* or Piedmontese chocolate pudding. And we can create a lovely dessert with nothing but fresh fruit and an aged, intense balsamic vinegar.

When we started Valentino, we had very ordinary desserts. For a long time, in fact, we bought them. Then, about sixteen years ago, we realized that we had to make an effort. We had our share of hits and misses until we solidified the concept of dessert. For those who still have an appetite when they get to dessert, we take our cue from the main kitchen, and try to reinterpret traditional recipes in an exciting way, or use traditional ingredients in a completely new recipe, like the chocolate tower with espresso granita.

Michelle Robie, the pastry chef who developed most of these recipes, is an American who understands how to incorporate Italian products into unique, creative desserts. We don't want you to have to take a five-mile walk after eating, or to feel that the dessert sits like a stone in your stomach. Our desserts are small, and we encourage people to play musical plates, so that everyone can taste all the desserts, one or two spoonfuls of each.

For those who want only a small sweet, there is the great Sicilian tradition of gelati. They are as versatile as spaghetti—there are so many flavors, so many mixtures and tastes. I like to combine a little piece of cake with mango ice cream, or an orange granita, something to give a last, refreshing memory of a meal. One of our most popular desserts is an assortment of cookies, gelati, and sorbetti, all made on the premises.

## DESSERT WINE NOTE

There are too many dessert wines out there to make many specific suggestions, but there *are* general rules. The only ingredient that has trouble with wine is chocolate, because of its intensity and bitterness. Chocolate shrinks your mouth with a tremendous sensation, so your safe bet is to give the chocolate something to fight. With chocolate, stay away from delicate wines likes Moscato or Sauterne. Instead, serve a sherry, a Marsala, a port.

For a sponge cake, ricotta, or fruit dessert, serve a fresh, simple white wine—Moscato d'Alba and Moscato d'Asti from the Piedmont region are absolutely fresh and very light in sugar and alcohol. Or you could serve a wine with a little more weight, something with some induced botrytis, or noble mildew. The Torcolato wines from Fausto Maculan are some of the very best in Italy. Or, from the south, try the Malvasia from Lipari Island. Pantelleria is another little island off Sicily that grows the sweetest grapes, zibibbo, which make Moscato Passito. *Passito* means that the grapes have been laid in the sun and dried so that they become very raisiny. You taste apricot, almonds, sugarcane, and ripe peaches—a great sensation.

For a rich dessert, have a very intense wine—a good Sauterne, a Tokaji Essencia from Hungary, or a California wine—a Dolce from Far Niente or a late-harvest Riesling from Phelps.

Or you can always serve champagne, from a brut to a demi-sec to a cremant. It's the sentimental choice for a perfect toast and a sweet finish.

## BUDINO DI MASCARPONE / Mascarpone Pudding

*4 servings*

Mascarpone cheese is very similar in texture to Philadelphia cream cheese and is pale white in color. You can find it in plastic containers in the refrigerated section of specialty stores, or sold by weight in fine cheese shops.

---

*1 ounce bittersweet chocolate,*
   *chopped into ½-inch chunks*
*1 egg white*
*Pinch of cream of tartar*
*2 large egg yolks*
*½ cup superfine sugar*
*2 tablespoons dark rum*
*½ cup mascarpone cheese*
*Pinch of salt*

Break up the chocolate into ½-inch chunks and melt in a stainless-steel bowl set over a pot of gently simmering water, or in a double boiler. Stir and remove from the heat. Set aside to cool to lukewarm.

In the bowl of an electric mixer fitted with the whisk attachment, whip the egg white with the cream of tartar for about 5 minutes on high speed, until soft peaks form. Add 2 tablespoons of the sugar and beat until stiff. Set aside.

Place the egg yolks in a large mixing bowl, gradually add the remaining sugar, and whisk until it turns a lemon-yellow color. Add the rum, and beat until all ingredients are well blended. Add the mascarpone cheese and a pinch of salt and beat until the mixture is light and smooth.

Fold the egg white into the mascarpone custard mixture. Spoon a fourth of the custard into a small bowl, and lightly fold in the cooled melted chocolate. Alternately spoon the remaining custard and the chocolate custard into 4 sherbet glasses. Swirl the chocolate with a fork, but do not blend the 2 mixtures. The pudding should be a predominantly white custard with streaks of chocolate. Cover each glass with a sheet of clear plastic wrap and refrigerate for later, or serve immediately.

# BIANCOMANGIARE

*8 servings*

I have grown out of this dish, but whenever I hear the word *biancomangiare* I feel a little tug of tenderness. My mother used to make it as a reward for when I was good. When I was three or four, it was the only dessert I knew. Now Mamma makes it for my boys.

---

FOR THE PUDDING

*2 cups milk*

*7 ounces almond meal (or ⅔ cups blanched almonds, finely ground)*

*¼ cup powdered sugar*

*7 tablespoons almond paste, available at specialty shops*

*1 tablespoon powdered gelatin, or 4 sheets*

*¾ cup heavy cream*

FOR THE CRÈME ANGLAIS

*2 cups heavy cream*

*4 large egg yolks*

*⅓ cup granulated sugar*

*1 tablespoon pure vanilla extract*

*2 tablespoons pistachio paste (optional), available at specialty shops*

*Sliced almonds, for garnish*

*Bittersweet chocolate, grated, for garnish*

*Powdered sugar, for dusting*

In a medium-size stainless-steel saucepan, bring the milk, almond meal, and powdered sugar to a boil, stirring continuously to prevent sticking. Add the almond paste, 1 teaspoon at a time. As soon as the mixture boils, remove it from the heat. Strain half through a sieve into a mixing bowl and add the unstrained half to it. Stir in the gelatin until dissolved. Cool to lukewarm in an ice-water bath.

Using an electric mixer fitted with the whisk attachment, or by hand, beat the cream to stiff peaks and add to the milk mixture. Pour into six 8-ounce custard cups and refrigerate for 2 hours.

TO MAKE THE CRÈME ANGLAIS: In a stainless-steel bowl, whisk together the cream, egg yolks, granulated sugar, and vanilla and cook over a pan of gently simmering water. Stir constantly, until thickened. Remove from the heat and chill. When cold, add the pistachio paste and mix well.

Preheat the oven to 325 degrees.

On a baking sheet, lightly toast the sliced almonds for about 7 minutes.

TO SERVE: Invert a custard cup on a plate, shaking gently to loosen the custard. Remove the cup. Spoon a few tablespoons of the crème anglais around the custard and top with the almonds and chocolate shavings. Sprinkle the plate with powdered sugar and serve.

## TERRINA DI RICOTTA SARDA / Ricotta Terrine

*4 servings*

Fresh sheep's-milk ricotta is very light and delicate, with a natural sweetness.

*6 large egg yolks*
*¼ cup granulated sugar*
*2 cups fresh sheep's-milk ricotta*
*    cheese, preferably from Sardinia*
*½ cup sweet Marsala wine*
*1 tablespoon ground cinnamon*
*1 teaspoon pure vanilla extract*
*Zest of 1 orange, finely chopped*

In a large mixing bowl, whisk together the egg yolks and sugar to a soft paste. Pass the ricotta cheese through a strainer and add to the yolk mixture. Add the wine, cinnamon, vanilla extract, and orange zest, and combine well.

Place the ricotta mixture in a terrine or loaf pan and refrigerate for a few hours before serving. Serve with a variety of honeys or fruit jams.

# CANNOLI

*Makes 40 cannoli*

Everyone in Sicily says they have the recipe for the best *cannoli*. My personal favorite is from Franco Ruta at Dolceria Bonajuto, in my hometown, Modica. It has a perfect, delicate flaky shell, and is filled with the best fresh ricotta I have ever tasted.

---

### FOR THE SHELLS

*1½ cups all-purpose flour*

*1 tablespoon granulated sugar*

*Pinch of salt*

*1 tablespoon plus 1 teaspoon olive oil*

*½ cup Marsala wine*

*2 quarts vegetable oil for deep frying*

### FOR THE FILLING

*½ cup granulated sugar*

*1 pound fresh ricotta cheese (about 2 cups), drained in a sieve overnight*

*1 tablespoon vanilla extract*

*2–3 tablespoons candied orange peel (see page 235)*

*3 ounces bittersweet chocolate, finely chopped*

*½ cup shelled pistachios, finely chopped*

*Powdered sugar, for dusting*

TO MAKE THE CANNOLI SHELLS: In the bowl of an electric mixer, sift together the flour, sugar, and salt. Pour in the olive oil and wine, and using the paddle attachment, mix on medium until the dough comes together and forms a ball. Wrap the dough in plastic and refrigerate for at least 2 hours.

Remove the cannoli dough from the refrigerator 30 minutes before frying to allow it to rest. Divide the dough into 4 pieces, dust lightly with flour, and roll the dough through a pasta machine, set at its widest position. Decrease the width of the rollers until you reach the lowest setting. Continue with the remaining pieces of dough. Set the long pieces of dough on a lightly floured surface and cut into 4-inch circles. Wrap each piece around a cannoli tube. Brush the edges with water, slightly overlap the ends, and press the edges gently to seal together.

In a large heavy-duty saucepan, heat the vegetable oil to 375 degrees. Add about 4 cannoli at a time (depending upon the size of the pan) and fry until golden brown. Remove the cannoli with tongs. With a towel in one hand, carefully grasp the cannoli shell and pull out the metal tube. Be careful—the tube will be very hot. Allow the tubes to cool and repeat the process for the remaining dough. Allow the cannoli shells to cool before filling.

TO MAKE THE FILLING: In a mixing bowl, combine the sugar, ricotta cheese, and vanilla. When smooth, add the candied orange peel and chocolate.

Place the filling in a pastry bag fitted with a large tip, and pipe filling into each end of the cannoli shell. Sprinkle chopped pistachios on both ends and dust with the powdered sugar. Serve immediately.

## CASSATA DI RICOTTA

*8–10 servings*

When I die and go to heaven, this will be my dessert of choice. It is an ancient Sicilian dessert, and we do many different versions—but the emotional sensation never changes. This is always my favorite. The ricotta, marzipan, and candied fruit are basic to the *cassata,* but other than that, you can mix and match the ingredients.

*2 pounds fresh ricotta cheese,*
    *drained in a sieve overnight*
*Zest of 1 orange, finely chopped*
*Zest of 1 lemon, finely chopped*
*2¾ cups powdered sugar*
*1 tablespoon pure vanilla extract*
*2 ounces candied orange peel*
    *(see page 235), finely chopped*
*2 ounces chopped torrone (Italian*
    *nougat, available at specialty*
    *stores)*
*2 ounces glazed chestnuts, chopped*
*½ cup shelled pistachios, chopped*
*2 ounces bittersweet chocolate,*
    *finely chopped*
*1⅓ cup heavy cream*
*3 large egg whites*
*1 Sponge Cake (see page 216),*
    *baked in a 10-inch round pan*
    *and cooled*
*1 pound marzipan*
*Candied fruit, for decorating*

*Preparation:* Over a large mixing bowl, pass the ricotta cheese, orange zest, lemon zest, and powdered sugar through a fine sieve. Stir in the vanilla. In a small bowl, combine the candied orange peel, torrone, chestnuts, pistachios, and chocolate.

In the bowl of an electric mixer fitted with the whisk attachment, whip the cream to soft peaks. Add the whipped cream to the ricotta mixture and mix well. In another bowl, whip the egg whites on medium-high to soft peaks. Add the candied fruits, nuts, and chocolate to the ricotta mixture, and gently fold in the egg whites. Transfer the mixture into a 1½-quart bowl that has been buttered and lined with plastic wrap—or into individual small bowls, if you prefer. Cut a thin piece of sponge cake and place it on top of the mixture. Wrap well and freeze overnight.

*The Dish:* Place a warm towel around the bowl of ricotta mixture to help release the cassata. Unmold onto a serving platter. Roll out a large, thin circle of marzipan and wrap it around the unmolded cassata. Trim off excess, and decorate with candied fruits.

✦ *"When I die and go to heaven, this will be my dessert of choice."*
*Wrapping the layer of marzipan around the cassata.*

## PAN DI SPAGNA / Sponge Cake

*one 10-inch cake*

1 cup plus 1 tablespoon cake flour

¾ cup plus 2 tablespoons granulated
    sugar

6 large eggs, separated

2 tablespoons water

½ teaspoon pure vanilla extract

¾ teaspoon cream of tartar

Preheat the oven to 350 degrees. Lightly butter a 10-inch springform pan.

Over a bowl, sift the flour and 3 tablespoons of the sugar. In the bowl of an electric mixer, whisk the egg yolks and ½ cup of the sugar on high, until very pale. Turn the mixer down to low and add the water and vanilla. Beat for 1 minute. Gently fold in the sifted flour and sugar and transfer to another bowl. In the clean and dry bowl of an electric mixer fitted with the whisk attachment, beat the egg whites with the cream of tartar on medium-high for 4–5 minutes, until soft peaks form. Gradually add the remaining sugar and continue to beat until stiff peaks form. Gently fold the whites into the yolk mixture, until all the whites are incorporated.

Pour into the prepared pan and bake for 30–35 minutes, until a toothpick inserted in the center comes out clean. Allow the cake to cool on a wire rack. Run a spatula around the edge of the pan and release the springform. Wrap in plastic.

# CREMA FRITTA AL GRAND MARNIER /
## Fried Cream with Grand Marnier

*Makes twelve 3-inch squares*

This recipe is out of memoryland, from my early days in Los Angeles. I supported myself through college working at The Marquis, where flambé was the house specialty and the entertainment. We finished a lot of products in front of the customers—deshelling shrimp scampi, mixing fettucine Alfredo. But the ultimate dish was the flaming dessert. It required a whole ceremony. First we perched the cooked custards on top of two bananas, like a little raft. In a flat copper pan on top of a can of Sterno, we squeezed fresh lemon and orange juice, melted some butter, added sugar, and, finally, added the liqueur. Then we set the whole thing on fire, finished the sauce, and poured it on top of the fried cream. That was me: I was a flambé guy.

---

*3 large eggs*
*6 large egg yolks*
*1¼ cups all-purpose flour*
*1¼ cups granulated sugar*
*¼ teaspoon salt*
*4 cups whole milk*
*1 cup (8 ounces) plus 1 teaspoon*
  *butter*
*2 tablespoons pure vanilla extract*

FOR THE COATING
*Vegetable oil for deep frying*
*2 large eggs, lightly beaten with*
  *2 tablespoons water*
*1 cup bread crumbs, finely ground*

FOR THE SAUCE
*¼ cup granulated sugar*
*2 tablespoons water*
(continued)

*Preparation:* Butter a 9 × 12-inch baking dish. In a large bowl, whisk the eggs and egg yolks together. Add the flour, sugar, and salt and mix to the consistency of a paste. In a large saucepan, bring the milk to a boil over medium-high heat. Add a few tablespoons of the hot milk to the egg mixture to temper it, stirring constantly. Add a few more tablespoons of the milk and continue to stir. Add the egg-milk mixture back to the rest of the hot milk in the saucepan and stir well. Add 1 cup of the butter, a few tablespoons at a time. Continue stirring, to prevent the mixture from burning. Remove from the heat and stir in the vanilla. Pour the mixture into the prepared baking dish. Spread the remaining teaspoon of butter over the top to prevent a skin from forming, and chill in the refrigerator for at least 2 hours, until very firm.

*The Dish:* Preheat the oven to 200 degrees.

Fill a deep heavy-duty pan with oil to 1½ inches deep. Heat the oil to 375 degrees on a candy thermometer. Cut the chilled cream into twelve 3-inch squares. Dip each square

2 tablespoons (1 ounce) butter
Juice of 1 orange
Juice of ½ lemon
2 bananas, sliced lengthwise
½ cup Grand Marnier

into the beaten egg and then in bread crumbs, to coat. Fry until golden brown, turning once. Place on an ovenproof serving dish, and keep warm in the oven until all the squares are fried.

> ✿ *Chef's Tip:* Don't overcrowd the squares in the oil, and make sure you bring the oil back up to 375 degrees before frying the next batch.

In a heavy-duty stainless-steel saucepan or skillet, stir together the sugar and butter. Over medium-high heat, cook the mixture without stirring, until it reaches a medium caramel color. Stir in the citrus juices. Add the bananas, top with a custard square, and coat with the sauce. Remove from the heat, add the Grand Marnier, and return everything to the heat to flambé the alcohol. Transfer to individual plates and serve.

## CROSTATA DI RICOTTA E CASTAGNE / Ricotta Chestnut Crostata

*8–10 servings*

I would eat ricotta *anything:* with pasta; in sweetened, fried ravioli; in *cannoli*—it is my tradition. Combined with chestnuts, it is one of my favorite things. Whenever I had a little money to spare when I was a child, I was at the *calda rostaio,* the corner chestnut vendor, getting my little cone of roasted chestnuts. Such a treat, especially after the movies.

---

FOR THE CRUST

*1 cup all-purpose flour*

*½ cup granulated sugar*

*1 large egg yolk*

*½ cup (4 ounces) butter, softened*

FOR THE FILLING

*2 cups fresh ricotta cheese*

*2 large eggs*

*½ cup granulated sugar*

*1 tablespoon pure vanilla extract*

*½ teaspoon almond extract*

*½ teaspoon lemon zest,*
  *finely chopped*

*1 cup candied chestnuts (available*
  *at specialty shops)*

FOR THE SAUCE

*1 cup granulated sugar*

*½ cup water*

*1 cup heavy cream*

*1 cup roasted chestnuts, chopped*

*Whole chestnuts for garnish*

TO MAKE THE CRUST: On a work surface, place the flour and sugar in a mound and make a well in the center. Add the egg yolk and butter to the well. Quickly, using your fingertips, work the flour into the liquid, being careful not to handle the dough too much. Gather the dough into a ball and refrigerate for at least 1 hour. On a lightly floured surface, roll the dough out to a large circle, ⅓ inch thick. Line a 9-inch tart pan and chill until ready to use.

Preheat the oven to 350 degrees.

TO MAKE THE FILLING: In the bowl of an electric mixer fitted with the paddle attachment, combine the ricotta cheese, eggs, sugar, extracts, and lemon zest and mix on medium for at least 15 minutes. Add the chestnuts and mix another 2–3 minutes. Pour the filling into the tart shell and bake for 45 minutes.

TO MAKE THE SAUCE: In a deep heavy-duty saucepan, combine the sugar and water. Bring to a boil over medium-high heat. Without stirring, cook the mixture until it turns a medium caramel color and remove from the heat. Add the cream and stir constantly with a wooden spoon. The mixture may spatter, so be careful. Return the pan to the stove over medium heat, and boil for 1–2 more minutes, stirring constantly. Add the chestnuts and let cool. Slice the crostata and serve with the sauce ladled over each serving. Garnish with extra chestnuts.

## TORTA DI CASTAGNE / Chestnut Cake

*4 servings*

---

*7 ounces chestnut puree (available
    at specialty shops)*

*5 tablespoons (2½ ounces) butter,
    softened*

*2 tablespoons rum*

*2 large eggs*

*5 tablespoons granulated sugar*

*¾ cup all-purpose flour*

*1 teaspoon Lievito Bertolini (Italian
    baking powder flavored with
    vanilla, sold in specialty food
    stores), or baking powder*

FOR THE CHESTNUT CREAM

*2 cups heavy cream*

*¼ cup granulated sugar*

*1 tablespoon pure vanilla extract*

*2–3 teaspoons chestnut puree*

Preheat the oven to 350 degrees. Butter a 9-inch baking pan.

In a large bowl, mix together the chestnut puree, butter, and rum. In another bowl, combine the eggs, sugar, flour, and Lievito Bertolini. Combine the 2 mixtures and mix well. Pour the mixture into the baking pan. Bake for 25 minutes.

Using an electric mixer, whip the cream with the sugar and vanilla until it forms soft peaks. Mix in the chestnut puree. Serve the cake with a dollop of the chestnut cream.

# CROCCANTE SEMIFREDDO

*8 servings*

This is the classic spumoni, revisited and cleaned up. It reminds me of *pezzo duro,* the hard ice cream that was such a treat when I was a kid in Modica. I bought it at the bar when I was sent to get wine for my parents, because they always gave me a little extra money for a treat. This is a grown-up version.

---

### FOR THE CIALDE (WAFER BASKETS)

*½ cup (4 ounces) butter*

*½ cup plus 2 tablespoons granulated sugar*

*½ cup plus 2 tablespoons all-purpose flour*

*2 large egg whites*

### FOR THE PRALINE

*½ cup whole almonds*

*½ cup hazelnuts*

*½ cup shelled pistachios*

*1 cup granulated sugar*

*½ teaspoon fresh-squeezed lemon juice*

*1 cup water*

### FOR THE SEMIFREDDO

*1 cup heavy cream*

*1 teaspoon pure vanilla extract*

*6 large egg yolks*

*¼ cup granulated sugar*

### FOR THE CHOCOLATE SAUCE

*1 cup heavy cream*

*4 ounces bittersweet chocolate*

*Preparation:* Preheat the oven to 350 degrees.

TO MAKE THE CIALDE: In the bowl of an electric mixer fitted with the paddle attachment, cream the butter and sugar on medium-high, about 3–4 minutes, until light and fluffy. Add the flour and mix well. Slowly add the egg whites and mix until combined. Refrigerate for 1 hour.

Butter a large baking sheet and line with parchment paper. Use a spatula or the back of a spoon to spread the batter very thinly into six 4-inch circles. Bake for 10 minutes, until golden brown. While the cookies are still warm, form them around a glass to create a basket shape, flattening them on the bottom so they will stand up. Set aside.

TO MAKE THE PRALINE: Preheat the oven to 325 degrees.

On a baking sheet, toast the almonds, hazelnuts, and pistachios for 10–12 minutes, until light golden brown. Rub the hazelnuts in a kitchen towel to remove skins. In a heavy-duty saucepan, combine the sugar, lemon juice, and water and stir to dissolve the sugar. Cook the mixture over medium-high heat, without stirring. When it comes to a rolling boil, turn down the heat. Continue cooking without stirring, until it has turned a light brown color. Stir in the toasted nuts. Remove from the heat and immediately pour the mixture onto an oiled sheet pan or Silpat nonstick mat. Allow to cool completely. When the praline is cold and hard, break into small pieces and finely chop with a knife or pulse in a food processor.

TO MAKE THE SEMIFREDDO: Using an electric mixer, whip the cream and vanilla until just stiff. Chill for 30 minutes to 1 hour, until cold.

In the bowl of an electric mixer fitted with the whisk attachment, whip the egg yolks and sugar on medium-high, until pale, about 3–4 minutes. Add 1 cup of the praline, then gently fold the yolk mixture into the chilled cream. Pour into a 9-inch round mold, cover with plastic wrap, and freeze overnight.

*The Dish:* When ready to serve, prepare the chocolate sauce. Heat the cream in a small heavy-duty saucepan. When almost boiling, turn off the heat, and stir in the chopped chocolate. Keep warm in a stainless-steel bowl set over a pot of gently simmering water, or in a double boiler.

Spoon the semifreddo into the wafer baskets, pour the warm chocolate over it, and sprinkle on a little of the remaining praline. Serve immediately.

## RAVIOLINI DOLCI ALLA CREMA DI CILIEGIE /
### Sweet Ravioli with Cherry Custard Sauce

*6 servings*

Mamma used to make ravioli on Sunday—marvelous, big ravioli stuffed with fresh ricotta and a touch of cinnamon. There was always some leftover dough and stuffing, so then she made smaller fried, sweet ravioli. I looked forward to these little pillows sprinkled with powdered sugar and stuffed with ricotta, so I have brought the dish into the present day. We use the same concept and make a different stuffing with dates, amaretto, chocolate, and hazelnut. And the dough is puff pastry. The only requirement is that the raviolini have to be very small. Otherwise they break.

---

FOR THE CHERRY CUSTARD SAUCE

*2¼ cups heavy cream*
*6 large egg yolks*
*½ cup granulated sugar*
*1 teaspoon pure vanilla extract*
*½ cup cherry preserves*

FOR THE RAVIOLI

*½ pound pitted dates*
*2 tablespoons amaretto liqueur*
*¼ cup hazelnuts*
*2 ounces white chocolate, chopped*
*3 tablespoons cream cheese*
*½ teaspoon ground cinnamon*
*9 ounces frozen puff pastry*
  *(defrosted according to*
  *instructions on package)*
*2 large egg whites, beaten*
*Powdered sugar, for dusting*

TO MAKE THE CUSTARD SAUCE: In a medium-size heavy-duty saucepan, bring the cream to a boil. In a large mixing bowl, whisk together the egg yolks, sugar, and vanilla. Whisking constantly, slowly pour about 3–4 teaspoons of the warm cream into the egg mixture, to temper it. Whisk in a few more tablespoons of the cream. Slowly whisk in the remaining cream and return it to the saucepan, stirring until it thickens, about 3 minutes. Do not allow it to boil. Strain and allow to cool. Stir in the preserves and chill for 2 hours.

TO MAKE THE RAVIOLI FILLING: Soak the dates in the amaretto until softened, about 30 minutes.

Preheat the oven to 325 degrees. Toast the hazelnuts on a baking sheet in the oven for 10–12 minutes and allow to cool. Rub the nuts together in a kitchen towel to remove the skins. Finely chop and set aside.

In a food processor fitted with the metal blade, puree the dates and liquid until smooth. Transfer the mixture to a large mixing bowl.

In a double boiler, or in a stainless-steel bowl set over a pot of gently simmering water, melt the white chocolate and stir until smooth. Add it to the date mixture and stir in the cream cheese, hazelnuts, and cinnamon.

TO MAKE THE RAVIOLI: Turn the oven up to 375 degrees.

On a lightly floured work surface, roll the puff pastry out to a large rectangle, about ¼ inch thick. Working with the longest edge closest to you, score the right half of the rectangle with a ravioli cutter, marking out 2-inch squares, without cutting through the dough. Brush the surface with egg white.

Spoon 1 rounded teaspoon of the date mixture into the center of each square. Fold the left side of the dough over the right side, sealing the edges together. Gently press down around the outer edge of the filling to eliminate air pockets. Use a ravioli cutter to form and cut out the squares. Brush the tops with egg white.

Arrange the ravioli on a nonstick baking sheet and bake for 10 minutes. Brush again with egg white and bake another 5 minutes. Brush one more time and bake until golden brown, about 5 more minutes.

When ready to serve, spoon the custard sauce onto individual plates, top with a ravioli, and dust with powdered sugar.

## PERE COTTE AL MASCARPONE /
## Poached Pears in Burgundy Wine with Mascarpone Mousse
*10 servings*

We first came up with this dish in 1985, at the first conference of the American Institute of Wine & Food, in Santa Barbara. I remember people were pleased with the originality of a dessert that combined a cheese course and a dessert course. It was our debut as a restaurant of quality—especially to people with good palates. In fact, two of the compliments I remember were from Julia Child and Alice Waters. They found it original and full of flavor, and an easy sensation, not overly filling. Now it's one of our traditional desserts, even though it's not that pretty to look at.

FOR THE POACHED PEARS

*8 cups Burgundy wine*

*5 cups water*

*4 cups granulated sugar*

*Zest of 1 lemon*

*1 teaspoon whole black peppercorns*

*2 teaspoons whole cloves*

*4 cinnamon sticks*

*1 vanilla bean*

*10 Bartlett pears, ripe but firm*

FOR THE MASCARPONE MOUSSE

*¼ cup heavy cream*

*1 pound mascarpone cheese*

*¾ cup granulated sugar*

*2 large egg yolks*

*Fresh mint sprigs, for garnish*

*Preparation:* THE DAY BEFORE SERVING: In a large stockpot, combine the wine, water, sugar, zest, peppercorns, cloves, and cinnamon sticks. Split the vanilla bean down the middle and scrape out the seeds. Add the seeds and pod to the liquid and gently place the pears in the liquid. Bring to a boil over high heat. Immediately turn off the heat and allow the pears to cool for a few hours in the liquid. Reserve 4 cups of the poaching liquid. Transfer everything to a smaller container, cover well, and refrigerate overnight.

In a small saucepan over medium-high heat, reduce the reserved liquid by half until it begins to thicken. Remove from heat and chill.

*The Dish:* Before serving, make the mascarpone mousse. Using an electric mixer, beat the cream to stiff peaks. In another bowl, beat together the mascarpone cheese and sugar by hand for 1 minute. Add the egg yolks and mix well. Fold the whipped cream into the mascarpone mixture, until smooth. Place in a pastry bag with a star tip, or use a spoon to spread the mousse.

Put 1 pear in the center of a plate. Pipe or spoon the mousse around half the pear. Spoon the reduced sauce on the other side of the pear and garnish with a sprig of fresh mint.

## TORTA DI FORMAGGIO CON FRAGOLE E VECCHIO BALSAMICO /
### Mascarpone Cheesecake with Strawberries in Balsamic Vinegar

*8 servings*

Cheesecake and apple pie were my favorite desserts when I got to New York. Sometimes after I was done working at the NYU cafeteria, I'd go to one of the little cafés in Greenwich Village and just have dessert and coffee. This is my variation on that cheesecake, with mascarpone added for its more distinguished flavor and lovely creaminess. Do not expect this to look like a mile-high New York cheesecake, though. Our version is smaller in scale: a slim layer of filling between the cake crust and the fruit. The topping of fresh strawberries and balsamic vinegar gives this dessert a unique identity; I like it much better than sweeter fruit sauces, because it provides an interesting balance.

---

*1 recipe Sponge Cake*
  *(see page 216), baked*
  *in a 9-inch round pan*
*1 tablespoon pure almond extract*

FOR THE FILLING
*½ cup cream cheese*
*¾ cup granulated sugar*
*1 teaspoon pure vanilla extract*
*½ cup mascarpone cheese*
*2 large egg whites*

FOR THE STRAWBERRIES IN
BALSAMIC VINEGAR
*1 pint strawberries, stems removed*
  *and cut into quarters*
*¼ cup granulated sugar*
*2 tablespoons balsamic vinegar*

Make the sponge cake according the recipe on page 216, substituting 1 tablespoon of pure almond extract for the vanilla extract. Bake according to the directions and let cool. Line the bottom of a 9-inch cake pan with a thin layer of almond sponge cake.

Preheat the oven to 325 degrees.

In the bowl of an electric mixer fitted with the paddle attachment, cream the cream cheese and ½ cup of the sugar on medium, 2–3 minutes, until smooth. Add the vanilla and mascarpone cheese, and mix to combine. Set aside.

In the clean dry bowl of an electric mixer fitted with the whisk attachment, whip the egg whites on medium-high, slowly adding the remaining sugar. Beat a few more minutes, until semistiff peaks form. Fold the whites into the cheese mixture. Pour or spoon the cheese filling into the cake-lined pan.

Place the cake pan in a water bath and bake in the oven for approximately 1 hour. Cool and refrigerate. A half hour before serving, prepare the strawberries. Put the cut fruit in a large bowl and toss with the sugar and balsamic vinegar. Allow to marinate for 20 minutes. Slice the cheesecake into individual portions and serve with the strawberries.

# CROSTATA DI PIGNOLI CON MORE E CONSERVA DI FICHI /
## Pignoli Crostata with Blackberry and Fig Compote

*8 servings*

---

*½ recipe Pastry Dough*
*(see page 228)*

FOR THE PINE NUT FILLING
*1 cup plus 3 tablespoons granulated*
*sugar*
*¼ cup plus 2 tablespoons cream*
*cheese, softened*
*2 large egg yolks*
*2 tablespoons plus 1 teaspoon*
*amaretto*
*5 ounces Traditional Amaretti,*
*crushed (see page 252)*
*1¼ cup pine nuts*

FOR THE COMPOTE
*1 pint blackberries*
*Zest of 1 orange, finely chopped*
*4 fresh figs, quartered*
*1 vanilla bean*
*½ cup granulated sugar*

Lightly butter a 9-inch tart pan. On a lightly floured work surface, roll the dough out to a 10-inch circle, ⅛ inch thick, flouring the surface of the dough as needed. Line the tart pan and chill for at least 30 minutes.

Preheat the oven to 350 degrees. Cover the tart shell with foil and fill with pie weights or dried beans. Blind bake the tart shell for 20 minutes. Remove weights and foil, and bake for another 20 minutes or until the crust is golden brown. Check frequently to avoid burning. Cool on a rack.

TO MAKE THE FILLING: In the bowl of an electric mixer fitted with the paddle attachment, cream the sugar and cream cheese on medium, 3–4 minutes. Add the egg yolks one at a time, and mix until fully incorporated, scraping the bowl with a rubber spatula to avoid lumps. Add the amaretto slowly and mix well. Place the crushed cookies on the bottom of the prebaked tart shell. Spoon the cream cheese filling into the shell and spread evenly. Sprinkle the pine nuts over the top. Bake at 350 degrees for 25–30 minutes, or until the filling is set. Cool. Keep the oven at 350 degrees.

While the tart cools, place the blackberries, orange zest, and figs in a nonreactive (stainless steel or glass) baking dish. Split the vanilla bean down the middle and scrape out the seeds. Add the seeds and pod to the fruit mixture. Sprinkle with sugar, cover the pan, and bake for 20 minutes. Remove the vanilla bean and serve the warm compote over each slice of the pignoli tart.

## LA PASTA FROLLA / Pastry Dough

*Enough for two 9-inch crusts*

1 cup (8 ounces) butter, chilled and
    cut into small pieces
1 cup granulated sugar
1 large egg
1 large egg yolk
¾ teaspoon pure vanilla extract
¼ teaspoon orange oil
3¼ cups pastry flour
Pinch of salt
¾ teaspoon baking powder

In the bowl of an electric mixer fitted with the paddle attachment, cream the butter and sugar on medium-high until pale in color. Add the egg and egg yolk, and mix well. Add the vanilla and orange oil and mix to combine. Turn the mixer off and add the flour, salt, and baking powder. Turn the mixer to medium-low and mix until the dough just comes together; do not overmix, or the dough will become tough. Flatten into a disk for one 9-inch, ¼-inch-thick crust, or divide the dough in half for two 9-inch, ⅛-inch-thick crusts. Wrap in plastic and refrigerate until firm, at least 1 hour or overnight.

Bake according to instructions in individual recipes.

## SEMIFREDDO AL LIMONE CON SALSA DI LAMPONI /
### Lemon Semifreddo with Raspberry Sauce

*6 servings*

---

FOR THE LEMON BUTTER

*½ cup fresh-squeezed lemon juice*

*¼ cup plus 2 tablespoons granulated sugar*

*10 tablespoons (5 ounces) butter*

*3 large eggs*

FOR THE RASPBERRY SAUCE

*1 pint fresh raspberries*

*¼ cup plus 2 tablespoons granulated sugar*

FOR THE MERINGUE

*4 large egg whites*

*¼ cup water*

*¼ cup light corn syrup*

*¼ cup plus 2 tablespoons granulated sugar*

---

*1 cup heavy cream*

TO MAKE THE LEMON BUTTER: In a stainless-steel saucepan, stir together the lemon juice, sugar, butter, and eggs. Over medium-high heat, bring the mixture to a boil, stirring constantly. Strain through a sieve. Cover the surface with plastic wrap, and cool in the refrigerator for at least 2 hours.

TO MAKE THE RASPBERRY SAUCE: In a food processor fitted with the metal blade, puree the raspberries and sugar. Strain to remove seeds, and refrigerate until ready to use.

TO MAKE THE MERINGUE: In the bowl of an electric mixer fitted with the whisk attachment, whip the egg whites on high, for about 5 minutes, until they hold soft peaks. In a small heavy-duty saucepan, stir together the water, corn syrup, and sugar. Bring to a boil and continue cooking until it reaches 250 degrees on a candy thermometer, just before it reaches the hard ball stage. Very slowly, with the mixer on medium speed, add the syrup to the egg whites in a thin stream. Once you've added all of the syrup, turn the mixer up to high and whip to stiff peaks, about 5 minutes, and re-frigerate.

Whip the cream to semistiff peaks and refrigerate.

Butter six 4-ounce custard cups or molds, and line them with plastic wrap. Gently fold the cooled lemon butter, meringue, and whipped cream together. Fill the molds or custard cups with the semifreddo and freeze overnight.

Remove the semifreddo from the freezer and invert onto plates. Remove the plastic and spoon the raspberry sauce over the semifreddo.

## BAVARESE CON FRUTTA DELLA PASSIONE, SALSA DI LAMPONI /
### Bavarian Cream with Passion Fruit and Raspberry Sauce
*6 servings*

---

*2 sheets gelatin*
*10–12 passion fruit*
  *(about ¾–1 cup puree)*
*¼ cup granulated sugar*
*3 large eggs, separated*

FOR THE SAUCE
*1 pint raspberries*
*4 tablespoons granulated sugar*
*4 tablespoons water*
*Juice of 1 orange*

Soften the gelatin sheets in cold water and drain. Cut the passion fruit in half and scoop out the pulp. Discard the peels. In a food processor fitted with the metal blade, puree the pulp until smooth. Strain out the seeds. In a stainless-steel bowl set over a pot of gently simmering water, or in a double boiler, combine the puree, sugar, and egg yolks. Whisk until they become a fluid cream. Add the gelatin, and mix until completely melted. Set aside to cool.

In the bowl of an electric mixer fitted with the whisk attachment, whip the egg whites on medium-high until soft peaks form, about 5 minutes. Gently fold the egg whites into the cooled egg yolk mixture. Place the mixture in a mold, and refrigerate for 3 hours.

TO MAKE THE SAUCE: In a food processor fitted with the metal blade, puree the raspberries and strain. In a small saucepan, dissolve the sugar in the water. Add the orange juice and raspberry puree. Spoon over the *bavarese*.

# MILLEFOGLIE DI PESCA CON FRUTTI DI BOSCO /
## Peach Millefoglie with Berries

*4 servings*

FOR THE WAFER

*¼ cup cake flour*

*¼ cup plus 1 tablespoon granulated
     sugar*

*1 large egg*

*2 large egg whites*

*¼ cup (2 ounces) butter, melted*

*1 teaspoon pure vanilla extract*

*1 pound ripe peaches, peeled and
     chopped*

FOR THE FRUIT TOPPING

*¾ cup plus 2 tablespoons granulated
     sugar*

*½ cup peach-flavored brandy*

*1 scant tablespoon unflavored
     gelatin*

*1 cup heavy cream*

*1 pound small mixed berries*

*Juice of 1 lemon*

*Powdered sugar, for dusting*

*4 small bunches fresh mint*

Preheat the oven to 300 degrees. Lightly butter 2 baking sheets, or line with parchment.

TO MAKE THE WAFERS: In a large mixing bowl, combine the flour and sugar. In another bowl, whisk to combine the egg, egg whites, melted butter, and vanilla. In a slow, steady stream, add the egg mixture to the flour mixture, mixing well until it is a smooth paste. Form a walnut-size ball of dough. Using an offset spatula or the back of a spoon, spread the mixture on the baking sheet until you have a 4-inch circle. Repeat with the remaining dough. Bake until golden brown, approximately 10 minutes.

TO MAKE THE FRUIT TOPPING: In a food processor fitted with the metal blade, puree the peaches with ½ cup of the sugar and the brandy, and strain. In a small bowl, combine ¼ cup of the puree with the gelatin. Set aside for a few minutes to allow the gelatin to dissolve. Transfer the gelatin mixture to a small saucepan and melt over low heat for about 30 seconds. Remove from the heat and whisk in ¼ cup of the cream. In the bowl of an electric mixer, whip the remaining cream until soft peaks form. Add the gelatin mixture to the whipped cream and continue to beat the cream until slightly stiff. Fold the remaining peach puree into the mixture and refrigerate until ready to serve, no longer than 30 minutes.

Pass half of the mixed berries through a sieve or puree

in a food processor. Add the remaining sugar and lemon juice and stir together to make a thick sauce.

TO SERVE: Dust the tops of the wafers with powdered sugar and place 1 on each plate. Spoon a few tablespoons of the peach puree over it and surround it with mixed berries. Top with another wafer and repeat. Garnish with a few mint leaves and finish decorating the plates with mixed berry sauce and the remaining fruit.

## SPUMONE D'ARANCIA / Orange Semifreddo

*6 servings*

*Zest of 4 oranges*

*¾ cup plus 2 tablespoons granulated*
*    sugar*

*¾ cup plus 2 tablespoons whole milk*

*2 tablespoons cornstarch*

*4 tablespoons Triple Sec or*
*    Cointreau*

*4 large eggs, separated*

*1 cup orange juice*

TO MAKE THE SEMIFREDDO: In a heavy-duty stainless-steel saucepan, combine half the orange zest, ¾ cups of the sugar, and all the milk and bring to a boil over medium-high heat. Dissolve the cornstarch in 2 tablespoons of the liqueur. In a bowl, whip the egg yolks and add the cornstarch mixture. Pour some of the heated liquid into the egg yolk mixture to warm it, and then slowly pour the remaining egg yolk mixture into the saucepan, stirring constantly. Simmer over low heat, stirring constantly, until the mixture thickens. Strain carefully and let cool.

In the bowl of an electric mixer fitted with the whisk attachment, whip the egg whites on medium-high until soft peaks form. Slowly add the egg whites to the milk mixture.

Place the mixture in an ice-cream mold or loaf pan and chill it in the freezer, covered with wax paper.

TO MAKE THE SYRUP: In a saucepan, combine the remaining zest, liqueur, sugar, and the orange juice. Let boil until it thickens.

To serve, cut the semifreddo into individual slices and pour a little syrup around the edges.

*8–10 servings*

*1 recipe Pastry Dough*
  *(see page 228)*

FOR THE FILLING
*6 tablespoons (3 ounces) butter*
*¼ cup plus 2 tablespoons granulated*
  *sugar*
*¼ teaspoon salt*
*2 large eggs*
*3 large egg yolks*
*2 tablespoons all-purpose flour*
*4 tablespoons fresh-squeezed lemon*
  *juice*
*2 tablespoons grappa*

Lightly butter a 9-inch tart pan. On a lightly floured work surface, roll the dough out to a 10-inch circle, ¼ inch thick, flouring the surface of the dough as needed. Line the tart pan and chill for at least 30 minutes.

TO MAKE THE FILLING: In the bowl of an electric mixer fitted with the paddle attachment, cream the butter, sugar, and salt on medium for about 3–4 minutes. Add the eggs and the yolks one at a time, mixing well between each addition. Mix in the flour, lemon juice, and grappa. Refrigerate until ready to use.

Preheat the oven to 350 degrees. Line the tart shell with foil and fill with pie weights or dried beans. Blind bake the tart shell for about 20 minutes, remove the weights and foil, and bake another 20 minutes until light golden. Allow to cool. Pour the filling into the tart shell and bake for 25 minutes, until set. Allow to cool.

## FRUTTA CANDITA / Candied Fruit Peel

*1 cup*

This should be eaten when you want to sin a little, at any time of the day. It reminds me of the caffè-bars of my youth, the places where you stop for your daily ritual of *espressi* (more than one, because you stop more than once a day). On the counter you always had *biscotti, cioccolatini Perugina,* and lots of *frutta candita,* especially where I grew up, in the south. Adding sugar in this way is an Arab influence—and wonderful Sicilian fruits are turned into a naughty, sweet morsel. Steal one whenever you can, particularly with coffee or tea in the late afternoon.

*3 whole lemons*
*3 whole oranges*
*3 cups granulated sugar*
*Water*

Peel the lemons and oranges, removing the white pith from the inside of the peel. Cut the peels into long, thin strips with a sharp knife. In a large saucepan, cover the peels with water. Slowly bring to a boil and then simmer for about 10 minutes. Drain. Repeat the process 3 more times. The fourth time, simmer in 1 cup of water and 2 cups of sugar. Cover, and let the peel simmer slowly until the syrup is absorbed.

Spread the pieces of peel on a platter to cool and roll in the remaining sugar. Store in covered jars for future use.

## POLENTA DOLCE ALLA NOCCIOLA /
### Sweet Polenta with Hazelnut Sauce
*4 servings*

Here are two essential Italian ingredients presented in a new way. When you sweeten cornmeal, or polenta, it can taste like a custard. Polenta dolce shows up in northern cuisine, often served with fruit compote or ice cream. The hazelnut sauce is a nice alternative, since *nocciola* are everywhere in Italian desserts, from nougat to custard.

---

FOR THE POLENTA

*½ cup (4 ounces) butter*
*½ cup granulated sugar*
*1 tablespoon pure vanilla extract*
*Zest of 1 orange, finely chopped*
*Zest of 1 lemon, finely chopped*
*2 large egg yolks*
*⅓ cup almonds, ground to equal*
   *½ cup almond meal*
*¼ cup semolina*
*1 tablespoon cornstarch*
*1 tablespoon Lievito Bertolini*
   *(Italian baking powder flavored*
   *with vanilla) or baking powder*
*4 large egg whites*

FOR THE SAUCE

*1 cup hazelnuts*
*1½ cups milk*
*1 vanilla bean*
*2 tablespoons Fra Angelico liqueur*
*4 large egg yolks*
*¼ cup plus 2 tablespoons granulated*
   *sugar*

Preheat the oven to 350 degrees. Butter a 9 × 13-inch baking dish.

In an electric mixer fitted with the paddle attachment, cream the butter, ¼ cup of the sugar, vanilla, and zests on medium until light and fluffy, about 3 minutes. Add the egg yolks one at a time, mixing well in between. In another bowl, combine the almond meal, semolina, cornstarch, and baking powder. Turn the mixer to low and add the dry ingredients in 3 batches, mixing well to combine.

In the clean and dry bowl of an electric mixer fitted with the whisk attachment, whip the egg whites on medium-high, about 5 minutes, until soft peaks form. Add the remaining granulated sugar, and whip another 1–2 minutes until semi-stiff peaks form. Gently fold half of the egg white mixture into the butter mixture. Fold in the remaining whites.

Spread the mixture into the baking dish, and bake for 30 minutes, until golden brown. When the "polenta" has cooled, invert onto a flat surface and cut into diamond shapes.

TO MAKE THE SAUCE: On a baking sheet, toast the hazelnuts in the 350-degree oven for about 10 minutes. Allow to cool a few minutes, rub the nuts together in a kitchen towel to remove the skins, and coarsely chop.

In a medium-size heavy-duty saucepan, warm the milk and ¾ cup of the hazelnuts. Split the vanilla bean down the middle and scrape out the seeds. Add the seeds and pod to the milk. Bring to a boil over medium heat. Turn off the heat, add the liqueur, and allow to steep for 30 minutes to 1 hour. Strain the milk and bring back to a boil. Turn off the heat.

In a large bowl, whisk together the egg yolks and sugar. Add a small amount of the hot milk to the yolk mixture, and mix well. Slowly pour this back into the hot milk. Stirring constantly, cook for about 5 minutes over medium heat, then chill over a bowl of ice. Serve the polenta with the sauce and garnish with the remaining toasted hazelnuts.

# TORTA DI RICOTTA CON SENTORI D'ARANCIO E CIOCCOLATO /
## Ricotta, Orange, and Chocolate Torte

*8 – 10 servings*

*1 recipe Pastry Dough
    (see page 228)*

FOR THE RICOTTA FILLING
*2½ cups fresh ricotta cheese
½ cup plus 1 tablespoon granulated
    sugar
3 large eggs
2 tablespoons all-purpose flour
Zest of 1 lemon, finely chopped
Zest of 1 orange, finely chopped
2½ ounces semisweet or bittersweet
    chocolate, chopped*

FOR THE ORANGE SAUCE
*1 cup fresh-squeezed orange juice
¼ cup granulated sugar
Zest of 1 orange, finely chopped
1 vanilla bean
2 ounces Cointreau
1 tablespoon cornstarch*

FOR THE GARNISH
*Candied orange peel (see page 235)
Fresh berries*

TO MAKE THE FILLING: Drain the ricotta overnight in a sieve.

In the bowl of an electric mixer fitted with the paddle attachment, combine the ricotta cheese and sugar and mix on medium. Add the eggs one at a time, mixing on medium until fully incorporated. Turn the mixer off, add the flour and zests, and mix on medium-low until incorporated. Fold in the chopped chocolate.

TO MAKE THE TART: Lightly butter a 9-inch tart pan. On a floured work surface, gently knead slightly more than half the dough. Roll it out to ⅛ inch thick, flouring the surface as needed. Run a thin metal spatula between the work surface and the dough and ease the dough onto a rolling pin to transfer it to the tart pan. Line the pan, making sure to press the dough into the corners. Remove excess dough by running the rolling pin over the edge of the pan, and reserve scraps for the lattice top. Fill the tart shell with the ricotta filling, cover with plastic wrap, and refrigerate.

Preheat the oven to 350 degrees.

On a floured surface, roll out the remaining dough into a circle about ⅛ inch thick. Using a pastry wheel or knife, cut into ½-inch strips. Remove the tart from the refrigerator and arrange the strips in a diagonal lattice over the filling. Bake for 40–50 minutes.

TO MAKE THE ORANGE SAUCE: In a stainless-steel saucepan, combine the orange juice, sugar, and orange zest. Split the vanilla bean down the middle and scrape out the seeds, adding both the seeds and the pod to the mixture. Bring to a boil over medium-high heat. In a separate bowl, combine the Cointreau and cornstarch. Using a small fine-mesh sieve, strain the cornstarch mixture into the juice mixture. Return to a boil, remove from the heat, and strain. Chill for at least 1 hour.

Spoon a few tablespoons of the sauce onto individual plates and place 1 slice of the tart on top. Garnish with candied orange and fresh berries.

## TORTA DI CIOCCOLATO ALL'ESSENZA DI AMARETTO /
### Chocolate and Amaretti Torte

*8 – 10  servings*

Here we have combined two of the most popular sweets, chocolate and amaretto, into what feels like a traditional rich Italian torte. It was created at Valentino about ten years ago.

---

FOR THE CAKE

*10 Traditional Amaretti (see page 252), crushed to equal ⅓ cup*

*2 ounces bittersweet chocolate*

*½ cup all-purpose flour*

*1 cup (8 ounces) butter, at room temperature*

*1 cup granulated sugar*

*5 large eggs, separated*

FOR THE MOUSSE

*3 cups heavy cream*

*¼ cup powdered sugar*

*½ cup cocoa powder*

FOR THE GARNISH

*1 pound bittersweet chocolate, broken into small chunks*

*2 cups heavy cream, whipped*

Preheat the oven to 375 degrees. Lightly coat a 9-inch springform pan with butter, and dust it with flour, knocking out the excess.

In a food processor fitted with the metal blade, process the cookies and chocolate until crumbly. Place in a medium-size mixing bowl and add the flour. Set aside.

In an electric mixer fitted with the paddle attachment, cream the butter on medium for 3–4 minutes, until light and fluffy. Slowly add the granulated sugar and beat until pale. Add the egg yolks one at a time and beat until smooth and creamy. Add the cookie mixture and combine until the texture is smooth. Transfer to another bowl and set aside.

In the clean and dry bowl of an electric mixer, beat the egg whites on high for about 4–5 minutes, until soft peaks form. Gently fold them into the cake batter, being careful not to overmix. Pour into the prepared pan. Bake for 1 hour, until the cake is a deep brown color and a toothpick inserted into the middle comes out clean. Cool for 10 minutes. Release the sides of the pan and allow to cool completely. Remove the bottom of the pan and slice the cake horizontally into 2 even layers.

TO MAKE THE MOUSSE: Using an electric mixer, beat the cream on high until very soft peaks begin to form. Add the powdered sugar and cocoa powder and turn the speed down to low. Whip until the sugar and cocoa are blended and the cream is stiff. The mixture should be firm but spreadable and smooth.

Spread the mousse on 1 layer of the torte, and place the second layer of cake over it. Spread the remaining mousse on the top surface of the torte and sprinkle with chocolate pieces. Serve with whipped cream.

**FOR THE CAKE**

*10½ ounces bittersweet chocolate*

*10 tablespoons (5 ounces) butter*

*⅔ cup granulated sugar*

*5 large eggs, separated*

*¼ cup plus 2 tablespoons*
*    all-purpose flour*

**FOR THE GANACHE**

*6½ ounces bittersweet chocolate,*
*    chopped*

*¼ cup heavy cream*

*¼ cup brewed espresso*

*2 tablespoons (1 ounce) butter,*
*    softened*

*1 tablespoon Triple Sec or other*
*    orange-flavored liqueur*

*Fresh raspberries, for garnish*

✷ *Chef's Tip:* The cake may be made up to 2 days in advance and kept in an airtight container at room temperature until you are ready to make the ganache and serve. For a more elegant presentation, cut the cake into 8 – 10 wedges and coat each individual serving with ganache.

TO PREPARE THE CAKE: Preheat the oven to 350 degrees and butter a 10-inch springform pan. Adjust the oven rack to the middle position.

Chop the chocolate and cut the butter into pieces. In a double boiler, or a metal bowl set over a saucepan of barely simmering water, melt the chocolate, butter, and sugar, stirring until smooth (sugar will not dissolve). Remove from the heat and cool to room temperature. Transfer the mixture to a large bowl.

Add the egg yolks one at a time to the chocolate mixture, whisking well after each addition. With an electric mixer, beat the whites until they just hold soft peaks. Sift the flour over the chocolate mixture and, with a whisk, fold in the flour and half the whites. With a rubber spatula, fold in the remaining whites gently but thoroughly. Pour the batter into the prepared pan, smooth the top, and bake 40 – 45 minutes, or until a tester comes out with moist crumbs adhering. Cool the cake completely in the pan on a rack.

TO MAKE THE GANACHE: In a double boiler, or a metal bowl set over a saucepan of barely simmering water, melt the chocolate, stirring frequently until smooth. Remove from the heat.

While the chocolate melts, in a small saucepan bring the cream just to a simmer and add the espresso. Add the cream mixture to the chocolate, along with the butter and liqueur. Stir until smooth.

TO ASSEMBLE THE CAKE: Remove the side of the springform pan. Invert the cake onto a large rack set over a shallow baking pan. Pour enough warm ganache over the cake to coat it, and let it stand for 5 minutes.

Scrape the excess ganache from the baking pan and pour it over the cake a second time. Let it stand at room temperature until the ganache is set, at least 1 hour, and up to 6 hours.

Just before serving, garnish the top of the cake with raspberries.

*Wine:* For this dessert, I'll make an exception and suggest specific wines: a Recioto della Valpolicella (Allegrini), with a high concentration of syrup and fruit, or a California Black Muscat (especially Andrew Quady's rose-scented Elysium).

## TERRINA DI CIOCCOLATO AGRODOLCE ED AMARETTI CON GRANITA DI CAFFÈ /
### Terrine of Bittersweet Chocolate and Amaretti with Espresso Granita

*8 – 10 servings*

---

**FOR THE TERRINE**

*3 ounces (about 20) Traditional*
*Amaretti, crushed (see page 252)*
*4 tablespoons Cointreau*
*1 pound bittersweet chocolate,*
*chopped*
*½ cup (4 ounces) butter*
*2 large egg yolks*
*1¼ cups heavy cream*

**FOR THE ESPRESSO GRANITA**

*4 cups water*
*1½ cups granulated sugar*
*1 cup espresso beans, ground*
*2 teaspoons lemon zest,*
*finely chopped*

TO MAKE THE TERRINE: Butter a 6-cup terrine mold or bread pan and line with plastic wrap. In a medium-size bowl, soak the crushed amaretti cookies in Cointreau. Melt the chocolate and butter in a stainless-steel bowl set over a pot of simmering water, or in a double boiler. Remove from the heat and cool slightly. Slowly whisk in the egg yolks. Whip the cream until it holds soft peaks and gently fold it into the chocolate mixture. Alternately layer the chocolate mixture with the crushed cookies in the prepared loaf pan. Refrigerate overnight.

TO MAKE THE GRANITA: In a small saucepan, stir together 1 cup of the water with ½ cup of the sugar. Over medium-high heat, bring to a boil and set aside.

In a large stainless-steel saucepan, bring the remaining water and espresso to a boil, then turn off the heat. Add the lemon zest and infuse for 5 minutes. Strain through a coffee filter. Stir in the sugar syrup and cool in the refrigerator.

Pour the granita mixture into a nonreactive baking dish and place in the freezer. When it begins to freeze, stir every 15 minutes, scraping the sides and bottom of the pan. When the granita no longer has any liquid in it, stir well and cover with plastic wrap. Store in the freezer until ready to serve.

TO SERVE: Unmold the terrine onto a cutting board. With a knife warmed in hot water, slice the terrine into 1-inch-thick pieces. Place 1 slice of terrine on a chilled plate and spoon the granita around it.

## SALAME DI CIOCCOLATO ALLO ZABAGLIONE /
### Salami-Shaped Chocolate with Zabaglione

*6 servings*

Romano Tamani owns one of the great restaurants in Italy, in a little town between Verona and Mantua. That was where I had my meal of many little courses that led to the idea for Primi. For dessert, he served something I couldn't believe, this *"salame"* made of chocolate, so appropriate to the divine rustic food his family reproduces daily. He, his sister, and his aunt live in a region of Italy that takes its food history very seriously. This dessert is a delicious step into the past.

*1½ cups (12 ounces) butter*
*1½ cups granulated sugar*
*2 large eggs*
*1 cup cocoa powder*
*1 cup espresso, finely ground*
*1 pound almond biscotti, chopped*
*1¼ cups almonds, finely chopped*
*4 tablespoons Calvados*
*4 tablespoons Grand Marnier*
*2 tablespoons crème de*
  *cacao liqueur*

**FOR THE ZABAGLIONE**
*3 large eggs*
*1 large egg yolk*
*¼ cup dry Marsala wine*
*½ cup Moscato wine*
*¼ cup plus 2 tablespoons*
  *granulated sugar*

*"A delicious step into the past,"*
*inspired by a dessert served at Romano*
*Tamani's divine restaurant in Italy.*

In a large bowl, combine the butter, sugar, eggs, cocoa powder, and espresso. Place the cookies and almonds in a medium-size bowl and stir in the Calvados, Grand Marnier, and crème de cacao. Add to the butter mixture, mixing until combined. Divide the mixture in half and roll into 2 very

large cigars or salami. Wrap each one very carefully in a sheet of parchment paper. Refrigerate for 12 hours.

TO MAKE THE ZABAGLIONE: In a stainless-steel bowl set over a pot of rapidly boiling water or a double boiler, whisk together the eggs, egg yolk, wines, and sugar until the mixture becomes a thick cream. Remove from the heat.

Slice the rolls into 2-inch-thick medallions and serve with the zabaglione.

## IL BONET / Traditional Piedmontese Chocolate Pudding
*6 servings*

I tasted this at a restaurant called Felicin, in La Morra, on my first trip to Piedmont. It's simple and full of originality—the signature of a region where tradition is a very big part of the cuisine. Piedmont is known for tagliarini pasta, truffles, Barolo wine, and *bonet,* the perfect finish. We haven't touched the recipe; certain things you leave the way they are, out of respect.

---

*1 cup granulated sugar*

*1 tablespoon cocoa powder*

*2 large eggs*

*4 large egg yolks*

*2 tablespoons rum*

*2 cups plus 2 tablespoons whole milk*

*8 ounces or 64 Traditional Amaretti (see page 252), crushed*

FOR THE CARAMEL SAUCE

*3 tablespoons granulated sugar*

*3 tablespoons water*

In a mixing bowl, combine the sugar and cocoa. Add the eggs, egg yolks, and rum and stir until thoroughly combined. In a medium-size saucepan, bring the milk to a boil over medium-high heat. Remove from the heat, and stir in the cookies. Set aside for 1 hour. In a large bowl, combine the milk and egg mixture and set aside.

Preheat the oven to 375 degrees.

In a small saucepan, heat the sugar and water over low heat. Without stirring, cook until it is a dark and glassy caramel. Immediately pour the mixture into the bottom and around the sides of six 4-ounce custard cups, swirling the molds quickly so that the caramel forms an even layer before it sets. Pour the custard into the cups and bake in a water bath for 30 minutes. Remove and cool. Invert the custard onto a serving plate, allowing the syrup to run over the custard.

*Wine:* A wine worth searching for is Forteto della Luja by Giancarlo Scaglione, a low-yield Moscato dried on the vine and then on racks before an extra year of barrique. It is a wine of delicacy, perfumes, and lingering scents.

## BUDINO DI ESPRESSO / Espresso Chocolate Custard

*6 – 8 servings*

Twenty-five-year-old Gianluca Fusta, the pastry chef at Valentino Las Vegas, comes from Milan. He is a scientist in the kitchen, always thinking about new flavor combinations—but his elegant desserts, like this smooth custard of chocolate and espresso, also reflect Italy's food history. He likes to serve it with mango sorbet, for a pungent counterpoint to the rich chocolate.

*1 pint heavy cream*
*¼ cup granulated sugar*
*1 teaspoon pectin*
*¾ cup espresso beans*
*6 ounces bittersweet chocolate,*
*    chopped fine*

In a food processor fitted with the metal blade, coarsely chop the espresso beans.

Bring to a gentle boil the cream, sugar, pectin, and espresso beans. Set aside, uncovered, for 30 minutes, and then strain. The mixture will still be warm.

Put the chopped chocolate in a mixing bowl. Slowly add the warm cream mixture to the chocolate a little at a time, mixing well after each addition. If the cream mixture becomes too cool to melt the chocolate, rewarm over low heat, stir, and continue adding to the chocolate. Continue this process until you have used up all the cream mixture, the chocolate has melted, and the custard is a thick, smooth paste. Place in individual molds and chill.

When ready to serve, unmold onto individual plates.

FOR THE AMARETTO TRUFFLE

*8 ounces milk chocolate*

*1 cup heavy cream*

*½ cup granulated sugar*

*2 large egg yolks*

*2 tablespoons amaretto liqueur*

*3 ounces bittersweet chocolate*

FOR THE GRAND MARNIER TRUFFLE

*½ cup heavy cream*

*6 ounces milk chocolate*

*3 ounces bittersweet chocolate*

*2 tablespoons (1 ounce) butter*

*3 tablespoons Grand Marnier*

*4 tablespoons cocoa powder*

FOR THE CARAMELIZED TRUFFLE

*7 ounces bittersweet chocolate*

*¾ cup granulated sugar*

*1 cup heavy cream*

*Pinch of salt*

*1 teaspoon vanilla powder*

*3 ounces white chocolate*

*Preparation:* TO MAKE THE AMARETTO TRUFFLE: Grate the milk chocolate into a bowl. In a heavy-duty saucepan over low heat, combine the cream and sugar, and mix with a wooden spoon until the sugar is completely melted. Remove it from the heat, pour over the milk chocolate, and mix. When cool, add the egg yolks one at a time. Add the liqueur and mix well. Cover the bowl and refrigerate for 3 hours. Grate the bittersweet chocolate in a separate bowl.

TO MAKE THE GRAND MARNIER TRUFFLE: In a medium-size saucepan over low heat, bring the cream to a simmer. Remove from the heat and stir in both chocolates, the butter, and the Grand Marnier. Cover and refrigerate for at least 3 hours.

TO MAKE THE CARMELIZED TRUFFLE: Grate the chocolate into a bowl. Pour the sugar into a small heavy-duty saucepan and let it melt over low heat. Cook until it reaches 320 degrees on a candy thermometer. It may spatter, so be careful. Remove from the heat and immediately place the pan in a bowl of ice water to stop the cooking. Add the cream, place the saucepan back on the heat, and mix until sugar is completely caramelized. Add the salt and vanilla. Pour this mixture over the chocolate and mix. Cover and refrigerate for 3–4 hours. Grate the white chocolate and refrigerate.

*To Form the Truffles:* Cover a large tray with aluminum foil. Prepare the truffle by scooping a walnut-size amount of the paste and shaping it into a ball with the palms of your hands. Roll the amaretto truffle in bittersweet chocolate. Sprinkle the Grand Marnier truffle with cocoa powder. Sprinkle the caramelized truffle with white chocolate. Place the truffles on the tray and refrigerate.

## BISCOTTI DI SEMOLINA / Semolina Cookies

*4–5 dozen*

1 cup (8 ounces) butter, softened

½ cup plus 1 tablespoon granulated
   sugar

1 teaspoon pure vanilla extract

3 large egg yolks

1½ cups all-purpose flour

½ cup plus 2 tablespoons cornmeal
   or semolina

Pinch of salt

In the bowl of an electric mixer fitted with the paddle attachment, cream the butter and sugar on medium for 3–4 minutes, until light and fluffy. Add the vanilla, and the egg yolks one at a time, mixing well between each addition. Add the flour, cornmeal, and salt and mix until just combined. Chill until firm, at least 2 hours, or overnight.

Preheat the oven to 325 degrees.

To shape each cookie, roll a small piece of dough into a log shape ½ inch thick and 2 inches long. Shape into a crescent and place on a buttered or parchment-lined baking sheet. Bake for 10 minutes, until lightly colored.

## BISCOTTI CARAMELLATI AL CIOCCOLATO / Dark Chocolate Fudge Cookies

*4 dozen*

½ cup all-purpose flour

Pinch of salt

¼ teaspoon baking soda

4½ ounces bittersweet chocolate

3 ounces unsweetened chocolate

6 tablespoons (3 ounces) butter

¼ cup light brown sugar

¾ cup granulated sugar

2 large eggs

1 large egg yolk

1 teaspoon pure vanilla extract

9 ounces chocolate chips, or
   bittersweet chocolate,
   finely chopped

1 cup shelled pistachios or walnuts

Preheat the oven to 300 degrees. Sift together the flour, salt, and baking soda and set aside.

Melt both chocolates and the butter in a stainless-steel bowl over a pot of gently simmering water or in a double boiler. Remove from the heat.

In the bowl of an electric mixer fitted with the whisk attachment, whip the sugars, eggs, egg yolk, and vanilla on medium-high, about 4–5 minutes, until the mixture holds its shape after you lift away the beater. Combine the melted chocolate mixture with the egg mixture. Add the sifted dry ingredients and mix to combine. Fold in the chocolate chips and pistachios.

Spoon the dough in tablespoons onto a parchment-lined baking sheet, spaced 2 inches apart. Bake for 10–12 minutes.

# TRADITIONAL AMARETTI

*20 cookies*

These are the crunchy cookies that are crumbled up in several of our recipes. If you want everything to be from scratch, this is the way to go. You can also purchase them at most Italian delis or gourmet shops.

*2 cups blanched almonds*
*3 egg whites*
*¼ cup (2 ounces) butter*
*1 cup granulated sugar*
*1 ounce almond extract*
*2 teaspoons flour, to sprinkle the pan*

In a food processor fitted with the steel blade, grind the almonds to a coarse meal. Beat the egg whites until stiff, and then gently fold in the almond meal. Add all but 2 tablespoons of the sugar and the almond extract. You should have a very stiff batter.

Butter and flour a baking sheet.

Place the cookie mixture into a pastry bag fitted with a #4 plain tip and pipe small circles onto the baking sheet, about 1 inch apart. Sprinkle lightly with the remaining 2 tablespoons of sugar. Allow to stand for 4 hours.

When ready to bake, preheat the oven to 350 degrees. Bake for 15 minutes, or until golden. Remove from the oven and allow to cool.

*64 cookies*

*1¼ cups blanched bitter almonds*
  *(available at specialty stores)*
*1½ cups blanched almonds*
*½ cup granulated sugar*
*3 large egg whites*
*2 tablespoons bitter almond extract*
  *(available at specialty stores)*
*Powdered sugar, for dusting*

✼   *Chef's Tip:*  If you cannot find bitter almonds or extract, you can use regular almonds throughout.

Preheat the oven to 350 degrees. Butter a baking sheet, or line with parchment paper.

In a food processor fitted with the metal blade, grind the almonds and 2 tablespoons of the granulated sugar to a fine meal. Transfer to a large mixing bowl and stir in the remaining sugar. In the bowl of an electric mixer fitted with the whisk attachment, whip the egg whites on medium-high to stiff peaks. Add the almond extract and mix just to combine. Fold the egg whites into the nut mixture.

Drop about 2 teaspoons of dough per cookie onto the prepared baking sheet, spaced 1 inch apart. Sift powdered sugar over the tops. Bake for 15 minutes, until puffy. Remove from the oven and let cool slightly. Using a spatula, gently lift the cookies away from the sheet and store in an airtight container.

## PANETTONE DI LUCIANO

*2 loaves*

At Christmas you have to have *panettone,* our dense, eggy bread filled with candied fruit. In Italy, at holiday time, everybody goes to the caffé-bar to have a piece, freshly baked. At the restaurants, we are always looking for new ways to serve it—with a sauce, stuffed, frozen, whatever we can think of. Luciano came up with the idea of scooping out the inside of the bread and filling it with ice cream. And the part you scoop out will be a great piece of coffee cake warmed the next morning.

FOR THE SPONGE

*2 teaspoons active dry yeast*

*½ cup plus 1 tablespoon warm water*

*1¼ cups bread flour*

FOR THE PANETTONE

*1 tablespoon plus 1 teaspoon active*
*dry yeast*

*½ cup plus 1 tablespoon warm water*

*2 teaspoons molasses*

*¾ cup granulated sugar*

*3 cups plus 2 tablespoons bread flour*

*8 large egg yolks*

*1½ teaspoons rose water*

*1 tablespoon salt*

*Zest of 1½ lemons, finely chopped*

*9 tablespoons (4½ ounces) butter,*
*at room temperature*

*1½ cups raisins*

*⅓ cup candied orange peel*
*(see page 235)*

*2 tablespoons (1 ounce) butter,*
*for crisscross decoration*

TO MAKE THE SPONGE: In the bowl of a heavy-duty electric mixer fitted with the dough hook, place the yeast in the warm water for a few minutes to dissolve. Add the bread flour, and knead on low for 1 minute. Turn the mixer up to medium and knead until elastic, about 10–12 minutes. Cover the bowl tightly with plastic wrap and let it rest overnight.

TO MAKE THE PANETTONE: In a large mixing bowl, dissolve the yeast in warm water, add the molasses, and let stand for 10 minutes to begin fermentation. Add the sugar and set aside for 20 more minutes. Add the mixture to the sponge and mix to combine. Add the flour, a little at a time, keeping the mixer on low until all of the flour has been added.

In a bowl, stir together the egg yolks, rose water, salt, and lemon zest. Add to the dough, a few tablespoons at a time, thoroughly incorporating each addition into the dough before adding more. Continue to mix on medium speed for about 12 minutes. Add the butter 1 tablespoon at a time. Knead the dough until all the butter has been incorporated, then slowly fold in the raisins and candied peel. Divide the dough into 2 pieces and shape into balls. Place them on a baking sheet and set aside in a warm place to rest for 30 minutes. Reshape and place in a special panettone paper mold. Cover with plastic and proof for 4–6 hours.

Preheat the oven to 325 degrees. Cut the panettone crosswise on top, place a little piece of butter over the center, and bake for 40–45 minutes.

When the bread has cooled, cut out the center core, saving an outer slice to put it back together. Fill the center with your favorite ice cream, place the slice back on top to seal, and cut into wedges. Serve immediately with cappuccino or a glass of Asti Spumante.

*Filling the panettone: "Cut out the center core, saving an outer slice to put it back together."*

*Filling the panettone: "Fill the center with your favorite ice cream, place the slice back on top to seal, and cut into wedges."*

The gentleman who was my godfather used to visit on Sunday mornings, and he always came with what we call *mani piene*—full hands. It is a tradition that when you visit a family, you have to bring something. They have to offer you coffee, and so you bring a little sweet. At Christmas, every *pasticciere*, every artisan who makes confections, has the Christmas log. I remember whenever we had a visitor, I always looked to see the shape of the package they brought. And at holiday time my godfather would bring a Christmas log.

---

*1 recipe Sponge Cake batter
(see page 216)*

FOR THE SYRUP

*1 cup water
3 tablespoons granulated sugar
½ cup cassis*

FOR THE BUTTER CREAM

*6 egg yolks
¾ cup granulated sugar
½ cup light corn syrup
2 cups (1 pound) butter
½ cup raspberry puree*

FOR THE GANACHE

*1 cup heavy cream
12 ounces bitter or semisweet
chocolate, finely chopped
2 tablespoons (1 ounce) butter,
softened*

FOR THE MERINGUE

*4 egg whites*

*Preparation:* TO MAKE THE SPONGE CAKE: Preheat the oven to 400 degrees.

Pour the sponge cake batter into a jelly roll pan and bake for 7–10 minutes. Cool on a rack.

TO MAKE THE SUGAR SYRUP: In a small stainless-steel saucepan, bring 1 cup of water to a boil over medium-high heat. Add the sugar and cassis and stir until the sugar is dissolved. Remove from the heat and set aside.

TO MAKE THE BUTTER CREAM: In the bowl of an electric mixer fitted with the paddle attachment, beat the egg yolks on medium until pale in color. In a small saucepan, combine the sugar and corn syrup and cook to dissolve the sugar over medium heat, stirring constantly. When the mixture comes to a rolling boil with big bubbles, transfer it to a glass cup to stop the cooking. Cool for 1 minute.

Pour about 1 teaspoon of the syrup over the egg yolks with the mixer off. Immediately turn the mixer to high and beat for 5 seconds. Turn the mixer off, add a few teaspoons of the syrup to the egg yolks, and again beat on high for 5 seconds. Continue until all of the syrup has been incorporated. Scrape the side of the bowl occasionally, and continue beating until the mixture cools. Gradually add the butter. Add the raspberry puree and mix to combine.

¼ teaspoon lemon juice

1 cup granulated sugar

3 ounces bittersweet chocolate,
    melted

FOR THE ASSEMBLY AND GARNISH

1 cup heavy cream, whipped with
    1 tablespoon granulated sugar
    and ½ teaspoon vanilla

1 pint mixed berries

6 grape leaves

TO MAKE THE GANACHE: In a small saucepan, bring the cream to a boil over medium-high heat. Turn off and allow to sit for a few minutes. Repeat the process 2 more times to thicken and reduce the cream. Place the chocolate in a mixing bowl and pour the hot cream over it, stirring constantly until the chocolate melts. Add the butter and beat lightly. Set aside to cool and thicken. Cover with plastic wrap.

TO MAKE THE MERINGUE: Preheat the oven to 200 degrees.

In a stainless-steel bowl, whip the egg whites with the lemon juice until the mixture has quadrupled in volume and has the consistency of a thick foam.

*"Pipe 8 caps and 8 stems. Bake . . . until dry. . . . Cut a small hole on the bottom of each cap. Dip the pointed end of the stem in chocolate, then attach the stem to the cap."*

Still whipping at high speed, gradually add the sugar. Continue to beat the meringue at high speed until stiff peaks form. Do not overbeat.

Immediately spoon meringue into a pastry bag fitted with a plain #4 pastry tip until the bag is three-fourths full, and twist the top to seal. Place a small dot of meringue in each corner of a baking sheet, then cover the sheet with a piece of parchment paper; the meringue will make it adhere to the sheet pan. Pipe 8 caps and 8 stems. Bake at 200 degrees until dry, about 2 hours. Remove and let cool.

When the meringue is dry, cut a small hole on the bottom of each cap. Dip the pointed end of the stem in chocolate, then attach the stem to the cap.

*The Dish:* TO ASSEMBLE THE CHRISTMAS LOG: Place the sponge cake on a kitchen towel. Brush the surface of the cake with cassis syrup. Spread the butter cream evenly over the entire cake. Roll the sponge cake up into a log and refrigerate for 30 minutes.

> *Chef's Tip:* To roll the cake tightly, place it on a kitchen towel, and pull up on the towel to begin rolling. Use a ruler pressed against the cake to tuck it into a tight roll.

With a spatula, spread the ganache on top of the log in a wavy motion (if the ganache has hardened, soften it over a pot of warm water). With a fork, comb the ganache to create wood grain and knots. Cut both ends off at an angle and place the end pieces on the sides of the log, with the longer cut edge attached to the main body. Decorate with meringue mushrooms, using whipped cream to attach them to the log, and with berries and grape leaves.

*Wine:* You ought to have a great glass of champagne with a Christmas log. This dish is about festivity, celebration, and memories, so have the best. For something other than champagne, try a Piedmontese Moscato, like Rivetti. There is also a wine made in the Veneto region of Italy that is absolutely delightful, called Acini Nobili, "noble raisins," made from the Torcolato grape infused with botrytis. It is a mouthful of golden sensations.

*"At Christmas, every pasticciere, every artisan who makes confections, has the Christmas log. . . . This dish is about festivity, celebration, and memories."*

## ❊ *The Past Becomes the Future*

All the important events in my life began in a kitchen—in Italy, in my grandmother's kitchen, where we spent so many holidays, and in my mother's kitchen, where I learned the importance of the family meal. Once I came to America, the drama continued in the same way. It was at the NYU cafeteria that I decided to take a chance with my life, and at The Marquis in Los Angeles where I chose the path I would take.

I met my wife, Stacy, because she liked the food that came out of the kitchen at Primi, my second restaurant; she was a regular lunch customer there, and finally I went over to her table to introduce myself. The kitchen at Posto represents my continuing education, and my link to the artisans back in Italy who helped define its menu.

The Valentino kitchen? That is my home for much of every day, the place where I try always to refine and improve the presentation of food and wine. For over a quarter century it has been my laboratory, a place to experiment with the new and to reinterpret the old.

This book started in a kitchen, too. I was at Karen's house for dinner, and as usual when I am a guest, I headed for the kitchen to look around. There was a large bookshelf full of cookbooks, but I could make no sense of the organization. They were not arranged alphabetically, not by country, not by author, not in any way I could understand.

When I asked about them, I got a practical answer: They were organized by use. The ones on the top shelf were most often consulted. So I began to page through them. Just by looking, I could tell which dishes made this family happy—there were splattered pages and scribbled notes in the margin of recipes that had become part of daily life in this house. It made me think of the foods that mattered to me, from Mamma's *cucina povera* to the beautiful foods of Valentino. By the end of the evening we had decided to create our own book, and make it as useful and fun as the ones on Karen's top shelf.

The recipes reflect my life's obsession: Italian food as a dynamic cuisine, rooted in the past but always open to change. I absorb American influences the way my ancestors borrowed from the

Arabs; I interpret the products that are available to me in a quintessentially Italian manner. My kitchens now are all about innovation, but not just for the sake of doing something new. We invent with a respectful eye on our heritage, never straying too far from the principles that guided my mother, and hers before. Anyone can think up new dishes. To do it with a nod to the past—to do it with the heart, not just the head—is what this book is all about.

# ✿ Suppliers

## CONVITO ITALIANO
1515 North Sheridan Road
Wilmette, IL 60091
Telephone: (847) 251-3654
Fax: (847) 251-0123

*Balsamic vinegar, olive oils, imported Italian meats, gourmet pasta, Italian wines.*

## CORTI BROTHERS
5810 Folsom Boulevard
Sacramento, CA 95819
Telephone: (800) 509-3663
(916) 736-3800
Fax: (916) 736-3807

*This gourmet food store, run by renowned wine expert Darell Corti, specializes in artisanal pastas, imported cannellini and cranberry beans, olive oils, balsamic vinegar, line-caught canned tuna from Portugal, canned tomatoes, and Italian pastries.*

## DANKO FOODS, INC.
P.O. Box 7013
Laguna Niguel, CA 92607
Telephone: (949) 249-8883
Fax: (949) 249-8925
Contact: Dan Ketelaars
Call for retail price list.

*Danko specializes in an international selection of seafood and specialty meats, including sturgeon, seppie, wild turbot, langoustines, oysters, mussels, wild Moulard duck, and Bresse pigeon.*

## D'ARTAGNAN
280 Wilson Avenue
Newark, NJ 07105
Telephone: (800) 327-8246
Fax: (973) 465-1870
Web address: www.dartagnan.com
Call for catalog, brochures, and retail price list.

*Specialties: foie gras, game, venison, confits, and homemade sausages and pâtés.*

## DEAN & DELUCA
560 Broadway
New York, NY 10012
Telephone: (800) 221-7714
Web address: www.deandeluca.com

*Imported wine, cheese, rice, and pasta.*

## A. G. FERRARI FOODS
Telephone: (877) 878-2783
(877) 87-TASTE
Fax: (510) 351-2672
Web address: www.agferrari.com
Call (877) 878-2783 for retail price list.

*The finest in imported Italian products, including olive oils, balsamic vinegar, tomatoes, and pastries.*

## MANICARETTI
299 Lawrence Avenue
South San Francisco, CA 94080
Telephone: (415) 589-1120
Fax: (415) 589-5766

*Rolando Beramendi, the founder, supplies an array of Italian products, and is a good source of rice, vinegars, and Latini pasta.*

URBANI TRUFFLES
29-24 40th Avenue
Long Island City, NY 11101
Telephone: (800) 281-2330
(310) 842-8850
Fax: (718) 392-1704
Web address: www.urbani.com
E-mail: UrbaniUSA@aol.com
Call for catalog, brochures, and retail price list.

*Imported truffles, caviar, dried porcini, San Daniele Negrini ham, Carpegna prosciutto, fresh foie gras, pâtés, and sausages. Poultry: quail, squab, free-range chicken, goose. Specialty meats: New Zealand lamb, suckling goat, veal, rabbit. Feathered game birds: pheasant, ostrich.*

VALRHONA CHOCOLATES
1901 Avenue of the Stars, #1800
Los Angeles, CA 90067
Telephone: (310) 277-0401
Fax: (310) 277-7304
Web address: www.valrhona.com

*Specializes in French chocolates.*

VAN REX GOURMET FOODS, INC.
2055 East 51st Street
Vernon, CA 90058
Telephone: (800) 542-2243
(323) 581-7999
Fax: (323) 581-1767
Call for catalog, brochures, and retail price list.

*Fruit purees, chocolate products, Tahitian vanilla beans, hazelnuts, almonds, amaretti cookies.*

WALLY'S
2107 Westwood Boulevard
Los Angeles, CA 90025
Telephone: (310) 475-0606
(800) 8-WALLY'S
Fax: (310) 474-1450
Web address: wallywine.com

*Fine wines, cheeses, and cigars.*

# ✿ Index

PIERO SELVAGGIO owns three restaurants: Valentino, in Santa Monica, California; Posto, in Van Nuys, California; and Valentino Las Vegas, at the Venetian Hotel in Las Vegas. At Valentino, he has twice received the James Beard Award—for Outstanding Service in 1996, and for Wine in 1994. *Wine Spectator* magazine named Valentino one of the top four restaurants in the country in 1996 and again in 2000, and has given its Grand Award for wine to the restaurant every year since 1981. In 1997 the Italian magazine *Gambero Rosso* named Valentino the finest Italian restaurant in the world.

Selvaggio was born in Modica, Sicily. He now lives in Brentwood, California, with his wife, Stacy, and their three sons, Giorgio, Giampiero, and Tancredi.

KAREN STABINER is a magazine journalist and the author of four books. An enthusiastic home cook, she has written about food for *Saveur,* the *Los Angeles Times,* and *Travel & Leisure.*

She lives in Santa Monica, California, with her husband, Larry Dietz, and their daughter, Sarah.

## About the Type

This book is set in Fournier, a typeface named for Pierre Simon Fournier, the youngest son of a French printing family. Starting with engraving woodblocks and large capitals, he made several important contributions in the field of type design; he cut and founded all the types himself, pioneered the concepts of the type family, and is said to have cut sixty thousand punches for 147 alphabets of his own design. Fournier was released in 1925.